SHAPING A NATION

A HISTORY OF WOMEN AS EDUCATORS
and EDUCATION INFLUENCERS

SHAPING A NATION

A HISTORY OF WOMEN AS EDUCATORS and EDUCATION INFLUENCERS

GAYNOR HALIDAY

PEN & SWORD HISTORY

AN IMPRINT OF PEN & SWORD BOOKS LTD.
YORKSHIRE – PHILADELPHIA

First published in Great Britain in 2025 by
Pen & Sword History
An imprint of
Pen & Sword Books Ltd
Yorkshire - Philadelphia

Copyright © Gaynor Haliday, 2025

ISBN 978 1 39903 215 5

The right of Gaynor Haliday to be identified as the Author of this work has been asserted by her in accordance with the Copyright, Designs and Patents Act 1988.

A CIP catalogue record for this book is available from the British Library.

All rights reserved. No part of this book may be reproduced, transmitted, downloaded, decompiled or reverse engineered in any form or by any means, electronic or mechanical including photocopying, recording or by any information storage and retrieval system, without permission from the Publisher in writing. NO AI TRAINING: Without in any way limiting the Author's and Publisher's exclusive rights under copyright, any use of this publication to 'train' generative artificial intelligence (AI) technologies to generate text is expressly prohibited. The Author and Publisher reserve all rights to license uses of this work for generative AI training and development of machine learning language models.

Typeset in INDIA by IMPEC eSolutions
Printed and bound in the England by CPI Group (UK) Ltd, Croydon, CR0 4YY

The Publisher's authorised representative in the EU for product safety is Authorised Rep Compliance Ltd., Ground Floor, 71 Lower Baggot Street, Dublin D02 P593, Ireland.
www.arccompliance.com

For a complete list of Pen & Sword titles please contact:

PEN & SWORD BOOKS LIMITED
George House, Units 12 & 13, Beevor Street, Off Pontefract Road,
Barnsley, S71 1HN, UK
E-mail: enquiries@pen-and-sword.co.uk
Website: www.pen-and-sword.co.uk

or

PEN AND SWORD BOOKS
1950 Lawrence Rd, Havertown, PA 19083, USA
E-mail: uspen-and-sword@casematepublishers.com
Website: www.penandswordbooks.com

Contents

Acknowledgements		vi
Introduction		vii
Chapter 1	The Early Educators	1
Chapter 2	Being a Governess	17
Chapter 3	Becoming a Schoolmistress	39
Chapter 4	Women's Influence on Education Gathers Pace	57
Chapter 5	The London School Board	69
Chapter 6	Unions and Associations: The Schoolmistresses' Battle	91
Chapter 7	The Elementary Schoolmistresses' Career Progression	99
Chapter 8	Secondary Education for Girls: The Discussions	117
Chapter 9	Secondary Education for Girls: The Struggle Begins	129
Chapter 10	Opportunities for Headmistresses	147
Chapter 11	Educated Women Exert Their Influence	161
Chapter 12	The Next Steps	183
Chapter 13	Education for Girls: The Capacity to do Things	190
Appendix 1: Examinations of Pupil Teachers in each Year of their Apprenticeship		205
Appendix 2: Qualifications of Stipendiary Monitors in each Year		208
Appendix 3: Education Code 1882: Teacher Classifications		210
Appendix 4: Endowed Girls' Schools Established 1871–1903		216
Appendix 5: Girls Public Day Schools Company Schools in 1894		220
Endnotes		222
Bibliography		227
Index		232

Acknowledgements

It is difficult to know where to begin with acknowledgements, but perhaps I might start with my own education at one of the first endowed girls' grammar schools, Bradford Girls' Grammar. I have always been appreciative of the LEA scholarship that meant I could be a pupil there and the lifelong friendships that ensued. Those first few weeks as we from the state elementary schools got to know the girls who had been at fancy preparatory schools, who thought themselves a 'cut above' and had already some grasp of French, were an interesting time as we all found our feet. Soon we were all in it together on a journey of education, following the ethos of the school's first head set out 100 years earlier, being given the confidence to follow any course we chose. We never thought of ourselves as inferior to men (well we weren't!) and (generally) believed in our abilities to succeed in the world. A few years ago, we had a reunion to celebrate our fortieth anniversary of leaving school and even though many of us had lost touch over the decades, there was genuine delight in meeting each other and finding out what everyone had done in the ensuing years. Sir Mathew Wilson MP, in a speech at the school's opening in 1875, had predicted such an outcome of affection and sincere regard through this bringing together of girls. Several former classmates were headmistresses and teachers; some were diplomats and senior civil servants; others were medical professionals, scientists, journalists, entrepreneurs; several, of course, were mothers too.

Many people have helped in my research for this book: those who researched and published theses on education; the archivists and transcribers who made archives searchable and available online; the education historians such as Derek Gillard whose website **https://www.education-uk.org** is a font of information that piqued my interest and sent me down many other rabbit holes of research. Particular mention should go to a friend of mine, John Jackson, currently writing a thesis on education in Bradford, who pointed me in the direction of some interesting theses and books; to Malcolm Tozer who provided me with his own research on Edward Thring of Uppingham School; to North London Collegiate School who granted me access to its online catalogue of school magazines and images; to the headmistress of Bradford Girls' Grammar, Mrs Caroline Foster, who welcomed me back to look through the school archives. And, of course, to Amy Jordan, commissioning editor at Pen & Sword, who said, 'yes, we'd like to publish that!'

And to anyone I've missed: thank you too.

Introduction

Apart from discovering I had ancestors who were teachers in the very early Board Schools, the inspiration for this book came partly from an unlikely piece of research into election corruption in 1868, when, after the election of Henry William Ripley as one of Bradford's MPs was declared void through bribery and corruption of the electorate, Edward Miall won the seat in the subsequent by-election. Although women had no vote, they did have influence; Miall was the object of so much female support that they organised a huge fundraiser to show their appreciation and even though Miall had been installed in parliament by the time of the presentation in May 1869, the women were not going to be thwarted of their plans for a big event.

Over 4,500 women attended, 'dressed gaily in crinolines and with their hair neatly got up in chignons'. So great was the crush and excitement at St George's Hall, Bradford that the doors had to be opened fifteen minutes early. The *Leeds Times* described it as 'Perhaps one of the most remarkable meetings ever held in the kingdom, and perfectly unique in its kind in every respect', a women-only event to which 'none of the hirsute sex' had been invited (apart from those taking part in the proceedings and the 'universally indispensable' men of the press – who had to make do with sitting on the legs of stools so arranged as to give temporary seating, when the women pushed them out of their seats in front of the orchestra).

Edward Miall gave a gushing speech and, as a sometimes-indignant woman of Bradford, I particularly like these extracts, which clearly demonstrate how in touch he was with those local women:

> I look upon these beautiful gifts of yours, in the first place, as the utterance of indignant womanhood in Bradford. Someone had taken liberty with your name, and woe be to the man who disposes of the will of a woman without having first asked her consent.
>
> It has been the fashion of man to degrade woman by lording over her, and of course he, to justify himself in doing this, has assumed that the political sphere is a sphere altogether apart from that in which a woman ought to move. But we have our first lessons in morality from the lips of our mothers, and our chief support in adversity on the arms and bosoms of our wives, and

he is the man who can accomplish little in this world, however he may set his heart upon the triumph of the right, who does not link with him the fond, pure, and affectionate counsels of woman. Happy will be the day in England – happy will be the day throughout the whole world, when woman takes up her real and proper position. ... Women of Bradford, take your part, let your benign and genial influence smile away, as far as it can, the asperities of party feeling; be present as it were, in the spirit at least, in all electoral contests, and diffuse your own sweet humour, as the humour which shall guide, and, as it were, sway the hearts of those over whom you have control.

Miall was right. Women have influence over their offspring from the day they are born, whether that be lessons in morality, support in adversity or counsel in decision making. What he perhaps had not appreciated was the influence women had and were to expand upon – their significance in educating future generations from their earliest schooldays – that women's soft power was to be the bedrock of developing hearts and minds for ever.

And perhaps we should also thank Bradford's other MP at the time, William Edward Forster, who pushed through the Elementary Education Act the following year, paving the way for compulsory and free education for everyone and giving women their first real opportunity to have their political voices heard by being elected to school boards.

Almost 130 years later, future prime minister Tony Blair stated his three main priorities for government were education, education and education and restated them when campaigning for his second term in office. He wanted to make Britain a learning society, to develop the talents and raise the ambitions of all young people, for them to gain the basic tools for life and work. Not only that, but 'they ought also to learn the joy of life: the exhilaration of music, the excitement of sport, the beauty of art, the magic of science. And they learn the value of life: what it is to be responsible citizens who give something back to their community.'

What he didn't acknowledge was that it was women who would continue to be at the forefront of all that. Today, around 80 per cent of primary school teachers are women. Children taking their first steps on their learning journey mainly do so under the guidance of nurturing and influential women who set them up with valuable life skills: literacy, numeracy and tolerance. That's some responsibility.

This book will cover not only the educators but also the women who strived for improvements in education, whether that be for the benefit of the children, other women, or that of the educators. I would add that although I have carried out many hours of research and disappeared down a multitude of rabbit holes of intrigue, this is not an academic work; the narrative is founded on stories that piqued my interest and supported my notion of women's great importance in shaping a nation.

Chapter 1

The Early Educators

The great advocate for women's rights, Mary Wollstonecraft (1759–1797), wrote of her opinion that all children (of all classes, rich and poor, male and female) between the ages of 5 and 9, should be provided with an education in schools organised nationally. She believed all should be taught together and treated equally in matters of curriculum, discipline and dress. A broad curriculum, taught in such a manner as to stimulate the children's curiosity, would encourage them to seek knowledge for themselves instead of simply accepting blindly what they were told in answer to their questions. In addition, the company of other children would enable them to enjoy a proper childhood instead of having to grow up too soon.[1] She was born too early to experience this herself; she attended a day school for a short period of time (in contrast with her brother who received an extensive formal education) and by her own determination, largely educated herself. Like many women who came after her, with her friend Fanny Blood and two sisters, she established a small school in order to make a living. After only a couple of years and Fanny's marriage and subsequent death, the school failed and Mary reluctantly became a governess to an aristocratic family in Cork, Ireland, the only other professional option for her at the time. This was a disaster; she returned to London and turned to writing, drawing on her experiences to pen (among other works) *Thoughts on the Education of Daughters: With Reflections on Female Conduct, in the More Important Duties of Life* in 1787 and *A Vindication of the Rights of Woman* in 1792, where she argued that women were not naturally inferior to men but only appeared to be so because of their lack of education. She died just eleven days after giving birth (to Mary Wollstonecraft Shelley née Godwin) on 10 September 1797. Had she lived longer, she could have witnessed at least some of her wishes around education coming to fruition.

***

Before the 1870 Elementary Education Act, for the majority of those who attended a school, primary education was mainly provided by voluntary or charitable bodies. Some children (from wealthier families) were taught at home by governesses, others attended private schools, frequently run by women. There were two main providers of elementary education, the largest being the National Society, founded on 16 November 1811, which aimed to establish a National School in every parish of England and Wales, usually next to the church. It was incorporated by charter in 1817 as the National Society for Promoting the Education of the Poor in the Principles of the Established Church throughout England and Wales.

The earlier British Schools, which started as the Society for Promoting the Lancasterian System for the Education of the Poor, in 1808, used the Lancasterian system (after Joseph Lancaster) to teach children. This was a monitorial system where older children with some education helped teach younger ones, meaning classes could be larger and education provided more cheaply. In 1814, the Society was (lengthily) renamed the British and Foreign School Society for the Education of the Labouring and Manufacturing Classes of Society of Every Religious Persuasion. British Schools were non-denominational (not all parents wanted their children schooled by the C of E and that included Nonconformists, Catholics and Quakers). On top of this, the Nonconformists established schools of their own, usually Methodist or Wesleyan. There was an active rivalry between the different types of school, but in essence, apart from religious doctrine, the teaching methods were similar in all. Education was not free, however; children had to pay their school pence to attend.

Education was free for destitute children at the Ragged Schools, developed from 1818 after John Pounds, a shoemaker from Portsmouth, started teaching children for free. The Ragged Schools' Union was established in 1844 by Lord Shaftesbury; it promoted the spread of such schools (there were 200 by 1852 and 350 by 1870) and was supported by benefactors like Angela Burdett Coutts (see Chapter 3).

In addition to this were the 'dame schools', run by women usually in their own homes to make a living. Here, for a small fee, girls could gain basic skills in reading and household tasks, depending on how well-educated the 'teacher' was.

***

The Directory, General & Commercial of the Town & Borough of Leeds for 1817 paints an informative picture of the provision for education in the town. It is clear that education provision was mainly for boys and what education there was for girls was very much focused on their future lives of domesticity; with very little in the way of career opportunities, a woman's only hope of avoiding a life of destitution seems to have been to marry and become a homemaker.

For the district's population of 62,534 (town: 35,951; villages: 26,583) it lists and describes the following schools under 'charitable institutions', and it is notable that nearly all these schools had a woman in charge:

Free Grammar School, founded 1552 by Reverend Sir William Sheffield, solely for purpose of classical education. Its head in 1817 was the Reverend George Page Richards A.M., Fellow of King's College, Cambridge and it was a boys-only establishment.

Royal Lancasterian Free School, Alfred Street. This building, capable of holding 500 boys, opened July 1812, supported principally by annual subscriptions and occasional benefactions. Here children were taught reading, writing, arithmetic at cost of 5s per year per pupil, 'a mode', the committee observed, 'the cheapest as well as the most effectual that ever was devised' [i.e. the monitorial system]. 'Much attention is paid to inuring the scholars to habits of decency, regularity, diligent attention and proper subordination [sounds ominous]. Required to attend morning and afternoon on Sabbath, whence they proceed to such places of worship as their respective parents are accustomed to attend.'

Girls' Free School, Assembly Court, Call Lane, 'is conducted on the same plan as the Lancasterian Free School of which it may be considered a branch and supported by subscriptions and benefactions'. Here, girls were taught to sew as well as read and write (seemingly not arithmetic though) and the number at the time was 173. Thursday morning was appropriated by religious instruction. 'Several ladies regularly visit the school.' Governess: Mrs Benjamin Stead.

National School, Kirkgate (erected on site of Tythe Barn) opened 7 February 1813 for instruction of 320 poor boys and 180 girls on Dr Bell's or the Madras system [monitorial]. 'Building is handsome and convenient.' Master: Mr Frederick Rayner; Governess: Miss Hannah Cowling.

The Charity School [Blue Coat] 'in the Lands near St John's Church and was built originally as chapel to Mr Harrison's hospital then converted to a school with £80 per year for the instruction of poor children of both sexes in reading, writing and arithmetic, and of girls the necessary arts of sewing, knitting and spinning etc.'

A comfortable blue cloth dress was given to each of the children. The school had been recently rebuilt in Gothic style and was intended solely in future for the reception of girls, the boys having been removed to the National School. It was in receipt of various benefactions and legacies. Governess: Miss Robinson.

Further information about the school may be gleaned from an advertisement for a schoolmistress to teach domesticity, discipline and religion at this soon-to-be all-girls' school, which appeared in the *Leeds Mercury* on Saturday, 16 November 1816:

> LEEDS CHARITY SCHOOL. WANTED a MISTRESS to instruct Sixty Poor Girls, or such other number as the Committee may Appoint, in Reading, Knitting, Sewing, and such other domestic Employments as the fund of the Charity may permit, according to a Plan which will be submitted to the Inspection of Candidates. The religious instruction and general Discipline, to be strictly conformable to those of the National Schools. The Salary Sixty Pounds per Annum, together with a neat Small House annexed to the School; several other Advantages will also be derived by a deserving Mistress from the Assistance of the scholars in the Care of her House. It is therefore hoped that the situation may suit some well-educated Active Female. A Widow will be preferred, and the Incumbrance of a Family deemed Objectionable. Applications to be made personally, or by letter post-paid, to the Reverend John Sheepshanks.

That the 'incumbrance of a family' was deemed objectionable is telling and may have been one of the considerations for imposing a marriage bar on women teachers.

In addition to these schools were three schools of industry in the town:

1. Mr Beezon's Yard, Briggate. Est. early 1799 and continues to be liberally supported by a number of benevolent ladies, twelve of whom undertake its management, attending each one month in rotation to assist in the school. Expenses annually around 40s but subscriptions and earnings in school exceed this sum so the surplus is applied at end of year in clothing the children. Number limited to 50 who are instructed in reading, sewing and knitting. Governess: Mrs Lydia Lee.
2. At Burley Bar founded 5 July 1802; fifty children taught as above, twenty-five in morning, twenty-five in afternoon supported by subscriptions and benefactions. Governess: Mrs Rebecca Knowles.
3. Clarkson's Yard, Quarry Hill; thirty girls taught as above for two hours every evening (except Saturdays and Sundays) [they were probably working during the day]. Governess: Mrs Hannah Whittaker.

These schools generally trained girls from poorer families so they could gain employment as domestic servants; it was to such an industrial school in Bradford that Patrick Brontë went in summer 1816, shortly after Charlotte Brontë was born, in search of a girl to help with the children and in their Thornton home. He chose

Nancy De Garrs, aged around 12, who stayed with the Brontë family for eight years, moving with them to Haworth and helping look after the family after their mother died, until the girls went to school at Cowan Bridge. Perhaps in testimony to how well Nancy did her job, her sister Sarah was later also to join the household.

Then there were the Sunday Schools. Their main aim may have been to civilise children, with a spate of Sunday School building taking place between 1812 and 1824, perhaps for political and social reasons. Juvenile crime was rife and there was a general fear of revolution due to the growing militancy of the working classes. Of course, because child workers could be educated without impinging on the working week, they grew in popularity.

The *Directory* reported:

Sunday Schools

Leeds has to boast of being the second town in the kingdom where this mode of instruction was introduced. The schools are now becoming very numerous; there is scarcely a place of worship in the town of whatever denomination, to which one is not attached. The teachers consist chiefly of young persons who devote their attention to this important work gratis.

A Sunday School Union was established in 1816 which has already been productive of much good. [It included 9 schools with a total of 358 teachers; 873 boys and 973 girls.]

A school also recently established for instruction of the numerous children employed at the Pottery, which intends to join this union. [Teachers 33; boys 60, girls 80.]

Of Sunday Schools not in Union: the Parish Church had 10 with 115 teachers; and 1,420 children; and the Methodists had 12 schools, 249 teachers and 1,841 children. [Note the ratio of teachers to children varied widely within schools.]

It summed up with: 'Total children who enjoy the advantages of this cheap and effectual mode of instruction are upwards of 5,000 and the benevolent persons engaged gratuitously as teachers above 700.'

By 1834, the number of Sunday Schools in Leeds had slowly expanded to include twenty in the Union and around twelve 'non-union', eleven Wesleyan Methodist and ten Wesleyan Protestant Methodist schools. In all, there were in excess of 1,000 teachers tutoring 10,600 children in equal ratio of boys and girls. The Wesleyans had also established four new day schools for which the scholars paid 2d a week for reading and writing on a slate (3d if they used paper to write on and 4d if grammatical instruction was added). Girls were also taught sewing and knitting for the same cost, but one might wonder if that was at the expense of losing some of the more academic instruction.

The benevolent persons so engaged in Sunday Schools were invariably women. One such woman was Ellen Rigg to whom a plaque was dedicated in Cartmel Priory. Ellen had died on 24 June 1852, aged 59, after thirty-three years as a 'constant teacher in Cartmel Sunday School'. That she had been a woman of independent means is without doubt; her will detailing numerous personal bequests to the people of Cartmel, plus a bequest of £100 for the repairs to the priory roof, and money to various other bodies, including the Sunday School, demonstrates this – plus she had the wherewithal to keep a servant and was described as a 'fund holder' in the 1851 census. The death notice described her as a 'constant and zealous teacher', one who died 'esteemed and lamented by all who knew her'.

Of course, Ellen Rigg was not the only 'woman of means' to put her time and money to the education of children. Schools were also financed by philanthropic estate owners, such as Lady Louisa Waterford née Stuart (1818–1891). Lady Waterford, who had spent her married life alongside her husband actively working to alleviate the suffering of their tenants at their estate at Curraghmore in County Waterford during the Irish Famine, was widowed in 1859 when her husband met with a hunting accident. She was left Ford Castle and its estate in Northumberland and it was here she commissioned and built a village school in the early 1860s. She was a talented artist and in 1863 commenced painting, in distemper, a series of pictures representing boys and girls mentioned in the Bible on twelve arched compartments on the walls of the schoolroom.

Earlier than that even, wealthy women were using their money for the betterment of poor children. One example is the bequest by Miss Ann Ludlam of Black House, Thurstonland, Yorkshire who left £300 in a trust for the erection and maintenance of a school, plus the salary of a schoolmaster, for the 'education of the poor of the township' in 1763. The school was free for instruction in reading to all children in the township, and the scholars were taught to write for a small quarterage. Admission to the school was by application to some of the resident trustees. The trust is still in existence and trustees meet to allocate grants, as was originally intended in the terms of the trust, for the purchase of books and teaching materials and to support the developing life of the school.

Educating girls for a career in education

As well as private education for girls of wealthier families, it seems certain professions saw the benefit of educating their womenfolk, particularly if they might have to support themselves in the future. One example is the number of schools set up for 'daughters of clergymen', probably the most notorious of these being the

Clergy Daughters' School at Cowan Bridge near Kirby Lonsdale, immortalised as Lowood Institution in *Jane Eyre*.

In 1823, the property at Cowan Bridge was purchased by a wealthy evangelical clergyman and landowner, Reverend William Carus Wilson. Wilson was a firm believer in the value of education and aware that the poorer clergy could not afford to properly educate their daughters. Priority was always given to providing any sons with an education (witness Patrick Brontë's insistence – or indulgence – in his only son, Branwell, having the money he needed), therefore Wilson resolved to establish a school for girls that would be affordable to the poorest of the clergy.

The stated purpose of the school was to provide:

> the intellectual and religious improvement of the pupils and to give that plain and useful education which may fit them to return with respectability and advantage to their homes or <u>to maintain themselves in the different stations to which providence may call them</u>.

In contrast to much of the available education for girls, the syllabus at Cowan Bridge was to include writing, arithmetic, history, geography (with the use of the globes), grammar, needlework and 'the nicer kinds of household work'. French, drawing and music were extras at £3 a year. By having a wider education than merely domestic instruction, the daughters of clergymen would be able to find paid employment as governesses or schoolmistresses.

A number of Wilson's friends who were also committed to education for girls were also benefactors, including William Wilberforce. With fees at £14 a year, half that of comparable schools, it is little wonder the running costs had to be subsidised by donations from far and wide.

Its chief patron was the Archbishop of York, and the president was the Bishop of Chester, with six bishops as vice presidents. It is interesting to note how many women from the nobility were listed as vice patronesses: the duchesses of Beaufort, St Albans and Gordon; marchionesses of Bute, Conyngham and Bristol; countesses of Liverpool, Lonsdale, Harrowby; Viscountess Galway; and twelve ladies. Interestingly, the last on the list is a Miss Currer. Was she the inspiration for Charlotte Brontë's pseudonym? The school opened in January 1824 with up to sixteen girls aged from 6 to 18. It is noted that the level of attainment on entering the school was generally very low; most could only 'read miserably' and very few could do any arithmetic.[2]

Patrick Brontë must have been satisfied with what he saw when he enrolled his two eldest daughters, Maria and Elizabeth, on 21 July 1824, because only three weeks later he brought Charlotte, then aged 8. Emily joined them, aged only 6, in the November as the forty-fourth pupil, the rapid increase in numbers showing there was clearly a demand for this type of school. It was probably the low fees that made it so attractive. Maria and Elizabeth had previously attended Crofton Hall School near Wakefield from September to December 1823, but Patrick was only able to afford the fees for that one term. Although Maria, Charlotte and Emily were to train as governesses, it seems Elizabeth, the more practical of the sisters, was to train as a housekeeper; Patrick did not pay the extra £3 for 'accomplishments'. The entry in the school register records Charlotte as being able to read tolerably, write indifferently and that she knew nothing of grammar, geography or history. Her needlework was neat but other 'accomplishments' (French, music and drawing) were lacking.[3] How (later) education changed her.

Much has been written about the terrible time the Brontë sisters had at the school; they stayed less than a year and the two older girls died shortly after returning home. Yet despite this, the school continued to be popular and by 1827 there were seventy-five girls at the school (drawn from places as far away as Africa and Australia) and a waiting list of twenty.

The school relocated to purpose-built premises in Casterton in the early 1830s, and it was to these that the Reverend Henry Venn Elliott, first minister of St Mary's Chapel, Rock Gardens, Brighton paid a visit in October 1833 to see his friend Carus Wilson. Elliott had issued a prospectus for his proposed School for the Daughters of the Clergy in 1832 and was clearly impressed by what he saw at Casterton:

> I offered up a little prayer that the Brighton School might receive a similar blessing when I saw, in going over all the rooms and offices of this Clergy Daughters' School at Casterton, how perfectly everything was arranged and with what looking up to God it was begun.[4]

A far cry from Carus Wilson's first school at Cowan Bridge.

The proposed school in Brighton was to accommodate 100 pupils each paying £20 a year for education, board and some clothing. Unlike Cowan Bridge, included in this cost was French and elementary music, but drawing and 'the finishing parts' of music were £4 and £3 per year respectively. The girls so educated would be qualified as governesses for the higher and middle classes. Of course, money was required for all this, but various benefactors were sufficiently impressed with the proposal and within a year £2,339 had been donated. The Marquess of Bristol gave an acre of land on the Downs; the architect George Basevi, whom Reverend Elliott had met during a tour of Greece, made a gift of the plans for the building; and Queen Adelaide became its royal patroness.

Although the school was not quite ready, it opened on 1 August 1836. Its lady superintendent was Miss Tomkinson, and Mary Bryan, Janey and Charlotte Cory were the first pupils. The reverend's wife, Julia, joined them and it is evident from a letter she wrote that this new venture was full of promise:

If you could but have seen us, and been with us, in the pretty little mullion-windowed room over the entrance. It looked so pleasant; a bright fire, the floor carpeted, the table spread with tea, happy faces round it, our hearts full of a thousand mingled emotions! It was the beginning of the accomplishment of hopes so long cherished, the dawn of a day that should go on in increasing brightness![5]

The register notes Mary Elizabeth Bryan, aged 14, as the daughter of Charles and Ellen Bryan of Woolaston near Chepstow who were 'deeply embarrassed in circumstances'. Janey Eliza (14) and Charlotte Eleanor (8) Cory were nominated by Robert Bevan Esq, Rougham, Bury St Edmunds – a donor of £50.

From a small start of just twelve girls, the number by Christmas was twenty-nine and in less than a year there were forty pupils, with five governesses besides Miss Tomkinson, two of whom were 'Parisian ladies'. By 16 October 1839, the hundredth girl, Mary Anne Morphew had been admitted.[6] Girls aged between 8 and 14 were admitted to the school and they had to be able to read and spell and to know the first four rules of arithmetic (addition/subtraction/multiplication and division). Donors of £50 (such as Robert Bevan Esq.), or subscribers of £10 per annum for five years, were entitled to nominate a child.

School records show that not every girl stayed the course. The seventh girl to be admitted, on 4 August 1836, was Mary Ann Jones, aged 16. After the Christmas holidays, her friends were requested to remove her and she left on 5 January 1837. It was noted that the influence of her conduct and character was judged undesirable in the school, and it was considered 'inexpedient that she should remain there'. She was not alone. A number of girls were removed 'by order of the Trustees' at various points in their education for 'Conduct and Character – most unsatisfactory'. Some left from ill health, others (mirroring the instances at Cowan Bridge) died at the school.[7]

In its first ten years, the school admitted 300 girls who would train to earn a living as a governess and it continued to expand. After twenty-one years at the helm, Miss Tomkinson resigned in 1857 and was replaced as Lady Superior by Mrs Ann Mills from Queen's College, Harley Street (see Chapter 2).[8] In 1861, the school was accommodating 100 pupils and 17 teachers, plus a large household staff, all female except for the porter.[9]

There are few notes, beyond 'destined for governess', in the 'remarks and subsequent history' column, but it is clear, even if not recorded at St Mary's, that some, such as Susan Carter, definitely went on to pursue the careers they were trained for.

Of course, this was not the only school for girls in Brighton; there were several close to the seafront, generally accommodating ten to twenty girls, and most had governesses from France and Germany. Speaking a foreign language was part of a young lady's accomplishments, and the girls who attended these schools were generally expected to make 'good marriages' rather than having a career.

***

After the Brontë sisters had left Cowan Bridge, it was some time before they ventured from home again and, like many of their generation, relied on their father to teach them. Charlotte's godparents later paid for her to attend Margaret Wooler's school at Roe Head near Mirfield and she was there as a scholar from January 1831 to May 1832, winning the school's French prize in December 1831. After imparting her knowledge to Anne and Emily in Haworth, and becoming superintendent at Haworth's first Sunday School in October 1832 (which was built at the instigation of her father, Patrick), in late July 1835 Charlotte returned to Roe Head as a teacher, with Emily as a pupil. After around eleven weeks, Emily's homesickness meant she returned to Haworth, and Anne took her place at Roe Head in January 1836. When Miss Wooler moved her school to Heald's Hall, Dewsbury Moor, eighteen months later, Charlotte and Anne went with her – Anne leaving through illness at the end of 1837, but Charlotte staying on to look after the premises, after Miss Wooler's father died, until May 1838.

Young ladies' schools as a source of income

For many women, running a school was a source of income. With no secondary education available for girls (the boys had the endowed schools) it is no wonder some women capitalised on the opportunity to educate girls of families who wanted better for their daughters. Even in 1817 there were around eleven of these schools listed in Leeds, generally providing education for girls aged 11–16. Some were day schools, such as those run by Phoebe Brook, in Hunslet Lane and Mary Wainhouse, St Peter's Square; others were listed as being boarding schools, including the one run by Jane Holmes, of Providence Row.

As commercial enterprises, it was vital that schools advertised, albeit in a genteel manner befitting their intended clientele:

Ladies Boarding School, Providence Row, Leeds

Mrs Holmes wishes to return grateful acknowledgement to her friends for their past favours and to inform them that her school will recommence on Monday 16th Inst.

Leeds Intelligencer, Monday, 9 January 1815

M. Wainhouse, St Peter's Square, Leeds. Very grateful for the liberal support she has for eight years experienced from her numerous friends, takes this method of returning her sincere thanks, and hopes, by sedulous attention to the improvement and morals of those young ladies intrusted to her care, to merit their future patronage.

She respectfully informs her friends and the public that her school will re-commence on Monday the 13th of January.
Leeds Mercury, Saturday, 4 January 1817

EDUCATION FOR YOUNG LADIES. MRS BROOK, grateful for the Favours she has received, begs Leave to inform her friends and the Public, that her SCHOOL will re-open on Monday the 28th Instant, when she hopes for a Continuation of their Patronage.
Leeds Mercury, Saturday, 26 July 1817

Some were frequent advertisers. Time and again, the Misses Thackray placed similar advertisements in the Leeds papers. They give a true picture of what was being taught to young ladies:

Boarding School for Young Ladies. The MISSES Thackray, High-Street, Knaresborough, take this Method of returning their sincere Thanks to their Friends, and the Supporters of their School, for the liberal Encouragement they have hitherto met with. They hope by a steady undeviating Attention to the Duties of their Situation, to ensure that Patronage, which it will ever be their highest Ambition to merit. The School will RE-OPEN, for the Reception of Young Ladies, on the 20th of January 1817. The Misses Thackray limit the Number of their Boarders to Ten, whom they carefully instruct in Religious and Moral duties and in every useful and fashionable Branch of Education. For References, the Misses Thackray would wish any one to apply to the Parents of those Young Ladies who have been last under their care. TERMS: Board, with Plain and Fancy Needle-Work £24, Writing and English Grammar £2 2s; Geography (with the Use of the Globe) £2 2s; French, Music, Drawing, and Dancing, the usual Terms.
Leeds Intelligencer, Monday, 20 January 1817

The Misses Thackray restricted the number of boarders to ten, but as there is no census available for this period, it is impossible to know how many were accommodated at other 'ladies' schools', though an examination of the census returns for Oakwell Hall near Birstall show that numbers fluctuated over the decades.

Oakwell Hall was an Elizabethan manor house and had been used as a school since a Mrs Wilks transferred her 'successful establishment for young ladies' from Dewsbury to its 'unusually large and airy rooms' in 1825. A sense of what was being taught can be gleaned from the advertisement in the *Leeds Intelligencer* on Thursday, 29 June 1826:

OAKWELL HALL, near Leeds. – Mrs WILKS'S ESTABLISHMENT for YOUNG LADIES will be Re-opened after the present Vacation, on Monday, the 24th July. A TEACHER Wanted, who understands French, Drawing, and Music.

It is not clear how long this school lasted at Oakwell, but the hall was advertised for rent by the owner, Joshua Walker, in 1833 and was taken up as a school by the Misses Hannah, Sarah and Elizabeth Cockill, daughters of a local dyer, who died in 1838. Elizabeth had been at school with Charlotte Brontë at Roe Head and Charlotte took a keen interest in the progress and success of the school, visiting on occasion (and later basing Fieldhead in *Shirley* on the hall). According to the 1841 census, the school had sixteen girls boarding (aged 8 to 17) with the three sisters as teachers. Another teacher had joined them by 1851, but the ladies' tenure ceased around 1853, after which Hannah married a solicitor in April 1854 and Elizabeth died later the same year.

The school was taken up by the Misses Upton (Sarah and Martha) for five years:

OAKWELL HALL, near BIRSTALL, LEEDS. The MISSES UPTON continue to receive PUPILS, to whom they offer every facility for the attainment of a solid English Education, together with instruction in Drawing, Dancing, and the French, German, and Italian Languages. The Musical Department is under the superintendence of Mr. Spark, of Leeds. The VACATION will TERMINATE Wednesday, August 3rd.

Leeds Intelligencer, Saturday, 2 July 1853

OAKWELL HALL, BIRSTALL, LEEDS. The Misses UPTON receive a limited number of Pupils, to whom they offer great advantages for the attainment of a solid English Education, and the acquisition of the French, German, and Italian Languages; with Instruction in Drawing. The Piano-Forte, Singing, and Dancing taught by First-rate Masters. Oakwell Hall is beautifully situated, at a convenient distance from Two Railway Stations, in a healthy and agreeable locality. Cards of Terms may be had on application.

Sheffield Daily News, Monday, 8 February 1858

It is interesting to note they cite first-rate masters as teachers; perhaps their clientele believed that being taught by a man was superior, or perhaps they were also taking boys at the school. After their cotton-spinner father died suddenly at Oakwell Hall in 1859, the sisters moved and by 1861 had relocated to Sydenham in Kent where they ran a ladies' boarding school for just eight pupils (half of whom were from the Dewsbury/Leeds area), with four resident mistresses (including themselves), a Belgian governess to teach languages, a visiting music teacher (German) and another visiting teacher. Martha continued to run a school in London and by 1891 the unmarried sisters were living together 'on their own means' in Chiswick. With a life of work came financial independence.

In the 1860s, Oakwell Hall became a boys' school under Henry Millard before returning to a ladies' boarding school by 1871, run by Susan Margaret and Catherine Elizabeth Carter:

> OAKWELL HALL, BIRSTALL, LEEDS. – MRS and the MISSES CARTER receive Young Ladies as resident pupils. Good music, drawing, dancing, drilling, and composition. Masters in attendance. A French lady resides in the house. Terms on application.
> *Yorkshire Post and Leeds Intelligencer,* Saturday, 29 June 1872

The Carters were daughters of Susannah and Edward Nicholls Carter, a clergyman, and Susan had been educated at St Mary's Hall, Brighton, entering the school aged 14 in August 1851. On the 1861 census, she is listed as a governess to a linen manufacturer's family at Dodworth Hall near Barnsley. The 1871 census shows the Oakworth Hall school under the charge of Ellen (the eldest sister) and Catherine, while Susan is at home with her parents, where a boarder was none other than Margaret Wooler. It is unlikely Susan had been a pupil of Miss Wooler, since she was born in 1835 and Miss Wooler had ceased teaching by 1841; perhaps she was seeking counsel about how to run a successful girls' boarding school. Ellen's role as a teacher was short-lived, as she married William Smith, vicar of Shadwell, Leeds, on 26 October 1871. Perhaps she was not really cut out for teaching: St Mary's Hall admission records show she entered the school on 5 September 1848, leaving in June 1851 without completing the training: 'Subsequent education – very little progress from want of ability and left in the 4th class. Conduct and character – most satisfactory.'[10]

Later censuses show Oakwell Hall school's numbers in decline. The Elementary Education Act and school-building programme is bound to have had an impact, as would the introduction of some formal secondary education for girls. Perhaps the Carters had to widen their net in thrifty Yorkshire by being less exclusively a girls-only boarding school:

OAKWELL HALL, BIRSTALL. Boarding School for Girls; Weekly and Daily Pupils also received; little Boys not objected to; Resident French Governess. Terms moderate. THE MISSES CARTER.

Dewsbury Chronicle and West Riding Advertiser,
Saturday, 15 January 1881

By 1891 only the Carters' nieces and cousins were boarding.

Schools like this, run by women for girls, when little else was available in the way of female education had served a dual purpose. Firstly, they had provided a career and financial independence for women who were unlikely to make 'good' marriage, and secondly, they had given girls the chance to do the same.

The Brontës could have followed a similar path and, for a time, this was their intention. As well as Charlotte's forays into teaching, Emily spent six months as a teacher specialising in music at Miss Elizabeth Patchett's seminary[11] for around forty girls at Law Hill, Southowram near Halifax in 1838/9, where she slaved from 6 a.m. to 11 p.m., before she returned to Haworth and her secluded life. Anne and Charlotte both had short stints as governesses in 1839 (Mrs Ingram's Blake Hall Mirfield and Mrs Sidgwick's, Stone Gappe, Lothersdale respectively), returning to Haworth before venturing out as governesses again in 1841. It was around this time that the three sisters discussed the possibility of setting up their own school along the lines of that at Oakwell Hall. It would have been a good model: three educated sisters teaching genteel girls (and of course Charlotte knew the Cockills). They pondered over how they could fund the start-up – Aunt Branwell offered them £150 – and how they could convince good families to entrust their daughters to their teaching; in the meantime, Miss Wooler offered to sell her school to Charlotte, but she declined in October 1841.

With Anne quite established as a governess for Mrs Robinson at Thorp Green Hall, Little Ouseburn, it was Charlotte and Emily who left for Brussels in February 1842, using money again offered by Aunt Branwell. They were described by the owner, Mme Zoë Heger, as 'daughters of an English pastor, of moderate means, anxious to learn with an ulterior view of instructing others', and as a consequence, M. Constantin Heger agreed a specific fee with all expenses included.

Emily's stay was short, her and Charlotte's return in October 1842 necessitated by the news that their beloved Aunt Branwell was dying. Emily was not to return to Brussels, but Charlotte continued at the Pensionnat Heger as both teacher and student in early 1843, attending French classes and teaching English to other girls. However, it seems she was not really cut out for a career as a teacher. She 'was known to be very clever, but she had no sympathy with young people and no authority over them', and it seems this lack of authority was scorned by her pupils who deliberately played up in class.[12] But how else was a woman of her station and means to earn a living?

On 1 January 1844, Charlotte left Brussels for good. That she was bi-lingual and had a diploma did not go unnoticed and it seems (from a letter she wrote to M. Heger) she was soon offered a lucrative post (£100 a year) at a large boarding school in Manchester (though which this was is unknown). Citing a need to stay home and look after her father, she turned it down.

Aunt Branwell had left the majority of her estate to the three sisters, each receiving around £300, and they discussed setting up their own school at the Parsonage once again, with Charlotte drawing up a prospectus and terms. In August 1844, Charlotte had cards printed for their proposed school at Haworth: Terms were £35 a year full board, with tuition in writing, arithmetic, history, geography, grammar and needlework. Extras in French, German, Latin and drawing would be a guinea per quarter and laundry was an extra too. Not cheap by the standards of the day (Claire Harman writes). She wrote to various suitable local families, but Mrs Busfeild of Keighley was sending her daughters elsewhere; the Whites of Stone Gappe had already placed their daughter, but recommended her to Colonel Stott; his daughters were off to Oakwell Hall, 'which was rather successful'.[13]

Ultimately, their half-hearted attempt at establishing a school as a source of income was abandoned. In any case, Aunt Branwell's legacy of £300 each was ten times the annual salary of Anne's position as a governess and, as history records, they followed their hearts' desires and used that money for another purpose entirely.

Competition in the private girls' school market remained intense and perhaps they would have never been able to attract the daughters of wealthy clientele to the far-flung bleak village of Haworth when schools such as this existed nearer the highly populated West Riding conurbations:

> Stourton LODGE. – MRS BEEVERS, who is assisted by resident Foreign and English Governesses and talented masters, and who has for a series of years successfully directed the education of a limited number of young Ladies, has two or three VACANCIES. In addition to sound mental culture and religious training, her pupils have the opportunity for acquiring every polite accomplishment, and the salubrious situation, extensive premises, and unusually liberal treatment not only ensure their health, happiness, and improvement, but the support of their parents, from whom the highest testimonials may be had. Stourton Lodge is a mansion seated in beautiful and very extensive pleasure grounds, three miles from Leeds, on the Wakefield road: the house is large, airy, and commodious, the rooms spacious and well ventilated; the general appointments and internal arrangements (*admitting that most important one* of baths, warm and cold) are in every respect

superior. The whole under the immediate superintendence of the Principal, Mrs Beevers, is peculiarly adapted to the purposes of a superior school. Prospectuses forwarded on application. Four little Girls can be received as weekly Boarders. Stourton Lodge, June 8th, 1853
Leeds Intelligencer, Saturday, 2 July 1853

And having attended such a school gave a young lady an advantage when looking for a position:

A Young Lady of the highest and of superior Education seeks a re-engagement as GOVERNESS in a Private Family. Address, J.S., Mrs Beevers, Stourton Lodge, near Leeds.
Leeds Intelligencer, Saturday, 15 December 1860

A young Lady, who has received a very superior education, open to engagement as a GOVERNESS. Reference, Mrs Beevers, Stourton Lodge.
Leeds Intelligencer, Saturday, 31 January 1863

By 1866, there were forty-seven girls' schools, of various sizes, run by ladies in the Leeds district. With regard to elementary education, the number of National Schools had increased from the one in 1817 to nineteen, plus there were a further six British Schools, all teaching girls and boys. Forty girls were being educated, clothed and trained to habits of industry at Leeds Charity School, so as to fit them for work as household servants; some girls were training at the mechanics' institution schools, others were at Marshall's Factory Schools, where Miss Jane Southern taught them, and some at a Ragged School where Ann Laycock was mistress.

The education on offer for the poor was a somewhat hotchpotch of religious, industrial or Sunday schools. Even this was not an option for many working-class girls; they were often forced to contribute to the family wage or help with household chores and childcare, and could rarely take advantage of the unregulated education on offer. Things were to improve, but it would take time and a good deal of effort.

Chapter 2

Being a Governess

The idea of having of a governess to educate children in the homes of the aristocracy stretches back centuries, although there were many changes to the English governess's position in society over those centuries. The rather sad, lonely, poorly dressed governess typified by *Jane Eyre* bears little resemblance to the status of governesses in previous eras.

Back in the fourteenth century, one notable governess was Katherine Swynford (née de Roet) who served as a governess to the children of John of Gaunt, Duke of Lancaster, son of Edward III, after the death of his first wife, Blanche. At that time, it was typically daughters of earls and baronets who represented the social position of most governesses; Katherine had married into that aristocratic class and held the title of dame. Stories about her vary in their timings, nonetheless it is known that she (widowed) and John (who had hastily remarried after Blanche's death) had a long-running affair. They spent fifteen years estranged after the affair was publicly disapproved of but, in Lincoln Cathedral in 1396, Katherine eventually became the third wife of her employer, elevating her from dame to duchess and into the royal family. Perhaps it was history such as this that caused the Victorians to fear their governess might wish to rise in social standing by marriage into the family that employed her.

Another well-regarded governess was also a Katherine – (Kat) Ashley née Champernowne – again from a titled family, who began serving Princess Elizabeth Tudor in the sixteenth century when the princess was just 4 years old. She was already the third governess but remained with Elizabeth throughout her life, continuing as First Lady of the Bedchamber to Elizabeth after she became queen. Katherine stayed in this position until she died in 1565.

It was not until the late eighteenth/early nineteenth century that families other than the wealthy and titled started to seek governesses for their daughters. Although they were not looking for ladies from titled families to provide education and social instruction, they did still want their employees to be 'ladies'.

One regular contributor to *Quarterly Review*, Elizabeth Rigby, who a few months after this contribution became Lady Elizabeth Eastlake, pompously defined ladies and their position as governesses in December 1848:

The real definition of a governess, in the English sense, is a being who is our equal in birth, manners, and education, but our inferior in worldly wealth. Take a lady, in every meaning of the word, born, and bred, and let her father pass through the *Gazette* [probably meaning listed as bankrupt], and she wants nothing more to suit our highest *beau ideal* of a guide and instructress to our children. We need the imprudences, extravagances, mistakes, or crimes of a certain number of fathers to sow that seed from which we reap the harvest of governesses. There is no other class which so cruelly requires its members to be, in birth, mind, and manners, above their stations, in order to fit them for their station.

In the same article, this rather opinionated lady declared her certainty that the Brontës were most definitely men. It seems though that Charlotte may have read the article, since Mrs Pryor, Shirley's former governess in the eponymous novel published in 1849, relates the haughty observations made by one of her first charges, Miss Hardman: 'We need the imprudences, extravagances, mistakes, and crimes of a certain number of fathers to sow the seed from which we reap the harvest of governesses.' Almost word for word.

Although the term 'governess' originally simply implied one who was responsible for the well-being of children – usually those of a royal or noble household – and directing their education, by the nineteenth century 'governess' had come to represent a private teacher who educated pupils in a family's home. However, the term was also used by ladies who educated children in private schools. Women who taught in elementary schools were invariably referred to as schoolmistresses; elementary schools being designed for, and catering to, lower-class children.

The girls' schools listed in the *Leeds Directory* of 1817 all have a governess in charge and the 1851 census lists around 72,000 women involved in teaching, specifying 21,373 governesses, 41,888 schoolmistresses and 5,259 female general teachers.[1] According to data on Ancestry, most governesses were under 30 years old and around 5 per cent were either French or German. Being able to teach a language was an advantage (hence Charlotte Brontë's desire to be bi-lingual, and schools advertising that French could be taught, albeit at extra cost). It is difficult to track the rise and fall of the numbers registering governess as an occupation; census reports vary from decade to decade in the way they recorded such information. From the records available, it seems that by 1861 the number of women in teaching had risen to around 80,000, outnumbering men 2.5:1, although the distinction between teacher and governess was not recorded in the reports – most women seeking positions as governesses during the Victorian period took positions in private homes or schools without great preference. Both occupations had increased by 1871, with 94,239 women in teaching (38,774 schoolmistresses and 55,246 teachers and governesses). As education opportunities increased for children, so teaching opportunities increased for women; by 1881, there were around 124,000 women recorded as teachers, and by 1911 the number was over 183,000, with around 168,000 recorded as unmarried, 11,500 married and 3,600 widowed.

Although being a governess was a way for an unmarried woman to earn an income and have a nice roof over her head, it was not an easy job. Those seeking governesses had high expectations of the abilities of their erstwhile employees:

> GOVERNESS WANTED in a Gentleman's Family, as Superintendent of Children, a Person of good Morals, Temper, and Understanding. She must know something of Music and the French Language. She must be a Gentlewoman, and have no Objection to Confinement. Letters, Post-paid, with Reference to Persons of Credit for the Character, addressed for G.M. Esq. at the King's Head Inn, Glocester, will be attended to.
> *Gloucester Journal*, Monday, 25 May 1801

> WANTED in a few Weeks; a well-educated Governess, from 24 to 34 Years of Age, in a Tradesman's Family, of an amiable Disposition, to instruct four Females, all under eleven Years; she must be competent to teach English and French grammatically, Music, reading, Writing, and Arithmetic. Letters, Post-paid, addressed to F.F.S. Post Office, Burslem, Staffordshire, with respectable Reference to Qualifications from last Situation, and stating the expected Salary, will be duly answered.
> *Aris's Birmingham Gazette*, Monday, 22 May 1820

They also sometimes did not want to pay much. The tone of this advert would discourage any woman with salary expectations beyond their station:

> WANTED immediately, at an Establishment in the Country, respectable Young Person as Teacher. To prevent unnecessary trouble, high salary will not be given. Apply (if letter, post-paid) at Mr. Jones's, No. 25, Langton Street, Cathay, Bristol.
> *Bristol Mirror*, Saturday, 21 April 1827

Women seeking situations were proactive and specified not only their abilities but their requirements too:

> A Young Lady is desirous of engaging in the above Capacity, with a Family where the Children are young. She is fully competent to teach the English

and French Languages grammatically, also all Kinds of fancy-work. The greatest Attention will be paid to those committed to her Care, and the most respectable References given. Letters addressed to C.A.B. No. 50, New Street, will be duly attended to.

Aris's Birmingham Gazette, Monday, 1 December 1817

LADY of liberal education, highly respectable connections, and great experience in teaching and forming the minds and manners of Young Ladies, in private families of the first respectability, is desirous of an engagement in a family or select Establishment. She is fully competent to teach Music, Drawing, Geography, History, English Grammar, Writing, Arithmetic, &c., and the usual branches of an accomplished and solid English Education, with some knowledge of French. The most satisfactory testimonials would be given as to her religious principles, moral conduct, and acquirements. Address (post-paid) to E.W., Highfields-house, Hales Owen, near Birmingham.

Cambridge Chronicle and Journal, Friday, 22 August 1834

YOUNG LADY wishes to meet with a Situation as GOVERNESS in a respectable Family, or in a genteel Establishment, being competent to give Instruction in the usual Branches of Education, including Drawing, and French which she teaches grammatically, and speaks with Accuracy. The most unexceptionable References are given by her Friends, and by the Lady of the Seminary she is about to leave, where she resided upwards of two Years. Salary moderate, as it is not so much an Object as a comfortable Home. Address (Post-paid) A.Z., Post Office, Darlington.

Newcastle Chronicle, Saturday, 23 June 1832

It is interesting to note this particular young lady, starting out in her career as a governess, was more concerned about having a comfortable home than any salary she might receive. Furthermore, it must have been an enormous wrench for any woman leaving a family and home where she had been happy when her services were no longer required. Not only was there a loss of income but also that nice roof over her head.

A LADY, who has just terminated her engagement, wishes to enter into another, in a Gentleman's Family. She has been accustomed to Teach all the branches of a plain Education, with Drawing, Piano-Forte, Singing, French, and Italian. Apply at Mr Douglas, bookseller and stationer, High Street.

Inverness Courier, Wednesday, 19 July 1843

A column in the *Taunton Courier and Western Advertiser* on Christmas Day 1839 referred to an article in *The Athenaeum* which questioned 'the real position of the domestic instructor'.

The column raised the issue of poor remuneration, stating the demanded and expected acquirements of a governess could only be obtained by considerable pecuniary outlay and asked why, when such knowledge in 'one poor head' had to be mastered sufficiently to be able to teach, drawing, singing, instrumental music of one or more kinds, two if not three foreign languages, ornamental needlework, 'geography, and the use of the globes', etc. etc., did some employers think it only worth around £20–£25 a year. Certainly, there were plenty of women, willing to take such low pay, who professed these qualities, but 'to promise and to perform are not often precisely the same'. Was it generous, just or honest, to the instructress or the pupils, to 'repay such services at a standard below that of the lady's maids and the footmen of the family?'.

The column continued:

> The low social position of the governess is still further determined by the coldness and the neglect of her employers. True, it may be, that the presence of a stranger and a hireling, at the domestic fireside, must often be an unpleasant restraint; if this be so, it is still but small tax to pay for those who cannot or will not educate their children themselves. Parents have no right to bring a cultivated and a sensitive female under their roof to mortify and degrade her: if they want her services, they must not rob her of any part of her just reward; and of this, comfort and respect are as much a part, as the stipulated board and lodging. If the governess be indeed fitted for her task, she will have sense and discretion to avoid becoming an unnecessary restraint on the heads of the family; and her acquirements will add to the pleasures of the domestic circle, rather than detract from them.

In many ways, the 'hireling' fell between two stools, neither entirely belonging to the family upstairs nor the servants downstairs. Banished to the nursery and schoolroom and therefore deprived of intellectual association and conversation, it could be a lonely role and perhaps a shock for those cultivated and sensitive females who exchanged the society of friends and relations for the house of a stranger and a master.

The column urged that governesses should be treated with 'all the delicacy and respect which custom exacts between well-bred equals'; not as a subordinate but as an associate of the mother – and that the children must acknowledge her as such for the benefit of 'their future characters as rational beings'. The recommendation was that when selecting a governess, rather than making 'your choice without pausing to ask whether she is worthy to become your own [companion] and denying yourself the great advantage of "that domestic intimacy with your children's intimate, which can alone make you certain that she is truthful, charitable, forbearing – that there is nothing low, mean, or narrow-minded in her character or conceptions"', to pay well and choose someone who can be your companion as well as executing her governess duties.

The governess deserved better:

> It is clear that inferior as the greater number are to what an enlightened parent must desire, they are on the average better perhaps than average parents deserve; ... in their ranks are to be found numbers qualified to fulfil more than is expected from them ... and who by nature and education are raised above an insensibility to the unjust harshnesses and hardships to which they are exposed. Neither is it enough that an impolitic coldness and neglect shall be adopted in the bosom of the family; it must be paraded in the face of day, and blazoned before the company in the drawing room. The dog or the parrot receive a larger portion of notice than the unfortunate governess, brought in with the children for the purposes of display.

The governess agency

For both parties, it was crucial to fit the right governess to the right family. One enterprising York-born woman embraced the opportunity.

Annie Burrows née Creser, daughter of a painter, young widow of a confectioner, set up an agency on Micklegate, York, and styled herself 'The Ladies Agent for Schools and Governesses'. Her business claimed to be established in 1864 (when she was 15 ...) and she was the authoress of *A Guide for Governesses English and Foreign Nursery and Finishing*. Printed in York in December 1875 and priced at 6d, the forty-eight-page booklet was 'full of sound advice' (*Educational News*) and 'perfectly unique' (*The Continent and Swiss Times*). Annie notes her little guide was 'intended to help principally young ladies who have had no experience in tuition' but that even 'experienced governesses may gain some hints from it', citing the following letter as an example of some of their (lack of) application skills: *Having seeing an advertisement in todays paper, I beg to offer myself as governess for three young pupils. I have had experience in teaching for the last eight years.* It was only one of many similar instances that had occurred among the 5,463 governesses she had had correspondence with; if the guide only enabled a few governesses to see their letters as others see them, and, therefore, improve their applications, 'one of the aims of the writer will at least have been accomplished'.

The guide covered three types of governess: the Nursery Governess (pages 1–9), the Finishing Governess (pages 10–32) and the Foreign Governess (pages 33–43). Her general advice to the nursery governess was not to spend too much time at lessons:

> A good nursery governess, who has been brought up by Christian parents herself, and knows the value of self-control, will do more for the benefit of children entrusted to her during the time she is playing with them than by any lessons.

And to be cheerful and pleasant:

> By the force of her example she will promote cheerfulness and prevent quarrelling. If any dispute arises, she will settle it quietly but firmly, and very quickly turn the children's attention to something else to prevent any recurrence to the forbidden subject.

She also had to know how to wash and dry a child properly:

> There is a real art in drying a child, although if she reflects upon the feeling caused by half drying her own hands, especially in damp or frosty weather, she will understand the feelings of a child who is indebted to her for a dry or moist skin, according to the result of her operations. It is very probable that chilblains, chapped hands, and even worse evils are contracted in that way, not through wilful neglect, but by careless ignorance. A governess who uses one towel to dry three or four children, will find the last child complaining, not unjustly, that it is wet. Mothers ought to see to this, and provide a plentiful supply of towels. Each child should be dried first with an ordinary towel, and afterwards with a soft fleecy towel, that will be sure to absorb all remaining moisture.

Good advice indeed.

A sense of the type of woman embarking on a career as a finishing governess may be gleaned from the following extract:

> FINISHING governesses are generally the daughters of clergymen or professional men who have not left enough money to provide for their daughters those home comforts they have, during their lifetime, so liberally bestowed. Sometimes they are daughters of gentlemen of fortune, whose

reduced circumstances bring them down to the governesses' mart, after having entered society on an equal footing with those they have to offer their talents to for bread. Sometimes they are driven from home by harsh stepmothers; very, very rarely are they governesses through choice, although nearly all profess to like teaching.

It is interesting to note Annie thought women were not governesses by choice but by reduced circumstance through (generally) the fault of men! She and her sister had been governesses, probably in the first instance because their father could not afford to support them. Later, when she was widowed early, she returned to governessing as a career, though in a different capacity (perhaps her own experience turned her away from actually being a governess). It seems she never remarried; she was financially independent through her own exertions.

Governess numbers increase

The 1851 census had revealed there were around ½ a million more women than men and there were 2.5 million unmarried women. Clearly, with insufficient available men to provide for them, women would have to find occupations outside the expected position of wife and mother. For an upper- or middle-class woman to earn a living, while maintaining her status as a genteel lady, being a governess in a 'good' home was the best option. Of course, with a surge in numbers following this example, supply outstripped demand and some families paid their governesses low wages and overworked them. With many governesses seeking employment out of financial necessity, rather than a desire to teach – around only 6–7 per cent of all middle-class women teachers had consciously chosen teaching as a career – both parties started to question the quality of education the governesses had received and were able to pass on.

With the UK experiencing economic growth and a sustained rise in income per head, the job market started to improve; more families began to hire governesses to teach their children – especially daughters, and especially in demeanour and manners – as served their new, wealthier positions in society. Industrialists and merchants, shopkeepers, military officers, and even farmers found the funds to afford governesses.[2] A family's desire to have daughters educated represented a clear indication by the family to prepare them for a future where financial security through successful marriages could not be guaranteed. To ensure the income they were dedicating to educating their daughters was well spent, families began hiring only trained governesses and, in order to improve their employment outlook, governesses looked to newly founded institutions to help bridge the gaps in their education.

Annie Burrows had sound advice on planning a good and lucrative career as a governess:

> The proper training for a finishing governess, is for her to be educated at a good school in the south of England, remaining there a year or two as governess pupil, and from there, going (if possible as pupil, but if not, as governess pupil) to Paris for a year to acquire fluency in speaking French; from France she should proceed to Hanover for a year, to perfect herself in German and music. On her return, she will be able to command an immediate engagement, even if only 20 years of age, of from 40 to 50 guineas per annum; supposing she holds that a year or two, she will obtain 60 in her next engagement, and 70 or 80 in her third situation, until she reaches the highest amounts given, from 120 guineas to 150. Is there any hardship in such a life? None at all, if the mind is well trained. A young lady so educated, and properly fitted for the duties of her profession, will find teaching a pleasure, and, because she has never entered society as a young lady of fortune, will never repine at her lot. She will be as independent as any professional man; and the true rights of women will be vindicated in her ability to provide for herself by a womanly occupation. The hardness of a governess's life consists in not being properly trained for it. A gentleman would find it equally hard if he were suddenly to have to descend from independent means, to teach what he had quite forgotten, or, perhaps, never really acquired. If parents, who know perfectly well that they cannot leave their daughters independent fortunes, were to look the matter boldly in the face, and resolve upon training them for teachers, they would do far more good than by giving them a smattering of French and music, with a slight introduction into society, a few fine dresses to attract partners that weigh the tinsel and turn away.

There is a sense in her guide that she was very much a campaigner for women's independence, negating the need to find a (rather scarce) suitable man to support you. Education was the key, but secondary education for girls had yet to make its mark:

> Educated women are as well paid as men, nay, very often better. Cambridge and Oxford men are engaged as tutors from 60, 80, to 100 guineas, after all the money that has been spent over their education; whilst as curates they earn at the most £150 per annum, non-resident; which is scarcely equal to a resident governess's £100 a year. Besides, the habits of extravagance acquired at the universities, renders men far more helpless in money matters than women ...
>
> There is an absurd idea that educated men are better paid, and better treated in every way than women, and that, if a woman can only attract a

lord of the creation, and so obtain a partner for life, she is better off than in any honourable calling she can pursue for herself; but in point of fact, out of ten young men in a town, perhaps not more than one is able and willing to maintain a wife. One may be a clerk in a bank, at a hundred a year; another in the civil service at a similar salary; a third, very delicate, and not able to work; a fourth, very wild and not willing to work; a fifth, has a mother and sisters to help; a sixth, struggling as a surgeon's assistant; a seventh, tried three or four professions and cannot succeed in any; an eighth, emigrated; a ninth, never could be taught any profession, is not quite *compos mentus*, poor thing! whilst the tenth, the solitary 'rising young man', generally a lawyer or a merchant, is so besieged with invitations, here, there, and everywhere, by hopeful mothers, that he either marries very quickly or becomes a woman hater. Men have been so often told that they are in the minority and becoming more and more valuable yearly, that they have become intolerably conceited, and regardless of the chivalry they once displayed towards the fair sex. The best cure for this state of things surely will be for ladies to be more content with their own sphere, and only strive to rise in it, instead of casting longing looks at careers they are not fitted for either by nature or training.

She had some foresight too:

Education is rising in value and in estimation. The Cambridge and Oxford examinations have greatly contributed to this result, and the day may come when women, properly trained, fulfilling their mission properly, may be held in the same estimation as successful professional men. The present real hardship seems to be that there are so many failures, that the successful women are scarcely believed in, and in social status do not hold their right position. Time, however, will rectify this, and other mistakes, as failures become rarer, and success more apparent. At present the Cambridge certificated governesses are much preferred, but have two drawbacks: youth and inexperience. Mothers who go much into society require experienced governesses of from 25 to 35, whereas the majority of the young ladies who have passed are under 21; but in a few years these drawbacks will disappear, and then they will take the first places, like the diplôméed foreign governesses: therefore, in all cases where a young lady is being trained for a finishing governess, it is desirable for her to be placed at a school where she will have the opportunity of passing her examination as early as possible; for it may be that the examiners who commenced with a poor opinion of the mental capacities of women, may pass to the other extreme, and make the questions as difficult to answer as they were at first easy.

With education so important to getting a good position in an increasingly competitive market, the guide lists twenty boarding schools 'selected as especially desirable for Young Ladies training for Governesses. All the English ones prepare Pupils for Cambridge or Oxford Examinations. All the Foreign ones have been tested by Pupils placed by the Ladies' Agent.'

Much of the rest of the guide revolves around how to apply for positions and how to dress for interviews ('don't wear a hat, wear a neat and becoming bonnet') and how to behave once appointed ('if a governess is paid marked attention by any gentleman in the evening, she will do well to courteously avoid it.'). Of course, being a 'ladies' agent', enterprising Annie advised of all the pitfalls of advertising or responding to advertisement – best to let someone else find you the right situation:

> There only remains one way of obtaining an engagement, and that is through an agent; and if care is taken in the selection, an agent will be better able to place a governess than any other person. She will, or ought to, be able to tell at once what salary a young lady should ask, what class of family she ought to try to enter, what sympathy there will be between the religious opinions of the governess and her pupils; and if her connection does not afford her a suitable opening at once, if she advertises for her, she ought to be able to acquire the information respecting the families who reply, that will enable her to feel confidence in placing a young lady in their home circle.

A young woman should know her worth too:

> Some people are fond of offering low salaries; but few meet with the rebuff a young high-spirited girl gave a clergyman's wife, who wrote to her offering her £25 per annum to teach five children of all ages, have two of them in her room at night, and speak French with a pure accent to them constantly. The reply sent by the Governess was headed: 'A labourer is worthy of his hire' ... and concluded: 'The engagement will not suit me.'

And, despite the advice to not respond to the attention of men, a governess was not denied the choice of 'making a match' simply by being a governess, if marriage was still her ultimate desire. In fact, her career was to her advantage:

> As a rule, governesses make excellent wives; they don't marry with the romantic ideas of love and bliss that girls who have never left home do. They have had opportunities of seeing in other families how much is required from a wife and a mother, and as 'lookers on' see most of the game, they profit by experience, and learn to avoid many rocks and shoals they might have

foundered on, if they had not had those opportunities of observation; besides, they learn more extended views of life, and after a few years of teaching, are better fitted to take the care and responsibilities of a household upon them. The rising young man an ignorant girl with £200 fortune could not have attracted, has had time to rise, whilst the girl has been learning and teaching; and the marriage will be all the happier for the maturity of mind and fortune attained. Therefore a governess, whilst she should by no means enter the profession as some do, with the idea of entering higher society than she would meet with at home, and making a good match, need not alarm herself with the idea of her being a governess preventing her making one in her own sphere.

Finally, Annie lists fifteen 'illustrative cases' of success – 'Numerous other cases could be added if space would allow' – including governesses who had progressed in their careers financially, some who had established colleges of their own, and those who had settled for a good marriage.

Becoming a professional governess

By using the term 'profession' to describe their work, women aspired to the prestige, those ideals of autonomy and independence, and the intellectual clout attributed to the 'learned professions'. The importance of training, examination and certification in their occupations complemented the new ideal of employment. As opportunities and the number of governesses increased, so did the methods to obtain needed knowledge and qualifications to get the best jobs. As well as the smaller, private schools, run by enterprising, educated women, larger, more dedicated colleges were created specifically for the purpose of training governesses.

One of the first serious ventures to make being a governess a profession was the boarding school, St Mary's Hall, founded in Brighton in 1836 by Reverend Henry Elliott. Built to accommodate up to 100 young women who would train for a career as a governess (rather than the job being a last resort for impoverished girls) it remained a girls' school (one of the oldest in the country) until 2009 (see Chapter 1).

The Governesses' Benevolent Institution and Queen's College

Despite their attempts at betterment, many governesses were so poorly paid it often led to financial difficulties, either through losing positions, being ill, or when retiring. This continued for decades.

The Governesses' Mutual Assurance Society, formed in 1829 to help alleviate the hardship suffered by governesses, especially in illness and old age, planned to make grants in cases of illness and assist governesses to purchase annuities from funds subscribed to by the general public. Unfortunately, it did not prosper and ended in 1838. A public meeting, in May 1841, proposed a two-fold institution comprising the Governesses' Benevolent Institution and the Governesses' Provident Fund, but this also failed. It was the third attempt, in 1843, by Reverend Frederick Denison Maurice, Christian socialist and professor of English at King's College in London, which resulted in the foundation of the Governesses' Benevolent Institution, after an appeal was raised by those who realised there was little financial support for governesses during times of unemployment, old age and sickness. It initially focused on providing needy governesses with financial relief – a ladies' committee administering payments almost immediately. A provident fund was established soon after, with governesses encouraged to buy annuities that they could draw in retirement. Funds were invested by the institution and annuities were subsequently allocated to successful applicants, the first in 1844.

A home for unemployed governesses was established in Harley Street in 1845, later moving to Cavendish Street in 1927. It closed in 1930. An asylum for aged governesses was opened in 1849 at Prince of Wales Road, Kentish Town.

A report in the *Morning Herald (London)* on Saturday, 8 November 1851 noted that out of a total of 118 applicants just 4 additional annuitants had been elected to receive £20 a year. The four were reported in the advertising columns: Miss Crew, with 11,065 votes; Miss Coates, 10,733 votes; Mrs Mechelin, 9,915 votes; and Miss Whitfield, 9,890 votes. It appears to have been a means-tested benefit, but the board of management agreed a reduction from £50 to £30 a year income being a level at which a lady was disqualified from being a candidate for an annuity. Applicants for annuities had to be over 50 years old and elections were held in May and November every year, subscribers casting their votes. The chairman congratulated these subscribers on the steps taken to benefit the 'important class of persons who were the peculiar objects of their generous care'. Large as the funds appeared, they were still insufficient to meet the demands being made and increased efforts in support of the institution would be put forth. There were forty-four annuitants registered in 1850 and eighteen inmates of the asylum. By 1861, those numbers had risen to 102 and 22. In total, with other help to governesses, in a ten-year period, 1852–62, around 4,700 applicants had been assisted in times of temporary difficulty; over 2,000 unemployed teachers had been received into the house in Harley St and over 9,000 had been provided with engagements without charge.

Alongside the financial support, unemployment was addressed with the establishment of an employment registry where governesses could enter their details, for free, in a series of books divided into columns representing skills or qualifications. Each governess had to have two satisfactory references. Families seeking governesses had a similar book in which to enter their requirements; this exchange of contact information helped both parties find what they were looking for.

Fifty years after its founding, the Governesses Benevolent Institution still provided the service of the free employment registry.

While it was F.D. Maurice who carried out the establishment of the institution, it was Mary Atkinson Maurice, his sister, who piqued his interest and persuaded him of the benefits of training women to be governesses or teachers. Mary had founded a school in Southampton in the 1820s, helped by her sister Priscilla. She continued her educational work after moving to Reading, this time assisted by another sister, Esther, for ten years, until Esther's marriage in 1844. At this point, Mary moved to London and became an active participant in the Governesses' Benevolent Institution. In 1847, she published a guide, *Mothers and Governesses*, in which she covered topics such as home education, governess history, treatment of governesses, general education, the difficulties experienced by governesses and remedial plans – not only to assist aged governesses 'past the power of labour' but also 'to have a right system of education brought within the reach of those, who undertake to educate others'. Mary cited the Prussian government's approach 'with every individual of empire under its eye':

> no portion of the empire is left without its due provision. No one can enter on the office of a teacher, without first obtaining a testimonial to his, or her, having gone well through a regular course of instruction; and until furnished with such a document, is not only unqualified to act, but is subject to a severe punishment for attempting it. This is in effect depriving him of the permission to teach at all, for a given number of years. The course of education in the schools is laid down, on a regular system, and the pupils must successively go through each class, and undergo strict examinations, in order that they may be thoroughly grounded in what they learn. This applies equally to all ranks of Prussian subjects, so that private governesses are under the same restrictions as those more publicly employed in schools.

No such system really existed in England, particularly where girls were concerned:

> Now, is it not, because there is no regular authorized plan for the education of teachers that so many who are unqualified, presume to enter on the office. Girls generally have no opportunity of obtaining really sound instruction, though some by the exertion of their own energies, and from a real desire of improvement, make the most of their advantages, and determine to master whatever they undertake; but in many of these cases the health has been sacrificed to the high principle and zeal, which enabled them to form the resolution. How then can these evils be remedied, for this is a question of great moment? The only efficient method seems to be that of establishing

regular training schools, under ecclesiastical superintendence, for the middling classes of society.

Each pupil must be bound to remain, for a stipulated number of years, during which time she must pass through a proper course of instruction, under the most competent teachers who can be selected.

She advocated strict quarterly examinations 'in every branch of study', that daily pupils as well as boarders should be admitted, and that a way to include eligible students whose friends could not pay the stipend should be sought:

Education should always be represented to them, as an honourable and dignified calling, next only to the sacred ministry of the Gospel. When such a system is thoroughly carried out, the condition of governesses will be altered – they cannot then any longer be looked down upon, for their education will place them in an advantageous position, and their help will be eagerly sought for.

Mary set out her plans for giving would-be governesses a good education, acknowledging it would not be an easy task but that among its many benefits:

These might be the means of raising the tone of education generally, and of leading to the formation of schools for girls, similar to the proprietary schools for boys, which are now become so universal. Let us then not be daunted, but rather stimulated by the apparent obstacles, which present themselves to carrying out that which would be really a national benefit. What good work at the onset did not meet with opposition and ridicule? It would be strange indeed, were it otherwise. But let us be convinced that it ought to be done, that there are means for doing it, and that it wants only energy and determination, to set heartily to the work, and we shall soon see female education in England, become the model for that of all other nations.

A year after publication, and with the enthusiasm shown for 'systematic education and certification', the Governesses' Benevolent Institution was expanded to include a college. Queen's College at 67 Harley Street, London opened on 1 May 1848, expressly for the improvement of governesses' education. It was the first public institution for the higher education of girls; its stated aim was to provide governesses with increased educational experiences and qualifications and remove those who were unqualified from the ranks seeking employment. By the time it received a royal charter in 1853, there were 200 women being taught by professors from King's College in a series of 'Lectures for Ladies', at the end of which the students gained a diploma. Older women, known as 'lady visitors', were in attendance as chaperones while the young ladies were in the presence of male lecturers. One of these lady visitors was Henrietta, Baroness Stanley of Alderley, whose campaigning work for women's education had many strands (see later).

The curriculum at Queen's College was tailored for governesses. A variety of subjects was taught, including mathematics and science, and this had expanded by 1872 to offer classes, through inter-collegiate lectures, in rigid dynamics, differential equations, optics, thermo-dynamics, astronomy, and dynamics of a particle, should governesses wish to attend.[3]

The Governesses' Benevolent Institution was well supported by donations from respected members of society and these helped fund free night classes (in addition to the general curriculum), for governesses only, through Queen's College. Almost 35,000 pupils attended these classes in a nine-year period between 1856 and 1865 and subjects included arithmetic, mathematics, geography, Latin, history, theology, and mental and moral philosophy. They were well attended and much valued; some classes had as many as seventy students.[4] The college's work brought nationwide attention to the work of middle-class women, although the board of governors denied it was bent on creating a distinct occupational group of governesses and schoolmistresses and opened its doors to girls aged 9–12, with a moderate fee for daytime attendance.

Governesses' self-improvement

This movement for betterment of governesses' education saw governesses being proactive in seeking out courses of self-improvement. The British and Foreign School Society's (B and FSS) Borough Road College, one of the first teacher-training colleges, founded in 1809 in Southwark by Joseph Lancaster for the education of male teachers in the 'monitorial system' had started admitting girls from 1814 to train in the monitorial system under Ann Springman, later Mrs McRae, who, apart from a period of ten years after her marriage in 1843, ruled 'the female department of the training school' until 1861). Between 1830 and 1850, as many as 13 per cent of applicants to the college were already private governesses and boarding schoolmistresses who recognised additional training and education would help them perform their current duties to a higher standard.

Liverpool had a Governesses' Institution at 31 Rodney St and delivered a series of Tuesday evening lectures. Its free inaugural lecture took place on 21 May 1850 and included geography and English grammar, followed by two lectures on mental philosophy.[5]

Governesses also obtained knowledge and qualifications through journals and magazines, sharing ideas and articles on classroom management, new lessons and lesson planning. In one particular magazine, *Work and Leisure: A Magazine Devoted to the Interests of Women*, one governess suggested a society for private governesses, an association of cooperation, asking:

> Why does it not strike us that there is a power in deeds which is not in groans? Why don't we set to work to help our own class, instead of whining over the unkindness of Fate? Is it really true that work deteriorates woman? If not, why can't – or rather, why don't – we do what males of all sorts are ready to do – what workless females, too, are ready enough for – why don't we co-operate?[6]

Although there were several 'governesses' institutions' in existence in different regions, the intent of this one was very much about sharing ideas and networking – a good idea in what was essentially a lonely job. Governesses and students were to write essays each term that dealt with issues related to teaching; these essays would be submitted to the society's secretary then circulated to other members for discussion. Membership was by subscription and as long as governesses paid their dues, they benefited from the society – wherever they might live.

Fulfilled expectations and the pioneers of girls' education

With Mary Atkinson Maurice's vision for women's education fulfilled, students from Queen's were able to expand their career options beyond that of governess. Among its earliest students were several who did not take up teaching. These include two poets, Adelaide Anne Procter and Jean Ingelow, and Sophia Jex-Blake who, with six others, campaigned for women to have access to university education and for them to be licensed to practice medicine. Two women who devoted their entire lives to girls' education were also formally educated at Queen's. Frances Mary Buss attended evening classes after her day's work teaching in her own small school (opened with her mother in 1845 when she was 18, at 14 Clarence Rd, Kentish Town, London) six nights a week in the first term (reducing to four after that) gaining college certificates in French, German and geography.[7] As a child, Frances had attended a mixed school until she was 10, then a 'higher' school, run by Miss Wyand, up to the age of 14, when she became a teacher at that school. She was too young and inexperienced to make much impression on her pupils; indeed, they took pleasure in making her cry. Instead, she took a 'select number of young ladies' at her home, to teach them 'the usual accomplishments with the essential points of a liberal education', but she was painfully aware of her own educational deficiencies. Leaving Queen's aged 23, she said its liberal atmosphere and learned instructors had opened a new life to her. With ambitious courage, she embarked on an independent venture and opened the North London Collegiate School for Ladies at the family home, by then in Camden Street, on 4 April 1850. The term 'collegiate' was used to distinguish the new style of girls' education from that of home-based governesses. Thirty-five girls assembled on its first day, daughters of retired gentlemen, doctors., artists, clerks and 'respectable' tradesmen.[8]

Dorothea Beale, four years Frances's junior, attended Queen's at the same time, but on a full-time basis and their paths did not cross until later. She had attended a boarding school until 13, and after removal from this school by her parents, her education was 'under the direction of myself', through access to libraries and home study and by attending lectures at Gresham College and Crosby Hall Literary Institution. At 16, Dorothea and her elder sisters were sent to a fashionable finishing school in Paris where she felt oppressed by the routine of learning by rote without the 'trouble of thinking'. Intellectually, the system was 'of a nature to induce atrophy of the thinking powers'. Fortunately, she did not have to endure it for long, as revolution in Paris forced the Beale sisters back to England. As with Frances Buss, Queen's College opened a new life for Dorothea. She was awarded certificates in mathematics, English, Latin, French, German and geography.[9] Her examiner in the 'Principles and Method of Teaching' said, 'she is likely to become an accomplished teacher,' and she was considered sufficiently accomplished to be offered a post on the staff, the first to be filled by a woman. She remained seven years, first as a mathematics tutor then Latin, and eventually head teacher at the school attached to the college. Her resignation in 1856 was due to her growing consternation about the lowering of entrance standards, meaning girls without the necessary educational grounding were being admitted. She feared it would lower the college's prestige. She was also not pleased that the already limited powers of women tutors (after a new principal had succeeded Reverend Maurice) were further being curtailed. Having brooded on her concerns, perhaps it was with some haste she had already accepted the position of headmistress at the Clergy Daughters' School at Casterton. Contrary to what Reverend Elliott (St Mary Hall) had thought about Casterton, despite its improvements after moving from Cowan Bridge, it was still a 'grim, unlovely place'. Perhaps things had deteriorated in the intervening twenty-year period; Dorothea found it not only ugly but rigid, narrow and full of petty restrictions, emphasised by a hideous uniform. A far cry from the liberal atmosphere of Queen's. Her pleas for reform were brushed aside by a committee of six clergymen. At her request, she had an interview with them where she told them that, 'an institution in which the government is entirely by punishments is not likely to produce the best moral effects.' Good behaviour and good work should be rewarded, not by prizes, but by 'distinctions, privileges, and the opportunity of doing good'. She implied she would resign if they did not make certain alterations. In December 1857, less than a year after taking the post, she received a letter from the chairman telling her the committee thought it best if her connection with the school ceased after Christmas and paying her a quarter's salary in advance. Shocked, she left, but not long afterwards heard that a number of her suggested liberalising proposals were being implemented.

Now unemployed, Dorothea sought a new position. She had heard there might be a vacancy at Cheltenham Ladies' College, but while she was waiting to hear, applied for several other posts and secured some part-time teaching at a school in Barnes. She had quite a wait. Eventually, she was summoned to Cheltenham for an interview on 14 June 1858. There had been fifty applications, but only a few candidates were even suitable for interview. Persuaded by her sisters to wear something other than her usual black or mouse-coloured gowns, she presented herself in a borrowed blue silk dress. Two days after the interview, she received notice she had been selected as the new Lady Principal.[10]

Of course, there were many young women wanting to prepare to become professional governesses and not all could go to London to do so. Individuals continued founding schools for governesses; one such woman was Mary Eliza Porter, later to become one of the great campaigners for secondary education for girls and one of the nine founders (including Frances Buss and Dorothea Beale) of the Association of Headmistresses in 1874 (see Chapter 9).

Having been a student at Queen's College in its early days, in the late 1850s Mary Porter, in her early twenties, took over a school founded by Miss Eloisa Heathcoat at Bolham near Tiverton, Devon, with the aim of educating her pupils (aged 16 to 20) to become governesses. Eloisa was the daughter of John Heathcoat, a renowned pioneer of industrial lacemaking (the business still exists; it made the fabric for a parachute for NASA's Perseverance rover landing on Mars in 2021!), who established an elementary school in Tiverton in 1843. In 1861, aged 25, Mary is listed as 'Head of Household' a teacher of English and Drawing. Also teaching with her are: 40-year-old German Emelia L. Sulser, teacher of German and music; Eliza Vicary, music teacher; Louisa Caldwell, 22, English teacher; and French girl Julienne Soulard, 18, teaching French. There were thirty-six scholars boarding, mostly daughters of professional men from various parts of the country, including Ireland, perhaps whose entrepreneurship had not been successful. On top of the academic subjects, they studied the art of teaching, which made Mary Porter's school somewhat unique. Some of her students already worked as governesses but signed up for classes in order to improve their skills and, by earning certificates for classes and lectures they attended, enhance their potential earning power. Mary's work in educating girls continued (see later).

Further improvements to the financial lot of the governess

Manchester's governesses' institution and home was established in 1864 at 90, Bloomsbury, Oxford Road. It provided accommodation for governesses who had been disengaged over holiday periods and had neither homes nor friends locally with whom they could stay. Other daily governesses made use of the home as a convenience for lunch, having morning and afternoon engagements at opposite ends of the city. The institution, like the one in London, had a system of free registration linking governesses with potential employers. At the first annual meeting in 1865, it was reported there were 135 governesses listed, of whom 46 had found situations through the institution. In addition, governesses – who paid for membership of the institution – had the advantages of protection, comfort, and companionship. Campaigner Josephine Butler, writing on governesses in *The Education and Employment of Women* in 1868, noted that both this institution and the one in London refused to register governesses who would accept salaries below £25 a year; that there must have been many such women can be demonstrated by the 500 applicants for a nursery governess position offering £20 a year and 300 for a position with no salary at all, save a home and roof over her head. Although work as a governess was the highest-paid position available to the working woman, a six-month register from the Manchester Institution in 1868 shows the following:

54 governesses who asked for £30 and under, per annum.
20   "   "   "   £40   "   "
19   "   "   "   £50   "   "
17   "   "   "   £60   "   "
10   "   "   "   £70 and upwards.

This was only an indication of expectations. In reality, nine out of ten earned under £50 a year (even though governesses registered at the Manchester Institution were 'the favourable specimens of the class' they were 'still glad to get a home on almost any terms'); above that amount was a prized salary, one in a family that probably required 'serious outlay on dress and personal expenditure' – governesses were always expected to dress as ladies.

Still, with many governesses finding gainful employment, the institution was meeting its aims and its success was attributed to the efforts of Miss Strongitharm and the ladies who had undertaken the management. Sophia Strongitharm was a farmer's daughter, born in Staffordshire in 1819 and was working as a governess in a small private girls' school in Marylebone in 1851. By 1861, she was a governesses' agent in Chorlton-on-Medlock, Manchester and in 1871, 'Lady Superintendent, Unemployed'. At some point, she found similar employment in London; a New Year's appeal in 1877 asked the benevolent to assist in supporting the Home for Governesses and Gentlewomen of Limited Means, Sunderlands, 25, Alexander St, Westhourne Park, London, through its Lady Superintendent, Miss Sophia Strongitharm.[11] It seems her campaigning for women's employment knew no bounds. In 1883, she wrote to various newspapers stating how difficult it was for women to find work in the over-populated UK and recommending they emigrate to the colonies. She was now female emigration agent for New Zealand and able to obtain free superior passage for suitable candidates, plus she was secretary to the Female Middle-Class Emigration Society, founded in 1861/2 by Miss Rye to promote the emigration of educated women. By the summer of 1885, Sophia had emigrated to Montreal, Canada, a 'near and accessible colony' and wrote to the *Manchester Courier*, saying there were too many teachers in the world, especially in the British Isles and that great opportunities existed in Canada and she would help find employments for 'England's surplus population' of women.

In a great example of economic migration, many governesses were reported as earning better salaries in the colonies. A newspaper article as early as February 1863 details that 400 governesses had arrived in Australia (140 sent by Miss Rye) and were being placed with families and paid 60–100+ guineas a year. Even better, an inexpensive plain dress and straw hat were perfectly acceptable attire.

Sadly, Sophia Strongitharm's work in Canada came to an early end. At the age of 67, she died 'at sea' aboard the *Lake Huron*, returning to Liverpool, on 30 August 1886.[12] The cause of death is given as 'senile decay accelerated by congestion of lungs', a sad end for such a dedicated campaigner for women's employment.

Women like Sophia, as is customary, had seen what needed to be done and got on with doing it. It is interesting to note that many of the poor governesses at the end of their working lives had little financial security after their years of toil when they asked the Governesses' Benevolent Institution for support. Their distresses were not the consequence of recklessness or self-indulgence, rather the result of kindness and self-sacrifice. One who had worked hard for twenty-six years had maintained a mother, three sisters, and a brother; another had devoted all her earnings to the education of five nieces; a third had supported her parents for twenty years; and a fourth had managed to save a little money, lent it to her brother – who then failed in his business. One forlorn statement after another by those who came 'cap in hand' to the institution.

One letter from a schoolmaster in the *Torquay Times, and South Devon Advertiser* on Friday, 9 September 1881 summed up the position of the private governess:

Why it is that an accomplished lady can command no higher remuneration than a peasant girl appears to be a social enigma. The one has received a long and expensive education; she is of ladylike presence and manners; she offers to impart to her pupils all the advantages of good breeding and culture which she herself possesses, and which society values highly. The other is … [not] … the domestic servant is frequently an object of envy to the poor governess. The servant who acknowledges her position of dependence is not only better paid, but is more comfortably and independently placed. The governess though professedly on a social equality with her employers, is poorly remunerated, and, moreover, is made to feel her state of dependency at every turn. How are we to reconcile this apparently anomalous condition of things, where society recognises the greater excellence and dignity of the mind as compared with the body and yet reward bodily far higher than mental arts? ... A French cook of any pretention to skill will cost some hundred pounds a year, but an excellent governess may be got for £30. Education is very well in its way, but who will compare it to good living?

Still, despite the difficulties experienced and the constraints imposed on women in the nineteenth century, it is clear that governesses worked hard to prove their profession was a valuable one – whether they were working privately in families or governesses in classrooms. By improving their own knowledge and teaching abilities they not only helped highlight teaching as a valuable and respectable career for a woman but also paved the way for following generations of women to further advance female education.

Chapter 3

Becoming a Schoolmistress

A little book, *The Schoolmistress; or, Instructive and Entertaining Conversations Between a Teacher and her Scholars*, published in 1824 in Dublin had this to say about the duties of a schoolmistress. It is interesting that she refers to the children using feminine pronouns:

> The Mistress of this School is expected to consider seriously and conscientiously what a responsible duty rests with her, as the teacher of a number of young children, whose future prospects in life depend on the instructions which they receive under her care. She should remember that now is the time to form good principles and useful habits, and to correct any bad ones they may have learned – that the parents rely on her to do all in her power to improve every child who comes to her to learn, and that therefore, if she do not make this her study, she actually defrauds those who employ her, of their children's time and services, for they might, probably, be much better occupied at home than idling in a schoolroom. The duties of her station are, first of all, to teach these children to love and fear that Divine Being who is the giver of all that we possess, and to whom we are accountable for all our thoughts, words, and actions, and that, to please Him, we must speak the truth, be strictly honest, and in every respect be virtuous in all our dealings. To needle-work she must be particularly attentive, for on her instructions (of course assisted by their own exertions) may depend, whether many a poor, friendless girl shall or shall not have the means of honestly supporting herself, and, if she becomes a mother, whether her children are to be in dirty rags or decent clothes, or brought up in idle or industrious habits.
>
> It may perhaps be the case, that some of the children who come to this school may be of a very early age, and the mistress may say to herself, 'that child is only six or eight years old, she has time enough to learn', but of this no one can ever be so certain as to make it a good excuse for delaying her education. Perhaps though her parents send her now to school, they may not be able to do so at a future time; or she might fall into bad health, and not be able to come; or her parents might remove to another place, out of the

neighbourhood, and then perhaps, when it was too late, the teacher might be sorry she did not teach her more while she had her. Let there be no idling, no neglect, no putting off of business in the school. There is one good and simple rule to abide by. In the morning think what is to be done: in the evening, think what ought to be done.

These were brief but comprehensive principles by which any elementary schoolmistress might abide, and there was to be ample opportunity to put them into practice.

Government money for education

After the 1833 Factory Act was passed, the government allocated £20,000 in grants for the two main (voluntary) elementary education bodies, i.e. the National School Society and the British and Foreign School Society, 'to be issued in aid of private subscriptions for the erection of schools for the education of the children of the poorer classes in Great Britain'. No application was to be entertained 'unless a sum be raised by private contribution equal at least to one-half of the total estimated expenditure ... and there is a reasonable expectation that the school may be permanently supported'. In addition, no public money was provided by the government until the amount of private subscription had been 'received, expended, and accounted for'. Nonetheless, a major school-building programme commenced. Clearly, the voluntary sector saw a need for educating children.

But with funding came audits, inspections and increasing demands from the new Committee of Council on Education, created in 1839 to oversee the distribution of funding, and the monitorial system came under intense scrutiny. More schools meant more teachers were required, but inspections found the skills of these new teachers were sometimes lacking.

In the committee's meeting of 25 August 1846, it was reported that many of the schoolchildren acting as assistants to the schoolmasters under the monitorial system were being withdrawn by their families at an early age in order to take up manual occupations. These children were from working-class families and needed to contribute to the household and it was suggested such scholars who could be 'distinguished by proficiency and good conduct' might be 'apprenticed to skilful masters, to be instructed and trained, so as to be prepared to complete their education as schoolmasters in a normal school'.

By December 1846, a formal government pupil training scheme had been proposed and comprehensive regulations for the Apprenticeship of Pupil Teachers and Stipendiary Monitors drawn up.[1]

Schools could select one or more of their most proficient scholars to be apprenticed to the headmaster or headmistress, but the application would only be approved if 'the master or mistress of the school is competent to conduct the apprentice through the course of instruction to be required' and the school was well furnished, well supplied with books and apparatus, and divided into classes where discipline was mild, firm, and conducive to good order. Instruction had to be skilful, and graduated according to the age of the children and the time they had been at school, 'so as to show that equal care has been bestowed on each class'. The number of pupil teachers apprenticed in any school was not to exceed one to every twenty-five scholars attending.

As to the candidates:

> The qualifications to be required of candidates and of pupil teachers in each year of their apprenticeship will be regulated by the following rules, in which the minimum of proficiency to be attained is precisely defined, in order to prevent partiality but their Lordships reserve to themselves the power to reward superior merit by shortening the term of the apprenticeship; or by awarding the higher stipends of the later years of the apprenticeship to pupil teachers whose attainments enable them to pass the examination of one of the later years at an earlier period.

Candidates had to be at least 13 years old and free of 'any bodily infirmity likely to impair their usefulness as pupil teachers'. Managers of schools connected with the C of E had to certify the moral character of the candidates (and their families) justified the expectation that the efforts of the school in instruction and training would be matched by the candidates' own efforts and example by their parents. In a wonderful example of education being an opportunity to escape the poverty trap, suitable apprentices from families where parental support was somewhat lacking were required to board in approved households.

Would-be pupil teachers had to fulfil certain educational standards: fluent and expressive reading; neat and grammatical writing; and understand the first four rules of arithmetic, simple and compound, to work them correctly and know the tables of weights and measures.

As well as the 'three Rs', they had to be able to point out the parts of speech in a simple sentence and have an elementary knowledge of geography. C of E pupil teachers had to be able to recite the Catechism and be acquainted with the outline of scripture history. In addition to all the above, 'girls should also be able to sew neatly and to knit'. Every pupil teacher was required to be clean in person and dress.

The pupil teacher apprenticeship lasted five years and, in recognition of the depth of education they would be required to teach, the subjects covered were wide ranging; at the end of every year, each apprentice was examined by a school inspector (see Appendix 1 for list of qualifications tested). In each year of examination, inspectors observed 'the degree of attention paid by the pupil teachers to a perfect articulation in reading, and to a right modulation of the voice in teaching a class'. A knowledge of vocal music and of drawing (especially from models) was 'much encouraged, though not absolutely required, because the means of teaching it may not exist in every school'.

At the end of the apprenticeship, having passed all the examinations and presented the required testimonials in each year, the pupil teacher was awarded a certificate.

In rural districts where all the general conditions required for the apprenticeship of a pupil teacher might be satisfied but where the schoolmaster or mistress was unable to conduct an apprentice, the committee introduced a stipendiary monitor scheme. This was to encourage managers (through a small stipend) to retain their monitors to the age of 17. This had to be with parental agreement and on condition the monitor was given extra daily instruction by the school's head. The rules and conditions of selection were similar to those for pupil teacher apprenticeships, but the yearly examinations were less intensive, reflecting the ability of the head to deliver instruction and the scheme was only four years instead of five (see Appendix 2).

After the yearly inspections and examinations, pupil teachers or stipendiary monitors were also required to present certificates of good conduct from the managers of the school, and of punctuality, diligence, obedience, and attention to their duties from the master or mistress.

Financial rewards

Once the inspectors were satisfied with everything, salaries for males were paid as follows:

	Pupil Teacher	Stipendiary Monitor
At the end of the 1st Year	£10	£5
At the end of the 2nd Year	£12 10s	£7 10s
At the end of the 3rd Year	£15	£10
At the end of the 4th Year	£17 10s	£12 10s
At the end of the 5th Year	£20	—

Female pupil teachers were paid about two-thirds of these wages.

The masters and mistresses who had delivered training and instruction were also rewarded: £5 for one, £9 for two, £12 for three pupil teachers, and £3 per annum more for every additional apprentice; and, on similar conditions, £2 10s for one stipendiary monitor, £4 for two, £6 for three, and £1 10s in addition in each year for every extra stipendiary monitor.

Some pupil teachers were destined to manage schools of industry and had been skilfully trained in gardening or in other suitable mechanical arts; female pupil teachers were instructed by the mistress in cutting out clothes, cooking, baking and washing, as well as sewing and knitting. For these subjects, masters and mistresses were also awarded an appropriate gratuity, 'proportioned to the degree of skill and care displayed'. The money was well deserved; all pupil teachers and stipendiary monitors were given instruction by the head for an hour and a half, five days a week, either before or after usual school hours. All monies were liable to be withdrawn if standards were not met.

After pupil teachers had completed their apprenticeships, they were eligible to enter an annual public examination from which those 'most proficient in their studies and skilful in the art of teaching, and concerning whose character and zeal for the office of teachers the inspector of the district could give the most favourable report' would be awarded £20 (women) or £25 (men) and denominated 'Queen's Scholars'. The funding gave them the opportunity to attend teacher-training college for three years, from which they would emerge as 'Certificated' teachers. Each year of training entitled them to a supplement to their salary and teachers were graded 1st/2nd/3rd class (with 3rd class being three years of training and therefore the highest grade).

Of course, many could not afford to take up the training – they needed to be earning money – so entered elementary schools as 'Uncertificated' or assistant teachers. Assistant teachers of three years standing and upwards could be examined for certificates of merit, but were not given any enhancements to their salaries.

The training colleges

Even before the formal pupil-teacher training scheme was introduced in 1846, the voluntary providers of elementary education had established training colleges. The two main ones were the B and FSS Borough Road College, Southwark (see Chapter 2) and the National Society's Central School, Baldwin's Gardens, Holborn, founded in 1812. Needing larger premises to accommodate the increasing numbers of trainee teachers, this college moved, first to Westminster and then, in 1841, to Stanley Grove, Chelsea, where it was renamed St Mark's College. Almost immediately, an equivalent college was sought for women. It was considered women would need a longer course than that currently being provided for men (a year instead of six months).

Whitelands, a house on the King's Road, Chelsea, was purchased. It included eight rooms to accommodate fifty boarders, plus a schoolroom, committee room, dining room, apartment for the principal and bedroom for the schoolmistresses. Women students paid £15 a year, in contrast to the charge of £25 for men at St Mark's. Its stated purpose was 'to provide a class of schoolmistresses higher in attainments than have hitherto been frequent among female teachers of the poor', and as well as focusing on religious and intellectual cultivation, the training included the works of female industry. Early reports describe its conditions as cramped and unsanitary, with students forced to work long hours with little or no leisure time.

It was not the only training college with poor conditions. Inferior accommodation, badly cooked food and pressure of work combined to cause frequent breakdowns, more so for women than men; women's college buildings and amenities tended to be poorer; staff to student ratios were lower, and they were expected to carry out more domestic duties. In addition, the women were more conscientious and compliant than the men.

The B and FSS college continued training both men and women until 1861 when its women-only college opened at Stockwell in south-west London on 3 April 1861, accommodating seventy-five students initially. An adjacent practising school was opened the same week.

Expanding beyond London

Of course, there was great need for training colleges for schoolmistresses outside of London, and the National Society, via its diocesan boards of education, set about establishing further colleges throughout the country. One of the first was in Salisbury in 1841, followed by Brighton, through the Chichester diocese, in 1842. Perhaps the idea of sending girls to train as teachers took some time to develop as it seems to have been undersubscribed, initially:

BRIGHTON DIOCESAN INSTITUTION FOR TRAINING SCHOOL-MISTRESSES.

On Thursday last the half-yearly examination of the pupils took place ... There was a great and general satisfaction expressed at the proficiency of the pupils in the scriptures both of the Old and New Testament, in the Prayer Book, Articles, &c., in History, Geography, and Singing ... It is highly satisfactory to be informed that there are now eleven schoolmistresses in various parts of the Diocese, all of whom have received their education in this institution during the three years that it has been in operation. There are ten pupils remaining; and as there is room in the house for sixteen in all,

it is very desirable that the clergy and landowners in the county should find out in their respective neighbourhoods such young women as may be likely to be approved by the Committee, and thus be received into the house for training. The day fixed for the examination of candidates for admission is Tuesday, August 15.
Brighton Gazette, Thursday, 26 June 1845

Even after the establishment of the government pupil-teacher scheme, Brighton was appealing to those who knew of young women with promising talent and able to afford the expense of their training to put those young women forward. As it was early in the scheme, no one would yet have been eligible for the Queen's Scholarship. It is interesting to note the college was urging suitable girls to take up a career as a schoolmistress rather than a servant:

BRIGHTON DIOCESAN TRAINING SCHOOL

The School is unquestionably in able hands; and we trust that it will have good success in its work. ... We are informed that those entrusted with the management of the School meet with some difficulty obtaining an adequate supply of candidates for admission; and we shall be happy if, by mentioning this circumstance, we succeed in drawing the attention of such as know of young women of promising talent, and are able to provide for the expense of their training, to this want of the Institution. There is in most parishes and parochial schools some girl distinguished by assiduity or intelligence, touching whom it will be felt that to limit her usefulness to a mere servant's function is to overlook in some sort her capability and calling. Is it not a duty, in such cases, to make an effort to introduce the individual into a larger sphere of usefulness and what sphere so readily presents itself as that of the schoolmistress? We trust that the Brighton Training School may soon be filled with pupils, the elite of our parochial schools.
Brighton Gazette, Thursday, 23 December 1847

Other dioceses were to follow the example of Chichester, and by the late 1840s and early 1850s, around twenty-five diocesan training institutions had been built by the National Society's diocesan education boards. Those solely for women included Norwich, Rochester (at Bishop's Stortford), Chester (St Elphin's at Warrington) Gloucester and Bristol (St Matthias's at Bristol), Exeter (for a college in Truro) and Lichfield (in Derby).

The *Derby Mercury* of Wednesday, 1 November 1848 reported on a number of meetings held in the diocese to discuss the provision of a training school for schoolmistresses in Derby to mirror the one for schoolmasters in Lichfield. To cover the requirements of Derbyshire, Staffordshire and Shropshire, 700 teachers were needed and therefore an efficient college of considerable capacity would be required. Interestingly, the report states that funds in some villages were so low they could not afford to maintain a schoolmaster, but they could afford to have a (lower-paid) schoolmistress, but countered this implied inferiority with the fact that 'in many respects the priority of claim in educational matters rested with the female'.

It was proposed to make the institution capable of accommodating forty pupils and eventually to give them two years' training, meaning there would only be twenty additional schoolmistresses to the diocese every year – and they could not, therefore, be charged with being extravagant in the matter of building the college. A site had been obtained, plans prepared, submitted to and sanctioned by the Committee of Council. With building costs estimated at £6,000, the diocese's expenditure would be £4,000, topped up by a grant of £2,000 from the government, which would also provide largely for the maintenance of the institution.

It believed that, with a very large number of young women now apprenticed in the government schools, those coming to the training institution would do so as Queen's Scholars with a grant of £20–£30 a year; once the institution was erected, the funding they would receive in this way would go a long way towards supporting it – and the females, when they had passed through these schools, would receive a certificate, 'accompanied by a liberal allowance from the government in the shape of salaries'. It was noted that 'the advantages of training were manifested in the success which had attended the operations of the harvest schools, a remarkable difference being perceptible between the schoolmasters and mistresses who had been under the superintendence of organised masters, and those who had not.'

A further report in the *Staffordshire Advertiser* on Saturday, 20 January 1849 again extolled the virtues of the training colleges for mistresses, citing the clergy and school managers' excellent reports of schoolmistresses who had been 'sent out' from Whitelands and Salisbury. Access to similar training was needed more locally, and especially since those institutions were full. Since the institute for schoolmasters in Lichfield was working well:

> ought they not to have a similar institution also for mistresses? Would it be said that it was less important to have good schoolmistresses than masters? Was there any one there who did not know the influence of female efforts, the influence of female character on the community, who did not estimate the good which was done by Christian women in their schools? Who could tell what effects in after-life would result from a proper training of those who were to have the training of those who would become the wives and mothers of our poor?

On Saturday, 23 June 1850, the foundation stone was laid to the merry pealing of church bells in celebration of the event. The institution officially opened on 1 October 1851 with fees set at 18s for the first year and 16s for the second and third years (including all expenses except clothing). Girls admitted at 16 would train for three years, those at 17 and upwards for just two. Fees for girls receiving a government certificate were reduced to 10s for the following year, so it paid to pass the exams.

By the end of its second year of operation in November 1853, there were thirty-six girls in residence, just eight of whom were Queen's Scholars. The girls had been examined and had demonstrated varying results of competence, particular mention being made of the bishop's examinations in the Holy Scriptures and in the history, meaning, and use of the Book of Common Prayer. Despite all the studies required by the pupil-teacher apprentice scheme, it seems that once at college, this particular committee was more focused on the young women's need to 'understand and be able to teach those practical duties of females which contribute essentially to the health, comfort, and morality of the working classes'. They were, therefore, 'instructed in all kinds of useful needlework, in cutting out every article of dress, in the economical expenditure of money, in habits of order and cleanliness, in the principles of ventilation, in cottage cooking and cooking for the sick, and in the peculiar duties of servants'.

Angela Georgina Burdett Coutts

Miss Angela Burdett Coutts, born in 1814, was the youngest daughter of Sir Francis Burdett, and on her mother's side was a granddaughter of the wealthy banker Sir Thomas Coutts. Through a slightly complicated inheritance, she became one of the wealthiest women in the country when she inherited her grandfather's fortune on the death of her step-grandmother in 1837, on condition she assumed the Coutts name. Taking her former governess, Hannah Brown (née Meredith), as her live-in companion, Angela forged a new life as an outspoken and dedicated philanthropist, dispensing large sums annually to various causes, particularly in London's East End. Many famous names can be connected to her work: Charles Dickens (with whom she founded Urania Cottage, a refuge for 'fallen women'); Florence Nightingale (to whom she donated funds to help improve sanitary conditions in hospitals in Crimea); and prime ministers Disraeli and Gladstone. Her philanthropy was wide ranging: she created Columbia Market and a social housing development for the most needy; gave financial support to those devastated by the Irish Potato Famine; commissioned the *Greyfriar's Bobby* statue in Edinburgh, supported the NSPCC and the RSPCA; and helped fund the building of the Royal Marsden Hospital. She was created baroness by Queen Victoria in 1871. When she was not travelling far and wide, her main residence was 1 Stratton Street, Mayfair. When Hannah died in 1878, Angela was grief-stricken.

Her subsequent marriage on 12 February 1881 caused a good deal of shock. At 30, her American-born secretary, William Lehman Ashmead Bartlett, was thirty-seven years younger than the baroness. She had known him since he was a 10-year-old recipient of one of her prizes at school and she had funded his education at Highgate School and subsequently at Oxford University. William took his wife's surname and continued her philanthropic work after her death in 1902. Angela Georgina Burdett Coutts is buried in Westminster Abbey.

Her work in furthering girls' education is less well documented, but it was one she was passionate about. An article, 'Project for Young Ladies as Schoolmistresses' in *The English Journal of Education* in 1858 includes her lengthy discourse on the merits of the profession and responding correspondence from Lord Granville, who, essentially, agreed with her views, though the journal's editor did not. *The English Journal of Education* was 'specially designed as a medium of correspondence among the heads of training colleges, parochial clergymen, and all promoters of sound education, parents, sponsors, schoolmasters, pupil teachers, Sunday School teachers etc.'.

Miss Burdett Coutts had 'ascertained with much surprise', when visiting pupil teachers in schools and trainee mistresses at Whitelands College, that they 'were children chiefly of parents whose condition in life was extremely humble; and on further inquiry, I was informed that this, as a rule, held good generally throughout the country. Such an extensive appropriation of these situations does not seem socially advantageous …'

Her proposal was for 'remunerative and honourable employment for the daughters of the middle classes', remarking:

> It has become a matter of general observation that, from amongst that large and respectable portion of the middle class upon whose means the burden of providing adequate education for their children presses heavily, few, comparatively, cause their children to be trained as National Schoolmistresses. The Government plan for educating and providing Mistresses for Elementary Schools appears generally overlooked, more especially by the friends and guardians of young persons left orphans, either wholly or partially, without any, or with but slender resources; for this class, which, unhappily always large, is fearfully and rapidly augmented during seasons of national affliction, of war, cholera, and other causes, such a provision in life seems peculiarly adapted. Not only is the remuneration larger, and the social position better, than that which many occupations confer, but there is also in the Teacher's offer a wide field for the exercise of ability for a good purpose, to promote which many young persons labour at the expense of much self-denial; and

although there exists a difference between teaching voluntarily for short periods and adopting it as a calling – a far greater amount of perseverance alone, as well as of information, and love of teaching also, being requisite in the latter case – the fact that persons often readily give their time gratuitously to this object may be taken as a proof that it is an occupation congenial to many minds, and one which young persons would frequently willingly follow, and in which they would find their talents usefully and beneficially employed. One of the causes of this neglect of an independent and honourable employment may probably arise from the fact, that so little is generally known of the system of education carried on in the Training Institutions of the country. This circular has been drawn up under the impression that a clear statement of the course of education given in Training Institutions, the means of fitting young persons for admission into them, and the facilities afforded to elder persons for obtaining the situation of Schoolmistress, would be useful to parents and guardians, and to others either seeking remunerative and useful employment for young persons or for themselves.

In the Report of the Minutes of the Committee of Council on Education for 1856–7, it is stated that the average emoluments [fixed for] all professional sources for Schoolmistresses are £71 per annum in the metropolitan district, and about £59 12s in the country. In more than half the cases houses are provided rent-free; and it will be seen that in certain cases retiring pensions are allowed by Government. But out of the ordinary resources, a careful person would be enabled to yearly lay by for the wants of after-life, or purchase an annuity according to a table prepared by the Government; especially as in more than half the cases houses are provided rent-free for Schoolmistresses. This usual provision of a house renders the position of the National Schoolmistress one of great respectability, and of a desirable character for well-educated persons.

Miss Burdett Coutts expands on the pupil-teacher apprenticeship and requirements for entry to a training college before adding:

Moreover, by a recent regulation of Government, the Committee of Council for Education have thrown open a limited number of Queen's Scholarships to all competitors capable of passing the necessary examination, whether they have been Pupil Teachers or not. Parents not desiring to place their children as Pupil Teachers in schools, or older persons desiring to qualify themselves as Teachers in schools, could obtain the preliminary knowledge by study, either under the care of a Certificated Schoolmistress who may be free to enter into such an arrangement out of school hours, or by receiving

> instruction at schools specially adapted to prepare candidates for admission into Training Institutions. Such schools would easily be found if required; and as the course of instruction provides a sound useful education, it would be suitable to every condition of life, and would qualify a person to teach in families, should that occupation be preferred to entering a Training School and taking charge of a National School. Tuition in private families must, however, only be regarded as an alternative before entering a Training Institution.
>
> The cost of training a female in a Training Institution is between £37 and £40 per annum. This sum, in the case of Queen's Scholars, is wholly and in all other cases to the extent of one-half, defrayed out of public or private grants, applicable only to the preparation of Mistresses for Elementary Day Schools; so that no person can enter a Training School except for this purpose.

She advocated making the scheme more widely known so women seeking employment would avail themselves of the opportunity for a superior career, instead of limiting their choice of employment to 'callings unsuitable to them'.

While Lord Granville of the Education Department concurred, the journal's editor pompously summed up his thoughts on the matter:

> Excellent as are the Training Colleges we doubt the wisdom of encouraging young ladies to seek entrance into them. In the first place, though the education now given in them is better and sounder than that which most young ladies receive in the highest ranks of life (few of whom could answer well even the papers on music or compete with the drawing accomplished every Christmas), still this would have its evil in the certainty that young ladies thus effectually educated, and also for the domestic purposes of life, would be admirably adapted for the wives of gentlemen both by mental and moral training, and none, or but very few, would ever remain in schools for the poor (they would marry the Clergyman or the Squire, or their sons, in nearly every parish they went to, or would probably be well married before they went at all). The only obstacle to this now, is the low birth of the present order of College-trained Schoolmistresses: and this Miss Burdett Coutts' plan would remove. It would obviously be a great abuse to allow public money to be used for educating the future wives of men of fortune. It could not be prevented. No woman can be pledged to celibacy.
>
> Miss Burdett Coutts is one of the most truly benevolent and excellent women engaged in the great work of public charity. We have the highest esteem for her but we must respectfully dissent from her views on this subject.

Moreover, her plan would deprive the girls of industrious poor parents of a post of usefulness which it must strike Miss Coutts they are specially fitted for by their own home life. It is for the same homes and stations they are intended to train their scholars; and they will do this all the more effectually because it is work in which their own lives have practically experienced them.

It seems an odd way of looking at things; it was envisaged that middle-class girls would make good marriages, so there was little value in training them for a good career, but working-class girls were expected to work.

Even more curiously, considering her views that girls should be educated, Angela Burdett Coutts had launched a prize scheme in 1855 for 'The Teaching of Common Things'. She offered three sets of prizes to the total of £50:

1. Schoolmistresses with pupil-teacher apprentices in National schools in Middlesex would be awarded first prize of £5, four second prizes of £4 and five third prizes of £3.

2. Second-year pupils at Whitelands (who had passed their first-year exams) were eligible for ten prizes at £1 each

3. Third-year female pupil teachers apprenticed in Middlesex National schools could compete for eight prizes of 10s each.

The merits of the candidates were determined by an examination, consisting partly of a paper of questions on 'common things', and partly of an essay. Angela Burdett Coutts also inspected the schools to ascertain whether, in regard to the teaching of common things, the practical efficiency of the teachers whose papers were most approved corresponded with the amount of attainments exhibited in their papers.

But what were these 'common things' being tested? Twenty questions were set, covering the most important points connected with running a home: food and clothing; general household arrangements; duties of servants; management of children; and treatment of the sick.

Examples included:

- Why is economy in the use of all articles a duty in every condition of life? Do you remember any passages in Holy Scripture which bear upon this subject?
- If at any time the supply of water should fall short, or if it could be obtained only with great difficulty, what could poor people do to promote cleanliness and health?

- Give an account of the different grains used for making bread; and give a good receipt for making a 4lb loaf, naming the weight of flour, &c.
- State what you know as to the comparative waste of boiled, roast, fried, and baked meats; and the different advantages of each mode of cooking.
- What simple remedies would you use in the case of a cold, cough, or sore-throat?
- Give an account of what you consider the necessary qualifications of a cook, laundrymaid, housemaid, or nurse. State the usual wages of such a servant; what articles of dress would be most suitable for her particular occupation; and how much you think she ought to save. If you were required to select a nursery-maid for a lady's family, what questions would you put to the children whom you thought most likely to suit for the purpose? What moral qualities would you deem most essential?
- Give full directions for making a man's shirt, a housemaid's apron, and knitting a stocking.

As many as eighty-three candidates – schoolmistresses, pupils, and pupil teachers – competed for the prizes in the competition's first year. It was reported that the answers were, on the whole, satisfactory, but nobody was outstanding enough to win first prize. Apparently, cookery was the subject with most room for improvement. In an account that could be as applicable today (but not solely to girls) as it was in the mid-nineteenth century, Angela Burdett Coutts observed:

> The answers to the [cookery] question were generally fair in regard to good, straightforward, and unvarying cookery, but showed little ingenuity in the preparation of food. There is so much variety, and many small luxuries, happily generally within the reach of the labouring man or artisan's family that the *Hints on Cookery* and the *Receipts* have been added, to show how much pleasant variety might be obtained by the exercise of a little thought and economy; and they may also serve to show that things are frequently thrown away or wasted in small kitchens which might be made valuable and attractive as food; and that a skilful use of many nutritious articles little regarded might add to the enjoyments and fireside comforts of the families of tradesmen and others who are above the condition of life of daily labour. To such families a knowledge of domestic economy, especially in the matter of food, must materially extend their ability to be useful to their poorer neighbours, either by actual help or as good examples. Moreover, the moral effects of good cookery are not to be despised, for, besides promoting economic habits, neat and well-prepared meals would keep many a working man from seeking as now, in the stimulating liquors of a public-house, for some consolation for the

ignorant, untidy, and unskilful cookery of his wife; they would conduce to domestic comfort, and thus foster the growth of domestic virtues. The good example ... should be followed by all who have the management or direction of schools for the poor in their hands; for why should not the daughters, sisters, and future wives of working men be taught how to perform the duties of their station? – why should they not learn at school how to bake bread and boil potatoes properly – how to choose a joint of meat and cook it afterwards – how to make cheap and wholesome pies and puddings – how to buy clothes, to mend them, and make them last long – how to make themselves and their families look respectable – how to light fires, to clean rooms, and keep their homes healthy and comfortable?

She also commented on the essays of the trainees at Whitelands, commending them for the sensible manner in which they had spoken of household work, teaching boys to knit, do needlework and on country matters. One she specially commended for her observations on the influence exercised by the 'head of the family'. The pupil had observed that after marriage, the man was 'head of the family' but it was entirely in the woman's own power whom she chose to marry and make the head of her family. Angela added that teachers would be doing a kindness to point this out to their elder girls, and advise them to observe carefully the habits of life and conduct towards others of the man who wanted them to enter into 'so serious and responsible an engagement' before committing.

Her interests in female teacher-training colleges extended beyond the bounds of London as a report regarding the annual examinations of students at the Derby Training Institution for Schoolmistresses in the *Derbyshire Advertiser and Journal* of Friday, 30 September 1859 reveals. Angela was on holiday in the Trossachs and wrote to say she could not attend the meeting as she had hoped:

Dear Mr Mundy,

As there is no chance of me now returning from Scotland in time to be present at the meeting, on the 22nd inst., at the Derby Training Institution, I have desired the prize books to be sent to you, which I propose giving to the young teachers recommended to me for their attention to, and proficiency in, industrial training. I sincerely hope that these prizes may in some degree aid the movement made by yourself and other ladies resident near Derby, respecting needlework; which appeared to me to be important not only locally but with reference to other training institutions. Her Majesty's Inspectors of Schools require that a much greater amount of attention should be now given to needlework and industrial training than formerly, and it is of the utmost importance that an interest, at the present moment, should be shown in the movement, and that their efforts should be seconded especially by ladies, under whose supervision girls' schools are mostly placed and who have complained pretty generally of the difficulty they find in procuring suitable schoolmistresses to teach in national schools. If the example set in Derby and in some other places were uniformly followed throughout the country, by ladies resident near to training institutions, it would do much towards remedying the want of which they complain. It would impress young persons with the importance of these parts of a woman's education, both as respects to themselves and others, and it would prove to them, whilst still under tuition, that a personal knowledge of needlework, and habits of industry and economy, are considered indispensable in a female teacher by those who employ them. This is generally becoming well known to schoolmistresses in charge of schools and to the managers of training institutions. They feel that a schoolmistress must become an object of imitation to the young children under her care; that her faults, virtues, and her habits, will be more or less reflected in their characters and habits, that she must be closely scanned by their parents, and that her influence will depend mainly not so much upon what she knows as upon what she is. All this is well known to every school manager, but it is not cannot yet be quite so fully understood by young persons who have yet to learn how powerful is the influence of habit and example; and, therefore, it is so very important that the essential qualifications, considered necessary in order for a schoolmistress to become useful, and to fulfil the duties of the station for which she has been educated in these public institutions, should be steadily kept before the minds of young persons qualifying themselves for position of national schoolmistresses, during the time they are under training. ...

For those reasons I have taken a warm interest in all the arrangements of the Derby Training School, and if the committee would like my prizes to be continued another year, I shall be most happy to do so, when I hope a few more may be recommended. I will beg you now only to present the two books which are for first class, and a volume for the others.

With my earnest good wishes and very sincere prayer that it may please God to bless their work when they enter on it, I am, yours affectionately A.G. Burdett Coutts.

Although it was important for girls to have an education and for schoolmistresses to be the imparters of knowledge, it seems women were still only expected to become housewives and mothers, even by the women who championed their education. The report lists the recipients of the prizes from the 'ladies of Derbyshire' and Angela

Burdett Coutts whose 'needlework and cutting out' and 'general usefulness' had gained them accolades. It is pleasing to see Ellen Poyser, who had prizes in both categories, later secured a position as schoolmistress at Yeavley near Ashbourne, Derbyshire, in 1861, where she lived in the school house. Even after her marriage to a local farmer, she continued her career for a least twenty years. Ellen Such, another prize winner, who also married, pursued her career for at least forty years and is listed on the 1911 census as a pensioner schoolmistress. Both came from relatively humble families and married ordinary working men.

The women teachers advance

The two main providers of education were rightly proud of their achievements, as were individual schools who had helped transform the girls of ordinary working families into schoolmistresses. They advertised their successes through newspaper reports:

> Christ Church Schools – At the recent Christmas examination, held at Whitelands Training College, under the auspices of the Committee of Council on Education, two of the former pupil teachers of the above schools, in this city, honourably distinguished themselves. Miss Margaret Hughes, daughter of Mr Hughes, of Backhouse's Walk, has succeeded in placing herself in the class list, amongst those who obtained certificates of merit of the first or highest degree; and Miss M.H. Atkinson, daughter of Mr Atkinson, of Cummersdale Mill, has placed herself in the second class. The former has lately been appointed mistress of an important school in Sheffield, and the latter of one at Lochgill-head, in Argyleshire.
> *Carlisle Journal*, Friday, 6 March 1857

> The Reverend W.F. Witts Girls' School – The following young persons, late pupils of the above school, having been students at Whitelands Training College the last two years, and passed their final examination last Christmas, have had awarded to them the following certificates of qualification by the Committee of Council on Education: Selina Anne Bowman (also a drawing prize) 1st class certificate; Amelia Faircloth 2nd class cert; Mary Ann Rayner 2nd class cert.
> *Cambridge Chronicle and Journal*, Saturday, 26 February 1859

> Queen's Scholarships – We understand that Miss Harris late a pupil teacher in the Bedminster British Schools, obtained a first-class Queen's Scholarship at the Christmas examination at Stockwell College. This is the seventh pupil

who has obtained a scholarship from these schools, a fact which must be encouraging to the teacher and very satisfactory to the managers of the institution. Miss M.C. Parfitt, late of the Clifton British School, succeeded in obtaining a Queen's Scholarship at the Christmas examination at Stockwell College. Miss Matilda Johns, late pupil teacher of St Michael's Infant School, obtained a Queen's Scholarship the late Christmas examination. Miss Ellen Greenfill adds another name to the list of Queen's Scholars who have from time to time been presented for examination from St Matthew's School.

Western Daily Press, Tuesday, 28 January 1862

Miss Annie Pleydell, formerly a pupil teacher in the All Saints and St. Clement's National School, has successfully passed her final examination Whitelands College, Chelsea, being eighth in the first college list.

Hastings and St Leonards Observer, Saturday, 22 March 1873

Shoemaker's daughter Harriet Annie Mary Pleydell was listed on the 1871 census along with more than 100 other young women training to be teachers at Whitelands. Not long after passing her final examination, she married clothier Stephen Chapman on 14 October 1874. Her marriage certificate names her occupation as schoolmistress, but for a time she put aside her career to raise nine children. By 1901, she had returned to her teaching career, as a 'Board School Governess', and was still teaching, in a London County Council school, in 1911. Her daughter Stephanie also became a teacher.

Many other girls were to follow similar paths and the opportunities for women to pursue an interesting and fulfilling career were about to increase significantly.

Chapter 4

Women's Influence on Education Gathers Pace

While it is clear that education provision was improving through better training of teachers and building of more schools, there was no compulsion for children to attend school and be educated. Working-class poor families sent children to work in paid occupations as soon as it was practical. Nor was education free; even if a child was registered on a school's books, attendance might be erratic. A report in 1868 had cited 'the ignorant condition of the youthful population', stating that of the 100,000 children aged 3–12 in Manchester and Salford, only 55,000 were on the school books, and average attendance was 38,000. A similar situation existed in Birmingham where just 15,490 of the 35,018 children aged 3–12 were at school. What education had been received was also deemed unsatisfactory, as around 45 per cent of people aged 12–20 still could not read or write and 75 per cent failed tests in arithmetic and general knowledge. This illiteracy is clearly visible in the number of people who were only able to sign the marriage register with a 'X her/his mark' and the spelling of their names was inconsistent.

The National Education League

Recognising improvements were needed, there were various discussions and resolutions in parliament and at union meetings around the country, and support from the trade unions for compulsory education for the working classes grew. In early 1869, the National Education League (NEL) was founded in Birmingham and expanded to 1,300 members, including many of the highest names in learning, literature and science. Of a provisional committee listed in September 1869, there was just one woman among the ninety prominent names: Lydia Becker. Lydia was to be the only woman on the twenty-strong executive committee of a Manchester and Salford branch of the league.

The NEL's objective was stated in succinct terms: 'The establishment of a system which should ensure the education of every child in England and Wales'. Its principles were more detailed:

1. Local authorities shall be compelled by law to see that sufficient school accommodation is provided for every child in their district.
2. The cost of founding and maintaining such schools as may be required shall be provided out of local rates, supplemented by Government grants.
3. All schools aided by local rates shall be under the management of local authorities, and subject to Government inspection.
4. All schools aided by local rates shall be <u>unsectarian</u>.
5. To all schools aided by local rates admission shall be free.
6. School accommodation being provided, the State or the local authorities shall have power to compel the attendance of children of suitable age not otherwise receiving education.

It added that nothing short of a system of national, unsectarian, and compulsory education would satisfy the requirements of the people of the United Kingdom.

What was meant by 'unsectarian' was clarified at the NEL's first general meeting in Birmingham's Exchange Rooms in October 1869: the teaching of catechisms, creeds or theological tenets of particular sects should be prohibited in schools. However, that was the extent of its prohibition: everything else was the decision of school managers, who, as the ratepayers' representatives, would follow the wishes of the inhabitants – 'the best guide in such matters'. It meant school managers had the authority to permit or prohibit the reading of the Bible during school hours, but if permitted, it had to be read without sectarian comment or note of any kind. In addition to this (and with similar caveats), the managers would have power to grant or refuse the use of the classrooms out of school hours for the purposes of religious instruction.

During the debate, it was noted that 'mixed education made muddle-minded scholars' and 'keeping distinct things separate was the shortest path to efficiency'. People had neither time nor money to spare and 'the State should adopt the speediest and cheapest transit to public knowledge' – adding that piety brought nothing to the workplace and even the most devout employer adjusted his wages according to the swiftness and expertise of the workman, not his religious knowledge. Some berated the worth of denominational teaching: John Charles Buckmaster (of the Department of Science and Art) denounced it as a barrier to progress, and campaigning 'firebrand' Nonconformist preacher George Dawson voiced that the only remedy was education – compulsory, maintained out of the rates, and secular – and education was the business of the nation, not the clergy.

The National Education Union

Understandably, the Church and others who had been providing elementary education for almost sixty years felt aggrieved at the assertions of the NEL; to oppose these views and promote their own, the Reverend William Stanyer and his associates set up the National Education Union. These men had already been considering the subject of education and planned to engage with the government as soon as the legislation was discussed in parliament. However, the formation of what they saw as a powerful body in support of secular education, and 'actively bent on eliminating religious and denominational teaching from the code of popular instruction', accelerated the formation of a union of those in favour of denominational teaching. The opinions of the defenders – as well as of the opponents – of the existing system, would be widely communicated.

From its headquarters in Cheetham Hill, Manchester, the NEU circulated a letter inviting interested parties to its proposed congress at Manchester Town Hall in early November.

In the letter, Stanyer outlined the purpose of the Union, which was to promote enlightened discussion of the question of education by those 'who had hitherto borne the chief burden of educating the working classes'. Although it was claimed they would facilitate, not obstruct, the legislation due to be considered in the next parliamentary session, they were clearly not in favour of introducing new schemes (i.e. those proposed by the NEL). Stanyer mooted that the English people did not respond well to the imposition of 'methods and systems foreign to their character' so any further legislation would need to harmonise with past legislation. He believed any changes should be approached by the earnest and zealous promoters of education under the present system, in a careful and practical spirit – and not left in the hands of 'doctrinaires and theorists'.

As planned, the congress took place in Manchester on 3 and 4 November 1869. The Union's stated objective was to secure the primary education of every child, by judiciously supplementing the present denominational system of national education and, to assist its aims, it had elicited the support of those already working in education to give practical and experimental opinions, not theoretical ones. Described (perhaps unkindly) as mainly a clerical synod in one newspaper, members included prominent defender of the Church of England, Dudley Ryder, 2nd Earl of Harrowby; Lord Edward Howard, chairman of the Catholic Poor Schools Committee; Lord Robert Montagu, MP for Huntingdonshire and former vice president of the Committee on Education; several school inspectors and several archdeacons, canons, bishops and vicars. All men.

Their rhetoric was often rather caustic. Naturally – as they had been the ones providing education – delegates were defensive of what they saw as an attack by the NEL. They dismissed the damning statistics put before the public as 'utterly fallacious' and 'absurdly exaggerated'.

The Dean of Durham, declaring it was very wrong of the NEL to propose anything which he called 'sweeping encroachment upon religious liberty', contended that a great deal had been achieved by England's clergy in the service of education. Landowners and clergy had contributed financially to children's schooling and it was a needless piece of extravagance to throw away the subscriptions derived from children's pence in National and other schools (the proposal at the time was for schooling to be free, paid for by ratepayers). He believed parliament would not entertain any such proposition.

The NEU had a point. Denominational societies had raised school buildings in every part of the land, and millions of men and women owed it all the (little) education they possessed. Even if it was lacking in some areas, it could be infinitely extended and improved at far lower cost than implementing a new, untried system.

But the NEL's argument was equally compelling. By introducing a new regime – a new start – legislation could make school attendance compulsory. Since it was difficult to force the poor to send their children to school if they were unable to pay the 'school pence', establishing a free school in every district, supported by either the Exchequer or by local rates, was a better way forward. And by making it secular, there would be no religious rivalries.

One thing was agreed: much needed to be done in order to keep pace with other nations. Multitudes of children were growing up uneducated and the available schooling remained 'unsuited to the future occupations and circumstances of those for whom it was intended if Britain was to succeed in the great industrial competition'.

With local branches of the NEL in all major conurbations, public meetings to discuss the future of elementary education elicited lively debate between those who identified as either Leaguers or Unionists. How should the industrial classes should be taught and how might their teaching be funded?

It seems compromise was the way forward. By mid-December 1869, the executive committee of the NEL had prepared heads of the National Education League Bill, to be introduced into parliament in the session of 1870. William Edward Forster, Liberal MP for Bradford, was to take the Bill through parliament. Although he shared many of the views of the NEL, he realised making education secular would create discord with the churches and that, in the short-term, making schooling compulsory was not practical – there were too few schools. When the Bill was introduced on 17 February 1870, Forster credited both George Dixon (NEL's chairman) and Anthony Mundella (who was later to push through the Act of 1880 making elementary education compulsory) with stimulating educational zeal.

Although the Elementary Education Act 1870 stands as the very first piece of legislation to deal specifically with the provision of education in Britain, demonstrating a commitment to schooling on a national scale, it was not perfect. When the Act was given Royal Assent on 9 August 1870, as well as not being compulsory, compromises and practicalities meant schooling was not free either, and the Act supplemented rather than superseded the voluntary schools, which carried on unchanged (apart from the British Schools which fell under the control of school boards after the 1870 Act). A system of school boards of locally elected bodies was established to build and manage schools in areas where they were needed; funding was from the local rates. Unlike the voluntary schools, religious teaching in the board schools was to be 'non-denominational'. This was restricted, in practice, to learning the Bible and singing a few hymns.

As well as money for new board schools, there was state funding of 50 per cent of the running costs of voluntary schools (though capital funding was not available). In response, the National Schools raised an astonishing £10 million and carried on building, almost doubling the number of its schools to 12,000 in fifteen years. Difficulties arose, however, in meeting the maintenance costs and the schools also suffered from competition with board schools. Eventually, many schools were closed or handed over to the school boards. These still thrive as voluntary-aided (VA) and voluntary-controlled (VC) schools.

The school boards

With its key aim of providing elementary education for all children aged 5–13, the Elementary Education Act 1870 stipulated that:

> There shall be provided for every school district a sufficient amount of accommodation in public elementary schools ... available for all the children resident in such district for whose elementary education efficient and suitable provision is not otherwise made, and where there is an insufficient amount of such accommodation, in this Act referred to as 'public school accommodation', the deficiency shall be supplied in manner provided by this Act.

Responsibility for providing these schools was essentially devolved to local councils. With a proviso that any strategy to complete and supervise a network of schools in their districts had to be affordable, from late August 1870 such councils across the country eagerly started discussing the establishment of school boards. Bradford, Manchester, Leeds and Sheffield all had boards established and working before Christmas; others were a little slower. Although women were yet to gain the parliamentary franchise, since the new Act allowed women to vote for and to be candidates to serve on the school boards, the opportunity arose for women to show they were capable of public administration nationally. Elections were as fiercely fought as any general election; still the majority of candidates were men and associated with one or other religious denomination. Bradford avoided an election by negotiating with one another who would form a fifteen-man board, although two women had been nominated out of forty-six candidates. Some councils argued as to whether to adopt the act at all, claiming they had enough school accommodation already and did not need to spend money building further schools. It was estimated the cost of providing new schools would add 4–6d in the pound on the rates, although it was acknowledged that investing in education would improve literacy and numeracy among manual workers.

Women are elected

Political conviction combined with the tradition of female philanthropy and, especially in the towns, school board politics provided an important field of endeavour for the women's movement.[1] Many women declared their interest in standing for election and were nominated and backed by men and, of course, they were supported by women keen to use their new vote. Eight were to be successful.

The first woman to be elected to a school board was Lydia Becker, in Manchester in November 1870. She was the only woman on the fifteen-strong committee, of which eleven were churchmen of one denomination or another. Forty candidates had stood for election and she was placed ninth in the number of votes cast. The *Manchester Times* of 26 November noted that, 'As a member of the Manchester School Board she has achieved a conspicuous and influential position which elevates her work and her words into a matter of undeniable public importance.'

With a note of caution, the *Manchester Evening News* reported:

> Miss Becker has got in the thin end of the wedge at last, and no doubt her return will greatly encourage the friends of the three ladies who are contesting the London School Board, and on behalf of whom even the Education League consents to modify its principles. Certainly Miss Becker's return is a distinct triumph, and we can hardly see how it can be helped as a strictly logical inference that a person qualified to sit on a school board is also qualified to exercise the franchise or even to legislate if returned by the electors. At the same time, however, it must not be forgotten that there are especial reasons why ladies should have a voice in questions of education, and it will consequently be as well if the women's rights party use their triumph in Manchester, and the triumph we hope they will win in London, with modesty and moderation. To cross the Rubicon is not, after all, to capture Rome.

The friends of the ladies contesting the London School Board on 1 December 1870 were, it seems, encouraged. Dr Elizabeth Garrett (later Anderson) was elected for the Marylebone division, taking 43 per cent of the total vote and Emily Davies was elected for Greenwich with 31 per cent of the vote. Mrs Maria Grey (née Shirreff), standing in Chelsea, was not returned.

In Brighton, Catharine Maria Ricketts polled the most votes of the thirty-one candidates for the thirteen places on its school board on 14 December 1870. In the list of candidates, Catharine is identified as a 'friend' (compared with the other twelve members who are listed by their various religious denominations), but that she had a religious motivation is indicated by her giving Bible instruction to pupil teachers in Brighton. One of her initiatives was to increase attendance rates by hiring women to visit mothers in their homes to explain the benefits of education. In 1878, Catharine left England to become the first missionary of The Women's Missionary Association, serving in the Shantou mission in China until her death on 28 December 1907, aged 65.

Other successes followed in early 1871: Marian Huth in Huddersfield; Eleanor Elizabeth Smith in Oxford; and Anne Frances Ashworth and Caroline Meta Shum in Bath. While some were already (and continued to be) suffrage campaigners and others had religious backgrounds, Mrs Huth, the only woman to ever serve on Huddersfield's school board, was the wife of a German-born wool merchant. The local newspaper described her as 'a lady, so cultivated and public-spirited' and asserted the Huddersfield School Board was all the better for her inclusion. Re-elected time and again, she proudly declared her occupation on the 1881 census as 'member of a school board'.

The campaigns

When it came to education, all were keen to ensure that girls were given the same opportunities as boys. These reports from the *Bath Chronicle and Weekly Gazette* in early 1871 serve as an example of how women campaigned and were supported:

> ELECTORS OF BATH. At the request of many of my fellow citizens – both men and women – I have consented to become a Candidate for a seat on the School Board. Seeing that there are as many girls wanting instruction as boys, and that mothers will be the first to feel the operation of the Education Act, I believe you will desire that Women shall take part in the work. Should I be honoured by your support, and obtain a position of great responsibility among you, I will endeavour to fulfil its duties with a single eye to the elevation of the untaught and neglected children of our city. ANNE FRANCES ASHWORTH. Bath, January 16th, 1871.
>
> TO THE ELECTORS. Ladies and Gentlemen, – HAVING been repeatedly and urgently requested by persons of various shades of opinion to allow

myself to be nominated for the School Board, I have at length and with much diffidence consented. The Legislature having provided a scheme for the universal education of the people, my exertions would be directed to produce such circumstances in the homes of the people as to render compulsory attendance at school practicable. It may not be unknown to some of you that the principal work to be done by the Board is one to which I have hitherto given my strength and time. Hundreds of the most neglected and miserable children of the city have come under my personal supervision; and their parents, homes, circumstances, and habits are perfectly familiar to me. I seek no merely personal honour at your hands; this kind of work was freely elected as my own when helpers were few and unhonoured. Should you elect me as member of your School Board, I trust that the honour thus accorded will enable me to prosecute more extensively the work I have hitherto been so much associated with. I am, Ladies and Gentlemen, Your obedient servant, CAROLINE META SHUM.

In February, just a day before the Bath School Board election, Dr Hathaway proposed the following resolution: 'That in the opinion of this meeting it is desirable that some ladies should be on the School Board to represent the girls who come under its control, and pledges itself to support Miss Ashworth's and Miss Shum's candidature.'

Invited by the committee to express her views, Miss Ashworth addressed the meeting, acknowledging that although she had lived in the city for many years, she was less well known than her fellow candidate, who was valued for her works of benevolence and usefulness. Her forthright and well-articulated address alluded to the notion that many objected to women speaking in public and, worse, having seats on the School Boards in equal council with men:

It is only from a strong sense of the necessity of saying a few words on this question from a woman's point of view that I speak today. Now I believe that people who have the very narrowest conception of what they are pleased to call a woman's sphere, will yet admit that to women is especially given the training of children (hear, hear). Therefore, I ask you, is it desirable that the education of children – of girls – should be solely under the direction of men? (applause). If you will let your thoughts go back to the past history of education in this country, you will find that the two sections of the community who have been most neglected, who have suffered most from the want of that great power – a cultivated, an educated mind – have been the working classes, and women of all classes. And why is this? It has been partly in consequence of the want of direct representation. No sooner had the electoral franchise been extended to men householders [1867] than the Education Act became absolutely necessary (hear, hear). Hitherto women have been denied all share, all participation, in anything outside their home that might be considered of a public character. But this question surely comes so near home to every woman that is it not the duty of some among them to come forward and claim a share in its direction? The House of Commons has recognised this claim, and has framed the Act with the intention that women shall take a direct part in carrying it out. I may remind you that many endowments which have been left in various parts of the country for the benefit of all have been hitherto appropriated for the benefit of boys alone. It is with great satisfaction that I have read the new scheme for the Bath Grammar School as prepared by the Endowed Schools Commissioners. In this it is proposed that hereafter two at least among the Governors shall be women, and that some of the funds may be devoted to the education of girls (hear, hear). Those parents who have known the inestimable privilege of an educated thoughtful mother will respond to my strong conviction that if there is more attention, more care, needed in the training of any portion of the community it ought to be given to the girls, the future mothers, the home educators of our nation (applause). I have been anxious for years past to do something to assist in the advancement of women – for their improved education, and to gain them some participation in public interests – because I am convinced that until women's actual influence is felt in everything relating to social life, we cannot hope for the elevation of the people (applause). All of us who have looked with hope to a system of compulsory education, have done so because we feel it is on this we must rely as a remedy in time to come for those great evils which afflict us so deeply, pauperism and immorality (hear, hear). If the minds of girls and boys are filled with useful knowledge they will gain in thoughtfulness and self-respect, and these qualities will be the surest to overcome temptations and tendencies to vice and degradation. It is not only more schools and more teachers that we require, but it is better schools and more efficient teachers – who will train and influence the minds of the children, and not be merely satisfied with giving them the slightest possible knowledge of writing and reading (hear, hear). I would have the teachers such that the children would come to them as to advisers and friends. In respect to the election which is to take place on Tuesday, I am not so unreasonable as to ask that all your votes should be given to Miss Shum and myself, but I trust you will consider that the lady candidates are not altogether undeserving of fair share of your support (loud applause).

Bath Chronicle and Weekly Gazette, Thursday, 2 February 1871

Sarah Emily Davies (for London), always known as Emily, and Eleanor Elizabeth Smith (Oxford) were already being recognised for their campaigning for higher education for women. Both had been called to give evidence in the Schools' Enquiry Commission in 1864, and in 1866 Emily Davies had published *The Higher Education of Women* in which she highlighted the differences between boys' and girls' education and made a case for access to university education in order to allow women to fulfil their potential and qualify for professional employment. Eleanor had moved to Oxford in the early 1860s where her brother, Henry John Stephen Smith, was a distinguished Savilian Professor of Geometry at the university. She had become well known for her learning and philanthropy both in the university and city through organising a series of lectures for women by professors affiliated with Oxford University and was to later serve as one of the original members of the council of Somerville College when it was founded in 1879.

In Exeter, there was much political wrangling over a lady nominee, Jennetta Octavia Temple, the Bishop of Exeter's sister. She was a worthy, well-liked and respected candidate and would have been a 'politically neutral balm' on a board comprised of men of opposing political loyalties likely to have 'no excess of love to each other'. Her nomination was 'shabbily opposed by one great political party [Tory] in the city and run shy of by the other [Liberal]' with claims being made that her nomination by two working men (a shoemaker and a carpenter) was 'illegal' because they ('by a stupid error') had named her on the form as 'Miss Temple' 'lady,' instead of 'Jennetta Octavia Temple' 'spinster'. Although she did have considerable support from a number of quarters and was likely to have polled well, she withdrew from the election on 26 January 1871:

> TO THE BURGESSES OF EXETER. Ladies and Gentlemen, I am informed that the Committee of Council on Education cannot decide the question of the formality or informality of my nomination. That being the case I do not think I ought to be on the School Board, as my legal right to be there might be called in question. I received official notice that I was nominated to the School Board; from report I learnt it was informal. Had the mistake been made by anyone to whom I had even spoken on the subject, I should have withdrawn at once, but I felt that those who had nominated me, although they did not know the technical rule with regard to my Christian name, did know whom they intended to nominate, and until I was certain the informality was without remedy, I was unwilling by my own act to refuse the nomination. I thank all those who wished elect me, but I beg them clearly to understand that, although my name may, as a matter of form, appear on the voting paper, I do not wish any votes to be given for me. I am, yours faithfully, JENNETTA OCTAVIA TEMPLE. January 26th, The Palace.

In the meantime, a week or so earlier, the parish of St Thomas the Apostle, Exeter had resolved it was expedient that a school board should be formed for the parish, to manage its numerous schools. On 21 February, the *Western Times* reported the eleven names put forward for five seats on the board; one of these was the now correctly nominated Jennetta Octavia Temple and this time her nominators were a ropemaker and a timber merchant:

> TO THE RATEPAYERS OF ST THOMAS. Ladies and Gentlemen – I have accepted the nomination to the St Thomas School Board, on the same ground I did that for Exeter, and can only repeat what I said then. School Boards have to regulate schools, not only for boys, but for girls, and I think a woman ought to be on the School Board, to assist judging what is good for girls, and upon that ground, and that alone, I wish to be elected. I am aware that, if elected, I must take other duties than this my own immediate object. I must be one of the Trustees for the Ratepayers, and for the parents of children who will come under the School Board. As Trustee for the Ratepayers, my duty will be to try that their money shall be spent honestly and efficiently. As Trustee for the Parents, I ask them to believe that I have but one wish, the good of their children, and that, whilst myself a Churchwoman, I honour with all my heart the right God has given parents over their own children, to teach them, or have them taught, to love and serve Him, as they think best. I am, yours faithfully, JENNETTA OCTAVIA TEMPLE. The Palace, February 23rd, 1871.

Again, she faced opposition:

> Miss Temple's committee have had certain local influences and many misstatements to fight against; but to the credit of independent clear-seeing electors, be it said, they quite admit the justice of the girls having one of their own sex to see that their education is properly taken care of. There are certain partisans, however, who not only oppose Miss Temple by 'putting on the screw' to the utmost, but besides this they have striven to defeat her by stating that she did not intend to seek election. The best contradiction to this is the admirable Address which this gifted lady has issued to the electors the parish, who will honour themselves by returning her the head of the poll tomorrow, and thus show their respect for this lady, and their admiration of the work she and her brother have done for education. In the words of one elector – 'She will be good as any three men on the Board, and do no end of good to the parish.'
>
> *Western Times*, Wednesday, 22 February 1871

Out of seven candidates who eventually faced the polls on 28 February, it was reported on 1 March that Jennetta Temple had been rejected. However, further scrutiny the next day revealed she had been successful, securing a place on the board by just one vote. That she was held in great esteem – by her fellow St Thomas board members at least – is demonstrated by her being invited to take the position of vice chair, which she declined.

As these first women began to make their influence felt on school boards, so their electoral experience and confidence developed. Others were encouraged to stand at subsequent triennial elections and make their mark – and so they did. By the end of the 1870s, there were seventy women on school boards across the country. Although greatly outnumbered, these women were able to campaign for improvements to school buildings and conditions, education, attendance, children's health and well-being. For example, Edith Lupton, the first woman elected to Bradford's School Board (in 1882) pushed for the removal of corporal punishment in elementary schools and against the half-time system in the 1880s. Sarah Ann Byles, another of Bradford School Board's women championed secondary education for girls (see Chapter 9). And we have to thank Margaret McMillan, elected to the same board in 1894, for highlighting the plight of under-nourished children in schools.

Chapter 5

The London School Board

It was the London School Board, the world's largest educational authority – with responsibility for 400,000 children – that played a vital role in setting the educational standards for other school boards to follow. Compared with other boards, which were limited to between five and thirteen members, the first London Board had forty-nine members and this was to rise to fifty-five by the mid-1880s.[1] Each of London's ten wards returned a number of candidates. During its period of existence from 1870 to 1902, twenty-nine women were elected to serve, with the 1879–1882 board having the largest number of women members (nine). In general, these women were already well connected and better educated than most; some were already activists and reformers – and they needed to be. It required a large amount of personal effort and expense to activate the political machinery. Halls were hired to hold public meetings; posters and handbills announcing meetings had to be printed and distributed; 'Address to Electors' leaflets were delivered house-to-house. It was, for these candidates, the equivalent of a parliamentary election, and – since London was the centre and symbol of imperial and national power – the letters MSBL (Member of the School Board for London) must have conveyed an additional sense of prestige and social status among them, even though it was an unpaid role. The range of responsibility might have been narrower than that of an MP, but the individual power within the sphere of the LSB was greater. For those already involved in the women's suffrage movement, it was also considered paramount to the success of suffrage that women should step forward to campaign for office and to prove their capacity for responsible and effective public service.[2] They campaigned hard, speaking in public halls, sometimes two or three times a night, dashing from location to location, hammering home the reasons for women to sit on the school board.

For successful candidates, work on the LSB was demanding. Members were required to attend weekly board meetings, usually a Wednesday from 3.30 p.m. until 6.30 p.m. or (quite frequently) much later. They were responsible for visiting schools in their own districts once a week, and for overseeing evening meetings of local managers who looked after the detailed work of small groups of schools. In addition, there were visits to other educational institutions such as the Cooking Centre or specialist schools.

In chronological order, these are the women who served. Many are better known for their other campaigning and reforming work and served only one three-year term on the London School Board; others stood and were re-elected time after time.

1. Elizabeth Garrett (Anderson), Marylebone 1870–73
2. Emily Davies, Greenwich 1870–73
3. Alice Cowell, Marylebone 1873–1876
4. Miss Jane Agnes Chessar, Marylebone 1873–1876
5. Mrs Alice Westlake (née Hare), Marylebone 1876–1888
6. Florence Fenwick Miller, Hackney 1876–1885
7. Mrs Elizabeth Surr, Finsbury 1876–1882
8. Helen Taylor, Southwark 1876–1885
9. Miss Rosamond Davenport Hill, City 1879–1897
10. Miss Edith Jemima Simcox, Westminster 1879–1882
11. Mrs Julia Augusta Webster, Chelsea 1879–1882 and 1885–1888
12. Miss Henrietta Müller, Lambeth 1879–1885
13. Miss Mary Eliza Richardson, Southwark 1879–1885
14. Frances Hastings, Tower Hamlets 1882–1885
15. Annie Besant, Tower Hamlets 1888–1891
16. Margaret Mary Dilke, Lambeth 1888–1891
17. Emma Knox Maitland, Marylebone 1888–1891 Chelsea 1894–1903
18. Margaret Anne Eve, Finsbury 1891–1903
19. Ruth Homan, Tower Hamlets 1891–1903
20. Alice Mary Wright, Westminster co-opted 13 July 1893–1894
21. Mary Bridges Adams, Greenwich 1897–1903
22. Eugenie Dibdin, Finsbury 1897–1902
23. Constance Elder, Westminster 1897–1900
24. Honnor Morten, Southwark 1897–1900
25. Ellen Courtauld McKee, City 1897–1900
26. Susan Lawrence, Marylebone 1900–1903
27. Hon. Agnes Maude Lawrence, Westminster, 1900–1903
28. Hilda Caroline Miall-Smith, Marylebone 1900–1903
29. Edith Glover, Chelsea Co-opted in place of Emma Maitland in January 1903

Elizabeth Garrett Anderson and Emily Davies served just one three-year term, not standing in the 1873 triennial election – other important matters and campaigns perhaps requiring more of their attention and time. Mrs Alice Cowell (Elizabeth's sister) took her place in Marylebone and Miss Jane Chessar joined her to represent the same ward.

Jane Agnes Chessar was born in Edinburgh in 1835, where she was privately educated with the view to becoming a teacher. Showing great aptitude, she travelled to London, aged just 16, to qualify more fully for her vocation by training at the Home and Colonial School Society's Training College for Schoolmistresses, Gray's Inn Rd. She was so successful in her Christmas exams that the committee sought to appoint her, so instead of taking up the post of governess in the Home for Daughters of Church of England Missionaries, as at first arranged, she took charge of one of the large training classes at the Home and Colonial Institution. There she remained for fifteen years, during which time probably more than a thousand young teachers were brought under her immediate influence. It was no easy task, especially in those first few days of a new year:

> The students, all newcomers, were with few exceptions, pupil teachers from various parts of England. Though well-meaning and sensible on the whole, some were decidedly rough in manner, and many possessed an exaggerated idea of their own abilities. But, before the end of a week, a marked change had taken place. By the power of her presence, by her scorn of pretentiousness, and by the high standard of manners and attainments set before them, the boldest and most conceited were subdued. Then came the all-powerful interest of the lessons, the sense of the justice of her rule, and the charm of a manner always graceful, but which became more gay and kindly as her pupils became more thoroughly loyal.
>
> *Educational Times*, Friday, 1 October 1880

Little wonder that, eventually, her already poor health was impacted and she resigned from the college in 1866. She carried on working as a teacher (she is listed on the 1871 census as a teacher of geography) giving private lessons and lectures on special subjects, chiefly physical geography, laws of health, domestic and political economy. These lectures were given in various parts of London and the provinces, for the National Health Society and other sanitary associations. She also taught these subjects in the Home and Colonial Training College, and in the North London Collegiate (founded by Frances Buss), and other high-class schools for girls. She gave evidence to the LSB in June 1871 that smaller classes were far better for teaching reading and arithmetic, and in November 1871 she was elected as a member of the College of Preceptors in Bloomsbury, an organisation founded in 1846 to ensure professional standards in teachers. Clearly, Jane was a perfect candidate for the LSB. In her campaigning election address she stated:

> For twenty years I have been practically engaged in education – during the greater part of that time in training teachers of Public Elementary Schools at the Home and Colonial College, Gray's Inn Road. I may, therefore, claim to have a large experience in the kind of education which it is the business of School Boards to extend. If I should be elected, the knowledge which I have thus gained may, I hope, be of service. Your choice of Mrs [Garrett] Anderson at the last election showed that you desired to secure the co-operation of women in carrying out the Elementary Education Act; and it seems reasonable to expect that the education of girls at any rate may best be promoted by the presence of women as members of the Board. I am of opinion that the benefits of education should be extended to all, and that a parent has no more right to starve the mind than to neglect the physical wants of his child. I am therefore in favour of compulsion in those cases where it is necessary. As a teacher I have found that the 'religious difficulty' is rarely a cause of embarrassment in schools. But, while I am decidedly in favour of scriptural instruction, I think it ought to be of an entirely unsectarian character. Should you do me the honour to elect me, I shall feel it my duty to give the necessary time and attention to the work with which I may be entrusted.
>
> *North Londoner*, Saturday, 15 November 1873

In her short time on the board (she was struggling with ill health and left the UK for warmer climes in 1875), she did much useful work in connection with the health and domestic training of girls. On 3 September 1880, still with a keen interest in education and still not well, she died suddenly from a stroke a few days after assisting at an educational congress in Brussels.

A colleague who had been with her in Brussels recalled:

> As is the case with all who have great personal influence, much of her work was of a kind which cannot be measured or recorded, which is even forgotten while its fruits are flourishing. She was identified with every important movement for the higher education of women, the training of teachers, and the spread of sanitary knowledge among all classes. But, in advocating a high mental culture for her sex, she was not one-sided. She never lost sight of the necessity for the domestic training of girls. She helped to organise classes for needlework and cookery, and urged that all girls should be taught, at least, the elements of household management and sick nursing. Many good works, now prospering in other hands, owe their existence to the faith and energy with which she supported them, when their success appeared doubtful. As a teacher, her work has this special feature – she widened the sphere of female education by showing that scientific subjects can be made interesting and

practically useful to girls of average intelligence; and she opened a new field of labour to highly cultured women, by proving that such subjects can be taught, and admirably taught, by a woman. She was a true friend to teachers, and many who are now happily employed in congenial work, owe their present position chiefly to her good advice, and to her untiring efforts to find useful and remunerative employment for those whom she thought properly qualified.

Educational Times, Friday, 1 October 1880

In 1876, four women were elected, including Mrs Alice Westlake (née Hare) for Marylebone, replacing the two previous representatives who decided not to stand. Alice was already 'at the core of the emerging mid-Victorian women's movement', before her marriage to barrister John Westlake (fourteen years her senior) in 1864, and in 1865 was one of the founder members of the Kensington Society, a discussion group of around fifty women. Membership of the society was by invitation only and it sought to pursue equality for women in various fields. 'None but intellectual women are admitted and therefore it is not likely to become a merely puerile and gossiping Society,' wrote Alice when inviting Helen Taylor, step-daughter of John Stuart Mill MP, to join the group. 'The object of the Society is chiefly to serve as a sort of link, though a slight one, between persons, above the average of thoughtfulness and intelligence who are interested in common subjects, but who had not many opportunities of mutual intercourse.' Looking at the list of members, it is clear that girls' and women's education and training would be some of the key topics discussed, as it included Emily Davies (educationalist), Francis Mary Buss (headmistress of North London Collegiate School), Dorothea Beale (principal of Cheltenham Ladies' College), Elizabeth Wolstenholme-Elmy (headmistress), Anne Clough (educationalist), Helen Taylor (educationalist), Elizabeth Garrett (medical student), Sophia Jex-Blake (medical student), Bessie Rayner Parkes (writer), Jessie Boucherett (writer), Frances Power Cobbe (journalist), and Barbara Leigh Smith Bodichon (artist).

Alice and her husband were instrumental in assisting Elizabeth Garrett in the establishment of the New Hospital for Women (where the medical staff were all women) at Seymour Place and from January 1875 at 222 Marylebone Road (Alice was treasurer). Alice took a prominent part in the movement for the better education of women, and their admission to different employments and to the suffrage. She remained a member of the LSB until 1888 and, as a member of the School Board Election Committee, was able to assist other women onto the school board.

During nine years as a member, she was one of the most frequent attenders at school board meetings, where she pursued Liberal party policies and instituted centres for teaching cookery. By 1882, she was on the central committee of the

National Society for Women's Suffrage. She was also an artist, exhibiting at the Royal Academy and the Paris Salon. She died at 3 Chelsea Embankment, London, on 11 August 1923.[3]

Also joining the LSB in 1876 was Florence Fenwick Miller. In October, she was invited by Reverend Stewart Headlam to become a candidate for the Hackney division. Motivated by what she described as the 'scandalous shortage' of women with the drive and ambition to pursue interesting careers in the public arena and keen to have influence in the education of the working classes, elementary school girls and women teachers, she accepted the nomination. Duly elected, she became the youngest woman, at 22 years old, ever appointed to the largest and most powerful organ of local government in existence at the time.[4]

Florence's own education had started at a dame school, following which she was home-educated by her mother until she was 6. She spent a year at a Young Ladies' Seminary before being sent to boarding school aged 7. At 18, Florence studied for a medical degree at Edinburgh University, shortly after The Edinburgh Seven had campaigned for women to be admitted to the course, later transferring to the London School of Medicine for Women, established in 1874 by a group of pioneer doctors (including Sophia Jex-Blake and Elizabeth Garrett Anderson). Florence married Frederick Ford, a stockbroker's clerk, in 1879, keeping her maiden name of Miller. She is listed on the 1881 census as Member of London School Board and lecturer in psychology and literature. As well as penning several teaching texts, during the 1880s she supported herself financially by writing for a variety of publications including the *Modern Review*, *Lady's Pictorial*, *Fraser's* and *The Governess*. The 1891 census notes her occupation as journalist and author, having left the school board at the 1885 election. From 1886–1918, she was a columnist for the *Illustrated London News*, editor of *Woman's Signal*, 1895–1899, and *Outward Bound*, 1890–1895. She was a delegate and speaker at the International Congress of Women, Chicago, 1893, and in 1902, elected first treasurer of the International Women's Suffrage Committee, Washington DC.

By 1879, women were really making their mark in London. The press reported of the 1879 London election:

> The ladies with seats on the late Board who offered themselves for re-election were all returned, namely, Mrs [Alice] Westlake in Marylebone, Mrs [Florence] Fenwick Miller in Hackney, Mrs [Elizabeth] Surr in Finsbury, and Miss Ellen [Helen] Taylor in Southwark. They are now reinforced by Miss Rosamond Davenport Hill for the City, Miss Edith [Jemima] Simcox for Westminster, Mrs [Julia Augusta] Webster for Chelsea, Miss [Henrietta] Müller for Lambeth, and Miss M[ary] E[liza] Richardson for Southwark.

Two other women, Jane Anne Simpson (Marylebone) and Helena Pauline Downing (Tower Hamlets), were unsuccessful.

Women's influence in London

When campaigning for votes to be elected to school boards, women's claims were that girls had quite different educational requirements to those of boys (physical, emotional and intellectual), so needed women in a position of influence in order to champion their interests and those of women teachers too. In light of that, the women on school boards were generally elected on to sub-committees to work on curricula, school attendance, and teachers' salaries, conditions and career opportunities.

Elizabeth Surr, seeking to be elected for the Finsbury Ward in 1876, published her 'Facts for Finsbury':

> THERE ARE 28,906 GIRLS, excluding Infants, and 858 FEMALE TEACHERS, Excluding Pupil Teachers, IN THE LONDON BOARD SCHOOLS.
>
> FEMALE VISITORS are engaged in each of the ten Divisions.
>
> The course of special instruction for girls includes NEEDLEWORK.
>
> CRECHES have been established where infants are taken care of, enabling the elder children to attend school.
>
> COOKERY is taught at present in four centres, and question of extending this branch of education must shortly come up for discussion.
>
> In the face of facts like these, can any doubt the desirability of returning A LADY FOR FINSBURY – THEREFORE, VOTE FOR MRS SURR, On Thursday, November 30th, Each Elector has SIX Votes, all of which can be given for Mrs SURR

Having been elected, the women faced social and political pressures and had to adapt to the unfamiliar demands of public office, including underhand political manoeuvring and financial obstacles to campaigning. They worked hard, many regarding their work on LSB as the main business of their lives. Florence Fenwick Miller, who was subject to some particularly harsh verbal assaults over her endorsement of a book on population control through contraception (deemed obscene by the puritanical Victorians), spent two or three days a week working from the offices on the Embankment and spent hours on committee work, particularly on the School Management Committee. Mrs Emma Maitland, who served in Marylebone from 1888 to 1891 and in Chelsea from in 1894 to 1903, worked Monday, Thursday and Friday and alternate Wednesdays. When they were not in the offices, both women spent time on constituency work, supervising local schools and engaging with teachers and ancillary staff, Emma playing a significant part in developing education for children with disabilities.

The longest-serving member of the LSB was Rosamond Davenport Hill, brother of Sir Rowland Hill (teacher, inventor and postal reformer). Rosamond's mother had suffered a great deal of ill health and as a result much of the housekeeping had fallen on Rosamond to perform. This first-hand knowledge was to prove invaluable when she was called on to organise the cookery, laundry and needlework departments of the LSB and in her first nine years on the board, she never missed a weekly board meeting. Prior to coming to London, from 1851 she had taught at and helped to run a Ragged School in Bristol, honing her administrative capacity and instituting practical reforms of considerable value, and giving both time and money when it was later transformed into an industrial school for girls. She served fifteen of her eighteen years on LSB as chair of the Cookery Committee and also joined the School Management Committee and the Industrial Schools Committee, taking the Industrial School at Brentwood under her immediate care. Rosamond was very much involved with practical instruction; she was chairman of the managers at Greystoke Place, Fetter Lane, the first school under the London Board to take up social economy as a regular subject. Here the children were instructed in the elementary duties and difficulties of the industrial life that awaited them, rather than more academic studies. It was said she spent the greater part of the meetings listening while busily knitting, speaking only when absolutely necessary. When one of her constituents challenged her in public, she wittily responded, 'This is the first time I have heard a woman complained of for using her hands too much and her tongue too little.'[5]

Influences on curricula

In May 1860, the Education Department of the Privy Council issued the Education Code – 'a document of very moderate length, but of very great importance'. It consisted of the minutes and regulations on education, distilled into a 'code', beginning with a preliminary chapter of definitions and first principles, followed by a series of divisions and subdivisions. It was noted that, 'Nothing can be more clear and simple than this statement of the law and practice upon a rather intricate subject.' It was revised annually, and usually contested by interested parties via newspaper correspondence.

Its primary purpose was to set out the conditions for the distribution of the parliamentary grant for public education in England and Wales. These grants were to aid in maintaining public elementary schools and training colleges for teachers, primarily based on attendance and the pupils' attainments in the subjects of instruction through examination, plus a merit grant (in 1882 this was 2s, 4s, or 6s per year for each unit of average attendance, according to whether the school inspector judged the school or class to be fair, good or excellent). Additional grants were specified for needlework and singing. Perhaps with Angela Burdett Coutts' mid-1850s values of girls being taught 'common things' in mind, the subjects taught to girls and boys continued to differ and failure to teach needlework to girls became one of the few offences for which an elementary school could lose its grant.

Seeking to improve teaching and outcomes in needlework, Louisa Ayscoghe Floyer, who had been appointed examiner in needlework to the London School Board in 1873, founded the London Schools' Association for the Improvement of Elementary Needlework in 1876 (and enlisted, among its patrons, Miss Burdett Coutts). Its primary objective was 'to encourage the teaching of the housewifely art of making and mending clothes' and to that end it held annual exhibitions at the South Kensington Museum, supported by various benefactors who distributed prizes for both teachers' and pupils' work. Forty schools competed in 1877, with 800 entries. In 1880, it was reported that:

> Pretty specimens of work can be easily attained, it appears; but the art of cutting out garments so as not to waste or misuse the materials is one understood by a comparatively small number of schoolmistresses, and the children have, in consequence, left the schools often able to stitch more or less neatly, but utterly unable to do that which, as the daughters or wives of poor men, it would be the greatest advantage for them to be able to do well.
>
> *Northern Whig*, Wednesday, 26 May 1880

However, it did conclude that progress was being made, with infants aged only 4 being able to neatly sew pinafores. Anthony Mundella, the MP whose Elementary Education Act 1880 was about to receive Royal Assent, making attendance compulsory for children aged 5–10, welcomed the news that an institution, the London Institute for the Advancement of Plain Needlework, had been opened and was now in operation in Connaught Street, Edgware Road, where instruction was given, and teachers and others who wished might learn all branches of the art. If, as he hoped, more attention should be paid to the subject, 'we should as a people be great gainers in the future'.

But was this at the detriment of other learning for girls? Some women board members helped to organise the agitation against the excessive demands of the needlework syllabus. In 1880, Henrietta Müller, at a meeting of the West Lambeth Association, suggested a meeting of the women teachers to discuss the needlework scheme, and later undertook to bring their resolutions and views before the board. She had support from three men on the board, Sir Charles Reed MP, Lynulph Stanley MP and Dr Gladstone, who alongside Henrietta, Alice Westlake and Edith Simcox met with Anthony Mundella and Earl Spencer on 20 July 1880.

Leading the deputation, Sir Charles drew attention to the increasing stringency of the needlework requirements in the third schedule of the latest Education Code, and urged that the fifth stage, which was due to come into operation, be suspended, saying needlework was the most difficult of all subjects to teach and the demands for such full and technical knowledge from children was as high as only women of mature years could be expected to obtain. There was reason to fear other educational subjects in girls' schools suffered from the pressure caused by the needlework requirements, and the pressure was severely felt by the teachers. Margaret, Alice and Edith and Dr Gladstone each urged their views, stating that girls who had passed through the fourth stage of the third schedule had mastered all that was necessary to make them useful and good needlewomen, and were sufficiently prepared for acquiring the further technical knowledge which was necessary to many of them in later life, and which could be gained after the completion of elementary education. Earl Spencer agreed to look into the important subject of needlework, but Mundella remained unconvinced it should be diluted. He thought:

> good needlework might be taught, and that was the opinion of vast numbers of school managers in the country. The manner in which very young children manipulated the threads of finest lace in warehouses convinced him that they were perfectly capable of doing needlework, and they did the work without the least mental strain upon them: and if the children began young enough there was nothing in the code which they could not attain without in the slightest degree interfering with their intellectual exercises in other studies.[6]

He was not to be swayed on the matter. Under 'Subjects of Instruction for which grants may be made' in the New Education Code of 1882, the compulsory subjects '(hereinafter called "the elementary subjects")' were listed as: Reading; Writing; Arithmetic; Needlework (for girls in day schools).

With perhaps the purpose of imposing the ideal family unit of male breadwinner and female full-time wife and mother, more traditionally female-only subjects were added to the curriculum. Theoretical domestic economy was made a specific, though optional, subject for girls in 1878, and in 1882 the government added grants for the teaching of cookery – although in the late 1870s, Alice Westlake had told female head teachers to reduce their workload by substituting cookery for classes in 'drawing and grammar'. Florence Fenwick Miller, Henrietta Müller, Elizabeth Surr and Helen Taylor all argued that since the teaching of cookery was done on gas cookers, quite beyond the reach of working-class housewives, it was also inappropriate to the realities of working-class life and not much use to them in 'an artisan's home'.[7]

Helen Taylor, attending the first Domestic Economy Congress (in Birmingham in 1877), stressed the value of a sound elementary education which would be the foundation of a later high-class system of cooking, adding that cookery lessons seemed better suited to mothers than to girls. Lydia Becker (of Manchester) restated the cause in 1881 at the third Domestic Economy Congress, objecting to compulsory domestic economy lessons in elementary schools, describing them as 'class legislation' and saying, 'Let the girls receive such an education as would make them intelligent women, and then they would be able to do anything which they had to do.'

In contrast to her colleagues, Rosamond Davenport Hill, as chair of the Cookery Sub-Committee, gave evidence to the Royal Commission on Elementary Education (Cross) 1887, which was investigating the effects and working of the Elementary Education Act (1870).

When questioned as to whether any of the girls become cooks or domestic servants she replied:

> We hope they do. I heard a little time ago that a girl had taken a place, and that her employer was quite delighted with her because she could cook the dinner while the family attended chapel on a Sunday morning.

Helen Taylor and Frances Hastings took up the baton again in 1885, unsuccessfully proposing a motion to reduce the number of cookery classes; Frances also argued against the amount of time girls spent sewing, stating that much of the practical instruction was unnecessary and girls should receive a foundation of general knowledge instead.[8]

Still, the differentiation continued and by the 1890s had expanded to include laundry work and housewifery. Some practical subjects were added for boys, but these were not equivalent in time applied to those being taught to girls. LSB members Jane Chessar, Alice Cowell, Emily Davies, Elizabeth Garrett Anderson, Frances Hastings, Florence Fenwick Miller, Henrietta Müller, Elizabeth Surr and Helen Taylor had all tried to limit this kind of training and campaigned for change but, generally, education provision for boys and girls was dealt with as though biology was destiny and that women would not be required to seek careers other than in domestic service.

Ruth Homan, who served from 1891 until the abolition of school boards in the early twentieth century, became vice chair of the Industrial Schools Committee in 1900 and also served on the School Management Committee. It was from this position she was able to mobilise support for a year-long pilot scheme to teach cookery to boys at the cookery centre attached to Bow Creek School, Poplar where she was manager. Being near to the docks, the lessons had an emphasis on naval fare, with the aspirations of employment at the seamen's homes and a modicum of success was realised when the 1902 Elementary Education Code allowed for the instruction of cookery to boys in 'seaport towns'.

However, prior to this, Ruth had been instrumental in the introduction of more domestic training for girls. In an interview reported in the *Woman's Signal* of 15 November 1894, as she was standing for re-election to the LSB, she related what had been accomplished and her next priorities:

> The teaching in connection with the cooking, needlework, and laundry has greatly improved. The needlework is much more practical since cutting out and mending have been added. I think the laundry work very important as a means of teaching girls how to manage a 'wash', without upsetting the whole house over it, which is so frequently the case. The fathers, too, are delighted that the girls can get up their collars so nicely. This appeals to the men wonderfully.

'Should I be re-elected,' continued Mrs Homan, 'I hope to introduce housewifery classes. I do not wish to add another subject, but to have practical lessons in housewifery conjointly with the domestic economy section, already existing ...'

Her 'rough plan' as she described it, was to establish centres in connection with a group of schools, where there would be two or three furnished rooms – parlour, kitchen, bedroom – to provide practical housekeeping lessons, plus a classroom where the theoretical part of domestic economy could be taught. The laundry and cooking could be amalgamated with the housewifery. In the classroom, instruction might be given as to the properties of food, processes of digestion, etc., under the heading of cookery. The properties of soaps, alkalis, and water would come under the laundry; and ventilation, sanitation, drainage, and sick nursing, under housewifery. So much for the academic educational progress of girls.

Issues of school attendance and punishment

In an article in *Macmillan's Magazine* (an Australian publication) in November 1880, Alice Westlake outlined some of the work being carried out on attendance levels. Local authorities prioritised the issue of school attendance because government grants and, until 1883, teachers' salaries, depended directly on average attendance levels. Of course, education was not free and in addition, many poorer families saw education as an intrusion that reduced the earning capacity of a family. With a great demand for juvenile labour, almost any child over the age of 10 could earn a few shillings a week, so the compulsory clause, requiring attendance from 5 to 13, was very tough on the poor. Nor did increased rents – because of increased rates to fund these schools – help the financial plight of the urban poor. Absenteeism was a persistent problem and girls' average attendance was generally lower and more irregular than boys'. This was not just confined to the metropolis. Thomas Allcott, writing in his school log book in Huddersfield on 7 October 1872, complained that 'fifty-six absentees had to be chased up and in most cases the children were employed at home in nursing younger siblings and running errands'. And again in November, 'A great number of children kept at home to nurse and fetch water. I find the parents who are always grumbling as to the progress of their children are the very people who invariably keep them home to do such petty jobs.'

In London, many women members prioritised this area of the Board's work. Girls were unlikely to receive corporal punishment for non-attendance (unlike boys); the method of getting them into school was more carrot than stick. To encourage the attendance of girls who were frequently kept at home to mind younger siblings, Helen Taylor, elected to the LSB in 1876, promoted the establishment of babies' rooms and in 1881 she and Elizabeth Surr persuaded the board to press for government legislation to provide for the establishment of nursery schools and were part of a deputation to the Education Department on the subject.[9] In another incentive, Henrietta Müller, also anxious over girls' non-attendance, sought (unsuccessfully) to encourage the girls by enabling them to qualify for a book prize on the strength of one, as opposed to two, complete attendance cards.

Their work brought some success; within eight years of the LSB's work on attendance, the number of children on the rolls of efficient schools in the metropolis had been doubled, and average attendance more than doubled. Alice Westlake reported that, 'From many an alley which the School Board officer could scarcely enter with safety, the children are now regular in attendance, and the parents who used to come to the school with abusive complaints are more civil, if not grateful.'

Of course, there were always children who skipped school. So great was the problem that in March 1876 the LSB formed an Incorrigible Truants Committee (by 1880, the Industrial Schools Committee), consisting of ten men to investigate and report on the situation, with a view to finding a solution. Its first meeting reported that these were the children of parents who 'sincerely desired to obey the law, but who, through feeble health, widowhood, or absence at work, cannot prevent the wilful and perverse truancy of their children' and in many cases the byelaws operated with harshness, if not injustice. Sending children to an industrial school for a long detention was disproportionate to the circumstances; they were not vicious or criminal, merely wilful; it disturbed family life and involved excessive public expenditure, and therefore the recommendation was to build a special school for truants. One idea was to follow a German initiative of a 'punishment school' whereby the errant child was subjected to the discipline of silence and not allowed any play (though exercise was provided through marching and drilling). First 'offenders' were to stay a week and the length of detention increased according to how many times the child had to be returned. Elizabeth Surr, as 'a mother of small children' was horrified at the idea, since 'play and talk were the very life of children'. On the other hand, Helen Taylor, who later in her career told the Metropolitan Board Mistresses' Association that she cared for the children 'from the point of view of a maiden aunt', supported the idea, saying that a forcible suspension of talk was a greater punishment to a strong person than flogging and that, as a rule, the incorrigible truant was of a robust constitution. Eventually, a truant school was established in an old building, Upton House, Homerton, where, in 1879, the conditions in which forty-six boys, 'rebels against civil authority', were being detained for up to two months (providing they behaved) created much cause for concern. By 1885, a new school to accommodate 100 boys had been built on the site, and it was reported that around 90 per cent of the incorrigible truants had returned to mainstream education and their attendance had been good. The example was followed by many other school boards.

However, all was not quite as it seemed. Elizabeth Surr, first elected to the LSB in 1876, gained a high public profile through her membership of the Committee on Incorrigible Truants. First reporting on the gross acts of cruelty inflicted on the boys by the assistants and demanding the sacking of the governor in 1879, she later challenged the assertion that there were no juvenile thieves at Upton House. Writing to the editor of the *Daily News* in June 1880, she detailed six of the twenty-four cases of which she had first-hand knowledge. Some had been at Upton House for over a year (far longer than had been initially proposed as a 'punishment school'), others, determined or incorrigible thieves, had been in prison for short sentences. Eight of the boys were due for transfer to industrial schools at the governor's request because they were exerting evil influence over the rest. Although not unsympathetic to their plight (agreeing they should be cared for and, if possible, rescued), Elizabeth contended that they were not the special class of children for which Upton House was purchased.

Working alongside Elizabeth in encouraging better attendance and less punishment was Helen Taylor. That a banquet had been given in her honour on her first being elected to the LSB shows how highly thought of she was. But, in a forerunner of what was to come, even on that occasion she contradicted the speaker when he asserted 'she brought power which, when employed as only a woman could employ it, was inestimable.' Her response was to disclaim the idea that women were only in their places superintending education of girls and infants:

> If that were so, women would be only the mothers of girls. Women and working men were received more readily on the school board than in more important places, but there were some who observed that the school board was not Parliament. She would remind men who prided themselves on superior powers of reasoning that the greatest logician for two thousand years [probably meaning her step-father] thought women's intellect equal to man's? It was not unwomanly to be interested in the education of boys, or to study the means by which they might rise in the future.

Helen Taylor caused a stir among other board members with more radical ways of encouraging the working classes to send their children to school. Already very comfortable at public speaking, from the earliest days of her career on the LSB she spoke openly about its work at various meetings, and was widely reported. Addressing meetings in Bermondsey, Blackfriars and Rotherhithe in late 1878, she expressed her regret that LSB's transactions, which had much interest to the ratepayers, were not better known to them. She told the audience many of the board's decisions did not meet with her approval, but rejoiced in a new initiative that was to open the school playgrounds to the public during the summer holidays and certain evenings in the week, 'providing a great boon' to the residents of crowded neighbourhoods. Unfortunately, her resolution to 'rid the Board of the disgrace of corporal punishment' had not been passed; she trusted it would eventually receive proper consideration and that her constituents felt the same. She opined it was:

> in the interest of the teacher to rid his school of irregular attendants and dull scholars, and by continuing the use of the cane they would accomplish that end. Those who did not learn received a tap [punishment], which prevented them coming again, and thus the poor, dull and stupid children were driven out, while the bright ones and those of well-to-do parents remained. The teacher of course found it much easier to teach the sharp ones, and consequently received greater credit. But that system, if carried out, would fill the board schools with the children of parents who were able to send them to other schools, while the children of the poor and destitute parents would find their way to industrial schools, where each child cost an average of £40 a year.
>
> *South London Chronicle*, Saturday, 30 November 1878

When asked for an explanation as to how this £40 was spent, Helen Taylor said, 'I only wish more ratepayers would ask that question, and I only wish it was easy to answer. I cannot answer it, for I do not know how the money is spent.'

Her outspokenness on Industrial Schools was to land her in trouble four years later, when she was tried for libel, having made several speeches accusing former fellow LSB member, Thomas Scrutton, former chair of the Industrial Schools Committee and founder of St Paul's Industrial School, Bow, of being morally guilty of the manslaughter of many children who had entered his school strong and healthy. Every kind of cruelty had been inflicted on these poor children over the years by the authority of a man who called himself a Christian and philanthropist, she said; he had supplied some of the miserable, adulterated food himself to the school, and she had little doubt the children were there only to make money by their work. After a four-day trial, where the most dreadful and sad cases of boys dying at the school were heard, the case collapsed; Helen Taylor was advised she could not support her justification for the libel and she should settle. Scrutton claimed his objective was attained and his character cleared. It was reported:

> That combative lady, Miss Helen Taylor, who seems to have more than the proverbial gift of her sex in speech, has at last paid dearly for her combativeness. Yesterday she agreed to pay a man whom she had libelled the tangible sum of £1,000, including costs. As the step-daughter of the late Mr John Stuart Mill, and member of the London School Board, the utterances of Miss Taylor have attracted more attention than they would otherwise have done. She is no doubt well intended, according to her lights, but the light that is in her is sometimes darkness. Perhaps if there were little more sweetness accompanying the light, it would be better for the lady herself, and the very good objects which she often champions. There may have been cause for sharp criticism of the management of the Industrial Schools (connection with which the libel arose), but it now appears that her zeal as a critic and censor has outrun her discretion.
>
> *Dundee Courier*, Saturday, 1 July 1882

This zeal and lack of discretion led some LSB colleagues to complain she was tactless and overbearing; men particularly nicknamed her the 'acid maiden'. Perhaps they felt the woman 'should know her place'. Elizabeth Surr, however, was totally supportive of her colleague (having given evidence against Scrutton in court and openly criticised him in the newspapers). She and other of Helen's friends and colleagues founded a small committee to organise public subscription to raise funds to cover the £1,000 payment.

Elizabeth and Helen were not the only women members to recognise and strive to help the plight of misbehaving boys. Florence Fenwick Miller also took a leading part in what she saw as a public duty to these children. The women were criticised by some men on the LSB, who claimed women ought not to have taken such a lead, to which Florence countered: '[we] had to lead, simply because the men would not undertake the task of censure which appeared to us necessary.'[10]

Taking up the mantle in the 1890s, Ruth Homan also fought moves to reinstate the ritual of flogging boys as a punishment for being sent back to industrial schools and, with Honnor Morten in 1898, attempted to ban the use of corporal punishment in the Board's reformatory schools. Of the eight women serving on the 1897–1900 LSB, only Emma Maitland disagreed that punishments were too harsh. Amendments to Ruth's proposal – by two men – resulted in the practice continuing, but in private rather than public. Ruth was subsequently promoted to vice chair of the Industrial Schools Committee.

Helen Taylor was the first woman to be promoted to a position of authority when she was elected to chair the Educational Endowments Committee in 1883. She had already been campaigning for money from the endowed schools to be distributed to the benefit of all children and had cited the example of the Queen Elizabeth School, which was originally endowed with 16 acres of land, and had a gross income of £5,000 a year. Helen recommended a letter be sent to the Charity Commission asking them to investigate just where that money went and asking that preference might be given to the children residing in the parishes of St John's, St Olave's and St Thomas's, and then, if there were any more benefits available in the said school, that preference might be given to the children of Southwark.

Her vociferous campaigning work for the poorer members of society also included calling for the abolition of school fees and suggesting the issue of shoes and stockings to those pupils who needed them, even providing them (and a midday meal) at her own expense via teachers and local committees in Southwark. She also suggested that smaller classes and larger expenditure on all things that were essential to both children's development and teachers' health.

She had a good grasp on value for money and was open in her criticism of the way the School Management Committee went about procurement, telling constituents at her annual address in Bermondsey Town Hall just how profligate the committee had been. In a story that could resonate with modern government spending she related:

> An example of how they paid for everything was to be found in the fact that they had paid £1 16s each for two tea jugs for an industrial school, while a lady member had bought the same day precisely similar articles at 4s each. ... Then they had the question of the payment of the architect. Those

who were for proper economical method of payment without commission of course did not carry their object; but when some of the members asked for increased payment for the visitors, the poorest men in the employ of the Board, the Board suddenly became stern and economical. They had just concluded a new contract with their printer to do the work of the Board at about 25 per cent higher than it could be done on small scale by any chance printer in London. Certain bills were charged at £1 per thousand which she had got printed at 25s per 10,000. With regard to the Board's new device for extravagance – viz., the enlargement of the Board's offices, at an estimated cost of £53,000 – it should be remembered that the ship Shaftesbury was only to cost £15,000, but that it ultimately cost £90,000; and there was no knowing to what extent this £53,000 would increase.

South London Press, Saturday, 27 October 1883

The women teachers' cause

It was primarily the women on school boards (elsewhere as well as London) who fought for the interests of women teachers, for salaries and other concerns.

As may be expected, women teachers' pay was far lower than that of their male counterparts. This inequality continued until 1961 when, finally, women teachers were paid the same rate as men for the same job (although there still appears to be a gender pay gap).

Promotion prospects were also an issue. It came to notice in June 1878 that a few men were being appointed as heads of boys' and girls' departments in board schools without due submission to the LSB for confirmation. This was contrary to the regulations, which required the name of every headteacher under consideration for a particular post to be put before the full board; instead, appointments were being passed by the School Management Committee. Florence Fenwick Miller rightly thought this was discriminatory and argued that if the situation was to continue it hindered the promotion prospects of women teachers, whose expectation was that they could progress to headships of girls' departments, meaning they could only ever be assistants and at lower salaries. There was suspicion that those in positions of power and authority (men, in other words) were more concerned with establishing a career path for men than for women.

Florence proposed a motion to forbid the School Management Committee allowing any male teacher in future to have charge of the girls' department of a school without special permission of the board having first been obtained. Citing a particular case, there was great debate about the merits of having a headmaster in charge of a school in localities where 'the people are of a somewhat vigorous and unlearned type', where the children might 'yield to the influence of a man and bow to his controlling power' (in a situation 'from which the majority of ladies might reasonably shrink'). The ladies taking part in the debate countered this by arguing that men were not fit for this work as they were not sufficiently gentle, although it was conceded this particular headmaster was of an unusually gentle type and looked up to as an adviser and friend by the local residents. Interestingly, the headship of the girls' department had been briefly taken off him and put under the charge of a mistress, at which point the department fell into 'palpable disorder' and the headmaster was put back in charge. That being so, this case was allowed to continue but Florence's resolution was carried, although some of the men 'more than insinuated' that it was a 'woman's rights' motivated cause.[11]

The marriage bar

Even more of a concern for the rights and careers of women teachers was the issue of the marriage bar. The argument that women should relinquish their teaching posts on marriage or on having children was raised on a perennial basis and one upon which even the women on the school board could not agree.

As early as February 1878, there was an attempt to ban the work of married women elementary school teachers with 'rapidly increasing families'. Elizabeth Surr successfully led the opposition, saying she 'feared this suggestion emanated from gentlemen who wished to introduce the thin end of the wedge for the ultimate exclusion of all female teachers from board schools'. In November the following year, Reverend J. Rodgers, quite reasonably, proposed that married women teachers give three months' notice of expected confinement in order a replacement might be found by the board. Florence said this was indelicate and that women would not submit to having their names and details of their confinements inserted on a register kept by young clerks. Elizabeth, described by the press as the eldest married lady on the board, concurred it was degrading. Helen Taylor, in usual combative form, suggested the board would be improved by one half if the men brought their better halves to the meetings. Despite their protestations, the motion was carried.[12]

The debates continued. In late 1881, Alice Westlake and Reverend T. Morse had put forward a motion that no married woman should be appointed a teacher for two years after she had given birth to a child, and that the teachers should be required to resign their appointments five months before an expected confinement. In response to this, Florence Fenwick Miller called a meeting at Saffron Hill Board School in May 1882 in order to found the Metropolitan Board Mistresses' Association. Around 200 married women teachers attended. Addressing her audience, Florence maintained:

that the [London School] Board had no moral or economical right to inquire into the private and domestic concerns of the teachers so long as the schoolwork was successfully done, while every teacher who failed in producing good results should be dismissed. The exclusion of mothers from among the teachers would injure the schools, both by removing a large proportion of the best teachers, by causing incessant changes of staff, by preventing clever girls from choosing teaching as the profession of their lives, and by taking away from the children precisely the teachers best qualified by their maternal experiences to manage and guide them. She believed the ultimate result must be to degrade the position of all women teachers, for the supply of competent women would be so diminished that men would be appointed heads over girls' and infants' schools, a course to which certain members were already much inclined.

Evening Mail, Friday, 5 May 1882

Other ladies, including Helen Taylor, also addressed the meeting.

Writing in *The Schoolmaster*, Florence also voiced that, 'it would be a great injustice to the teachers who had spent years of life in acquiring their profession to condemn them to leave the occupation in which their intellectual and moral vigour were in full exercise to become household drudges.'

It is clear that without the support of other women on the LSB, many of the issues facing women teachers would not have found an advocate. Writing in *The Lady's Pictorial* in 1885, Florence described the work she and other women members had done on the LSB and which could be replicated elsewhere: overseeing girls' education and the schoolmistresses' work and conditions. Women teachers made up two-thirds of the LSB teaching strength and:

The women teachers, too, need some women on the Boards to help and advise with them individually in their manifold troubles and difficulties, and also to look after their interests in the making of the rules and regulations by which the School Boards manage those institutions that are under their care.

Women teachers must have appreciated this sisterly support. Although Florence did not cite any examples of aid to schoolmistresses in individual cases in the article, one example of female board members being able to listen to schoolmistresses' grievances comes from a case of hardship reported to the LSB in 1882. Helen Taylor told the members of a schoolmistress calling on her one weekend when the headmaster of the school had, out of temper and spite, withheld the wages of the assistant teachers for a fortnight. The teacher had no means to support herself so Helen Taylor advanced her some money to provide for herself temporarily.

The debate on whether married women could continue in their profession rumbled on over the years, but was roundly defeated (in London at least) in June 1888. The Hon. Conrad Dillon was derided by his colleagues for his ridiculous motion: 'That no female teacher who is married be appointed by the Board; and that any female teacher who shall hereafter enter the service of the Board shall, upon her marriage, terminate her engagement with the Board'. In support of his views, he opined that:

> he was perfectly convinced that justice was not done to the children in schools where there were married female teachers. He quoted from a report of one of HM Inspectors to the effect that the children had been neglected in a certain school where the female teachers were all married, owing to the absence of these teachers. Then if female teachers found that they would lose their salaries if they married they would not be in such a hurry to marry, and many improvident marriages would be prevented. He believed one of the greatest evils we suffered from was young people marrying too soon.
>
> *Tablet*, Saturday, 30 June 1888

In response, Reverend A. Drew said if Dillon knew anything about the working of girls' and infants' schools he would have thought very seriously before he put on the paper such a motion as this. If there was one class of teachers more valuable than any other it was the class of married female teachers, especially as head teachers of girls' and infants' schools. He hoped the board would give a decided vote on this ridiculous proposition, which was the most absurd thing he had heard since he had been a member.

Others agreed. Mrs Julia Augusta Webster said no one but a married woman could properly understand the many reasons why it was extremely desirable they should have some married women in their schools. If a proposal were made that none but married women should be head teachers of girls' and infants' schools she might hesitate, but she could not hesitate about this. If they turned out the element of motherhood in their schools they would be acting dead against nature; and if they turned out the mothers she should certainly propose that they should turn out the fathers also. Mr Endean said the board could congratulate itself that the laws of nature were not under the control of Mr Dillon, who, in reply, said he had not expected to raise such a tempest, or to meet with so much personal abuse – for he could not call it anything else. He was perfectly prepared to admit the force of Mrs Webster's arguments, but he thought the matter was one for serious consideration.

He had once heard a coalheaver boast his wife had never had to do a day's work for her family, and he thought this was a manly view to take. Dillon's proposal lost by 27 votes to 3.

Florence, now retired from the LSB, wrote:

> The fact is that a very large proportion of the best and most successful teachers under the Board are married women. When I was member of the Board, I once, in order to crush this vexatious perennial motion for the dismissal of mothers from the teaching staff, showed that every mistress mentioned as model teacher that year by the inspectors was without a single exception, married. The reasons for this are not difficult to perceive. The married women are, as a whole, the elder teachers, and, therefore, the more experienced; they have that special management for and sympathy with all children that the touch of her own baby's lips gives to a true woman; and they are likely to be more settled to their duty than the young single ones, having drawn their lot in the great chance of a woman's life, and found that it includes for them the desirability of wage-earning. For these reasons, the married women teachers ought to form a large proportion of the best mistresses in our schools; and, as a fact, they do so.
>
> *Illustrated London News*, Ladies' Column, Saturday, 7 July 1888

She hoped the overwhelming result would permanently settle the question and prevent the married mistresses being periodically harassed by such a motion in the future. It did not and it was a national concern, with each authority making its own judgement – generally that it would not employ married women as teachers – but this changed from time to time; sometimes they would and sometimes they would not.

Chapter 6

Unions and Associations: The Schoolmistresses' Battle

After the Elementary Education Act was introduced in parliament in February 1870, the various local teachers' associations that were in existence were affiliated under the National Union of Elementary Teachers (NUET) in June 1870. The name was changed to the National Union of Teachers (NUT) in 1889 and existed as such until 2017. Only one woman, Christine Blower, was ever its general secretary (2008–2016).

The first membership lists of 1871 showed 59 associations and over 2,000 members and by 1881 this had increased to 13,000 members in 314 associations. A few associations restricted membership to certificated teachers, but most had no such restrictions and were keen to add women teachers to their numbers, although women did not join in substantial numbers until around 1900. Figures show a quarter of male certificated teachers were NUET members in 1871, but only a tenth of the female teachers had joined (though the numbers had increased to 52 per cent and 30 per cent respectively by 1881). Despite being relatively few in number, women were fairly well represented throughout the NUET, even in 1871, with only nine out of the fifty-nine associations having an all-male membership; in seven associations, women made up more than half the membership and this had increased to eighty-three by 1881. Social mores of the time may have meant women were reluctant to speak out at first, but by 1875 many schoolmistresses had acquired particular authority on prominent issues: the ridiculous demands of the needlework schedule; the introduction and increase in scope of domestic subjects being taught to girls; and developments in infant education. Their causes of complaint spurred more women into joining associations and many were encouraged to take part in proceedings. Although it was more usual for a man to read a woman's paper for her, occasionally they did read their own proposals, known as 'stray leaves', often being allowed to remain seated rather than standing to face the chair.

The growing number of schools required an increasing number of teachers and although the Education Department retained the requirement that the principal teacher should be a certificated teacher, it lowered the standard of the certificate.

Of course, many of the schoolmistresses now certified had come up through the ranks of assistant teacher and gained certification through examination and probation in a school (rather than at a college) and it has been suggested they were content to accept an inferior role in the schools in which they taught and not get involved in teachers' politics. Consequently, it was mainly college-trained mistresses who initially joined the NUET (making up 82 per cent of the female members) although by 1882 the ratio of college- to non-college-trained was more or less 50:50. Salaries and career opportunities were, as usual, one of the key issues facing schoolmistresses.[1]

One such schoolmistress who was not college trained but had risen through the ranks from being a pupil teacher was Miss Elizabeth Haliday. She was appointed mistress at St Luke's Infants' National School in Chorlton-on-Medlock, Manchester on 20 December 1870, aged just 20. The school, established in 1864, remained under the Church of England Diocesan Board rather than the Manchester School Board, which took over its first two voluntary schools in 1875, and the department had around 150 pupils. The government inspections, introduced after the voluntary schools had been given funding after the 1833 Factory Act, continued. It was soon reported the school (having been 'going on fairly' under her predecessor) was now 'going on very creditably' and Elizabeth was responsible for the training of a monitress and three second-year pupil teachers. On 16 July 1872, she noted in her log book, 'Miss Haliday receives her parchment this day. Second division of the second year, the report on the certificate is as follows: E. Haliday gives a lesson to the infants with skill and has her infants' school in a creditable state.' It was signed by W.S. Kennedy, HM Inspector.

As well as running the school and teaching, Elizabeth faced various trials and tribulations with her cohort of pupil teachers. They were frequently off with illnesses (bear in mind this was pollution-stricken 1870s Manchester); some offered themselves as candidates but then found the work not to their liking and withdrew (or their parents withdrew them) shortly afterwards. Some were excellent, passed their yearly exams and were awarded their pupil teacher certificates, but after three years of their five-year apprenticeship (just as they might be becoming useful to Elizabeth), the school managers transferred them to the girls' department and they were replaced by first-year pupil teachers.[2]

On 10 December 1872, Elizabeth received a letter from Reverend W.A. Darby, honorary secretary of the managing committee. She transcribed this letter into the school log book:

Madam,

I am instructed by the management committee of St Luke's Daily Schools to inform you that it appears plain from this statement of accounts for this year that as the expenditure of the schools [this would be the infants', girls' and boys', not just an overspend by Elizabeth] has increased from £372 19s 6d to £519 2s 0d, they are compelled to readjust the arrangement heretofore made with the teacher.

Resolved that the existing arrangements with the mistress in reference to the school pence will be altered to the following: that from 1 January 1873 they be allowed all school pence over 25 shillings per week not as formerly over 20 shillings per week. The arrangement of the capitation grant to remain in force.

In effect, it was a reduction of 5 shillings a week. A few days later, Mr Kennedy inspected the school again, paying particular attention to the pupil teachers' lessons and wrote on the mistress's parchment: 'I found good order and the infants are carefully taught.'

But there was more trouble from Reverend Darby:

Madam,

I laid your letter before the committee and after consideration they passed the 'Final Resolution' which I am instructed to convey to you.

Resolved that Miss Haliday's salary for the year ending 30 November 1873 be a fixed stipend for the current year of £75 together with her furnished rooms, as heretofore to be paid in quarterly instalments of £13 15s and the remaining £20 to be paid at the time of the capitation grant in January 1874. That the surplus of any school pence (over the £13 15s a quarter) to be paid to the treasurer at the end of each quarter.

With reference to the question of whether the committee are bound to give you three months' notice before altering your arrangements they will not discuss the point with you but if you require it they will pay you at the last year's rate for the three months but your salary will be reduced in the remaining three quarters so as to make the total payments for year ending 30 November 1873 £75.

Elizabeth noted this letter was in response to one she had sent, in which she had also stated that they might have considered her proposition of offering to pay for a third pupil teacher before making the resolution of 10 December 1872.

After the Christmas break, the school was again inspected and again 'Miss E. Haliday's school is in a very creditable state in all respects,' but it does seem as though at some point the number of pupil teachers had been reduced to two, hence Elizabeth's offer to pay for a third. Another letter was received from Reverend Darby advising that the committee could not alter the resolution it passed on 14 December respecting her salary. Elizabeth had written, begging (her words) the managers to reconsider this salary limitation as it decreased her salary from £83 to £75. However, disgruntled, she continued another year, and, dedicated to her vocation, undertook further training, attending Saturday morning science classes held in connection with the Union of Lancashire and Cheshire Institutes. Out of seventy students (principal, assistant and pupil teachers) she was one of only three women studying science and was presented with a certificate for animal physiology, elementary, first class on 6 December 1873.[3]

Whether she was a member of or had the support of the Church of England School Teachers' Association for Manchester, Salford and District (inaugurated in March 1870 and merged with two other associations to become the Manchester and District Union of Teachers a year later), is not known, but by the end of January 1874, this strong-minded young woman had had enough – noting in the log book: 'Mistress sent to the managers her resignation as mistress of St Luke's Infants' school.' Her reasons? 'Because the managers make it a rule to remove all pupil teachers who have completed their second and third years to the girls' school and supply their places with candidates or first-year pupil teachers.' She gave three months' notice and left on 30 April. Miss Mary Ann Booth replaced her but it seems that standards slipped. She was replaced in September 1876 by Miss Hannah Sharples, at which point the HMI report recorded that, 'Miss Sharples has only been here a fortnight and is therefore not responsible for the state of the school.' In November it had improved slightly, although 'this department is still suffering severely from the supineness of the late mistress and Miss Sharples has a great deal of work to do ...' Perhaps she was not up to the requirements either, or perhaps the unwillingness of the school managers to pay a reasonable salary did not attract a good calibre of teacher, but when Miss L.B. Moss took over in August 1878 she found the children in 'a very backward state indeed'. The school only possessed one set of slates for all classes and most of those were broken. There were not enough reading books and no animal pictures for the object lessons. All the children in Standard 1 had failed reading and writing and just three had passed arithmetic. She also noted (on investigation of why children were turning up late for lessons) that the former mistress had told parents it was fine if they got to school for 10 a.m.

Elizabeth Haliday, meanwhile, had found a new position. The creation of new board schools nationwide meant there were ample opportunities for schoolmistresses of good calibre, and Elizabeth, having given her notice, would have been confident of finding work. On 30 March 1874, the Huddersfield School Board had drawn up a shortlist of two candidates for headmistress of Moldgreen Infants' School and on 14 April Elizabeth Haliday was appointed at 'a salary of £100 per annum, payable monthly, the engagement to date from the 4th May, 1874, and to be terminated by a written notice of three months on either side'. Elizabeth left one job on the Thursday and started a new, better- (and more frequently) paid one, in a new town, in a better-funded school, on the Monday morning. It was a move that was to change her life. Thomas Allcott, headmaster of Moldgreen Mixed School had been recently widowed, his wife (also a former teacher) dying shortly after childbirth in November 1873. It is easy to imagine that Elizabeth and Thomas were kindred spirits in the field of education. He was a dedicated and considerate headmaster, and a great campaigner for better education and conditions. Reader, she married him – on 22 July 1875 in Manchester. His occupation as schoolmaster is noted on the parish register; hers as a schoolmistress is not. The HMI report of August that year states Moldgreen School Infants' department 'is in a most satisfactory state. The infants are very carefully taught; great pains have evidently been taken with the reading of the first class during the year. The order of the children is also very good, and they are very lively and intelligent.' Clearly Elizabeth's dedication and good work had continued in her new position.

On 23 April 1876 (nine months and a day after the wedding), their first child, Emily, a half-sister for Agnes, was born. It is probable that Elizabeth had to give up her career as a schoolmistress due to Huddersfield School Board's decision, made some time pre-1879, not to appoint married women as teachers; other school boards made similar restrictions, but it seems a shame that the career of such an able, trained and dedicated schoolmistress had ended. However, Elizabeth kept her involvement with education, founding and teaching at a mothers' class at the Congregational church where they became members after moving to Great Harwood in Lancashire in 1881. She was a great support to Thomas and their five children (all three daughters and one of the sons became teachers) throughout their fifty-four-year marriage – Thomas was involved in many organisations: chorus master of the local choral society; president of the local NUT; lay preacher, among others. Although she took no part in public life, her obituary in November 1929 noted Great Harwood had lost a well-known and highly respected resident. Thomas died just four months later.

Had she not eschewed her career to pursue the life of a housewife and mother, Elizabeth might have been one of the schoolmistresses who outnumbered schoolmasters in the Lancashire NUET associations; perhaps even one of those women who were determined to have an association where, in contrast, the men 'were apathetic' (though not Thomas Allcott, it may be supposed).

Still, it was men who initially ran the associations; where women were invited to serve as officers, all declined. Perhaps it was a reluctance to enter 'the bellicose and semi-political arena' of the committee room that had been described by men in debates about whether women should be included. After 1874, a few took up the office of treasurer of their particular association and gradually schoolmistresses began to take on more responsibilities. These tended to be fairly minor roles: librarian; secretary of benevolent funds; offices of pupil-teacher schemes; and many were elected onto association committees.

In 1876, the first women, Miss N.S. Wilson and Miss Jagger from Huddersfield, attended the NUET conference in Liverpool and spoke out – Miss Wilson seconding a motion to 'extend the mixed school system of instruction', supported by Miss Jagger – 'both ladies being received with great cheering'. As it had been in London, the issue of needlework was raised here, with George Gaunt (Huddersfield headmaster turned Huddersfield School Board inspector) moving that the teaching of needlework was now not sufficiently remunerated (given its new requirements) and requesting the executive of the NUET, when considering alterations to the Education Code, direct their attention to the subject. The motion, seconded by Miss Jagger, was carried.

The first report on the Educational Condition of Huddersfield by the town's new school board in 1871 was very telling in its attitude to girls' education, specifying under 'Subjects for Instruction' that:

> Elementary Social Economy, Elementary Domestic Economy, the Principles of Bookkeeping, Plain Needlework, Mending and Cutting out are introduced into the curriculum for girls, for there is no doubt that if the condition of the working classes in this country is to be ameliorated, this in no small measure depends on cheerful homes, clean and neatly mended clothes, and palatable food, which are the objects of a thorough instruction in the above subjects to accomplish.

Needlework, being a compulsory subject for girls (only) in elementary schools, along with reading, writing and arithmetic, was a huge drain on girls' education and the time of the women who taught it. With four to six fewer hours per week for other subjects, girls were subject to the same 'code' examinations as the boys and teachers were measured (and grants paid to schools) on their success. Despite the instruction from HMI for inspectors to be more lenient with girls' examinations, schoolmistresses maintained the inspectors would not or could not make any modification to the girls' examinations.

Undertaking to defend schoolmistresses from these unreasonable new syllabus requirements, the NUET appointed a special committee of ladies to produce a draft scheme for teaching needlework, but the new syllabus published by the education department in its Third Schedule of the Code in 1877 met with condemnation from all associations nationally:

Law of the Needle in School – The new schedule of needlework is causing great excitement among managers and mistresses. At a meeting of some 30 mistresses at Richmond, Surrey, after a long and animated discussion, resolutions were unanimously passed that the syllabus, as a whole, is impracticable, particularly those portions of it which relate to infant schools and the upper schedule in ordinary girls' schools. Other meetings protesting against the requirements [being] too severe have been held in different parts of the country. The objections seem mainly to be (1), that only half a grant is accorded to so important and expensive a subject as needlework; (2) that 'position drill' has nothing to do with needlework; (3) that 'simple' and 'counter' are terms not intelligible to infants, and ought not to be required in Standard 1 make any garments; (4) that 'pleating' ought not to be required the lower standards, and that for it 'gathering' should be inserted; (5) that no particular garments should be named in the standards (as they go out of fashion), but only garments containing the stitches required in the standards; (6) that herring boning should not be taught till Standard 4; (7) that Swiss darning and grafting are not generally known (8) that knotting and feather stitch are fancy-work stitches.

Western Times, Tuesday, 27 March 1877

The hostile response from these and other schoolmistresses did have some effect as the adoption of the needlework syllabus was postponed until 1879, but the London Schools Association for the Improvement of Elementary Needlework (see Chapter 5) pressed on with its needlework exhibitions, though it was reported in *The Schoolmaster* that these were unrepresentative of other London schools and of the work of children.

By 1885, needlework was recognised as a 'class subject', i.e. not compulsory (but still only for girls). It joined English, drawing, geography and elementary science as one of the maximum of three subjects from which the school could choose to teach; history was also available for the higher (older) classes. The three most commonly selected subjects were English, geography and ... needlework.

This teaching of needlework to girls and the demand on both teachers and pupils continued to be contentious but in 1895, at the second conference of the National Federation of Assistant Teachers:

Miss Webster (Sheffield) moved, and Miss Brookes (Sheffield) seconded: 'That this conference welcomes the addition of Note 5 to Schedule III (Needlework) of the Code (1895), which allows teachers to formulate their own needlework syllabus, subject to the approval of the managers of the school and the Education Department and urges upon all teachers the desirability of rendering the note operative, with a view to the adoption of schemes of more educational value, and practicability than Schedule III' – Miss Hardwick (Burton) and Miss Crabtree (Halifax) spoke in support of the resolution, and it was carried.

Burton Chronicle, Thursday, 31 October 1895

It seems some success had come from the campaigning and that decisions on the extent, at least, of needlework tuition would be made at a local instead of national level. The new education code (the code was revised annually in March) restricted the choice of class subjects to just two from English, geography, elementary science, history, and, for girls only, needlework and domestic economy, hence the resolution of the conference to adopt 'schemes of more educational value'.

Chapter 7

The Elementary Schoolmistresses' Career Progression

As well as allocating grants for the pupils' passing of exams and for attendance in schools, the Education Code (under Article 31) sought to classify teachers as follows:

a. Pupil teachers
b. Assistant teachers
c. Provisionally certificated teachers
d. Certificated teachers
e. Evening school teachers

and further described exactly what this meant for each classification (for example see Appendix 3).

The code applied to males as well as females, but there was segregation, with Article 35 stating that:

> A pupil teacher must be of the same sex as the principal teacher of the school in which he or she is engaged. In mixed schools under masters, female pupil teachers may be engaged, and may receive instruction from the master out of school hours on condition that some respectable woman, approved by the managers, be invariably present during the whole time that such instruction is being given.

There was a clear career progression and there was more than one route to becoming a certificated teacher, meaning the profession was open to candidates of all classes, regardless of whether they could afford to take time without pay to attend college full-time for two years. There was also opportunity for already certificated teachers, previously 'untrained', to attend college for the second year of the course without having to sit an examination first.

A clear illustration of a good career progression is that of Louisa Haliday, four years the junior of her sister, Elizabeth. In 1871, her occupation is noted on the

Manchester census as a 'pupil teacher in C of E School'. This does not appear to be the same school as where Elizabeth was head (St Luke's, Chorlton-on-Medlock) as there is no mention of her in the log book. By the mid-1870s, she had joined her sister in Huddersfield (perhaps at Moldgreen, but it is not certain). Unlike Elizabeth, she never married and pursued a long and well-respected teaching career with the Huddersfield School Board and, subsequently, the borough's education department.

Huddersfield School Board reported in its first triennial report of 1874 that:

> The Principal Teachers of the Board Schools in Selection of operation are either certificated, or have passed an examination entitling them to a certificate after 2 years' probation. The selection of teachers has particularly been regarded by the committee as a matter of primary importance. Teachers of recognized ability and experience, who have obtained very favourable reports from the Education Department have been engaged.

Of course, women teachers of 'recognized ability' were only worth 65 per cent of what they were prepared to pay men:

> The Scheme of Education fixes minimum salaries for the teachers but the Board on the 3rd June, after report from the General Purposes Committee found it necessary to fix the maximum salary of the principal masters at £200 and Mistresses at £130. Accordingly, Principal Masters and mistresses have been appointed at these rates [which they claimed were similar to those of other authorities].

Thomas Allcott's salary in 1874 was increased from £150 to £175 against Elizabeth Haliday's £100 at the same school, although it may be supposed there were more pupils under his charge in the juniors' department.

The first record of Louisa's employment in Huddersfield is in August 1876, when she was transferred from Stile Common Girls' School to the school's infants' department. The foundations for this new board school had been laid on 29 November 1873 but building contractor delays meant it did not open until 12 August 1876. In the meantime, a provisional school for 170 pupils had been accommodated in rather unsatisfactory premises. The brand-new school had 306 infant places and 277 for each of the boys' and girls' departments – 860 in total. Miss Bertha Ann Bray from Burton upon Trent had been appointed head of the girls' school in November 1875 but resigned due to ill health in January 1876. Her place was taken by Miss Mary Mellor of Farnley near Leeds at a salary of £100 a year. Louisa, now the same age as her sister when she was already a headmistress, was probably an assistant teacher. By

January 1877, she had transferred to Moldgreen Infants' School (although by this time her sister was no longer teaching) and was awarded a salary increase to £50 a year. In April 1878, the school board approved her salary increase to £65 a year as a certified assistant at Moldgreen. A year later, she was appointed to her first headship, Almondbury Infants' School, at £80 a year. From this point she went from strength to strength as her experience, skill and reputation as an excellent teacher grew. Her salary increased from £80 to £90 in 1881 and again to £95 in 1882. She moved back to Stile Common Infants' in early 1884, as an urgent replacement for Miss Jesse Fraser who died suddenly at her father's house in Scotland. Jesse had been with the school board for a number of years, transferring from Shelley Infants' to be headmistress at Stile Common at the same time as Bertha Bray had become head of the girls' department in November 1875. Louisa would certainly have known Jesse, having worked together at the school and as heads of their respective schools, and is likely to have felt her loss as keenly as the members of the Huddersfield School Board did.

Into Louisa's shoes at Almondbury stepped another Louisa, Louisa Gott. Interestingly, she was employed at a much lower salary than her predecessor had enjoyed, just £55 a year. This was not necessarily a reflection on her abilities; it may have been a reassessment of salary against school size. By the end of the year, Louisa Gott had taken up a headship of another school, Deighton Infants, at £80 a year (increased to £85 after two years) and was replaced by Sarah Jane Taylor at £70 (perhaps the board realised £55 was too low) and she was replaced two years later by Eliza Waite at £75. By this time (June 1886) Louisa Haliday's salary had increased from £100 to £105. At the end of that year, it was announced Louisa had been appointed headmistress of Mount Pleasant Infants' at Lockwood at a salary of £115, commencing in March 1887. She replaced Annie Shires who, after just a year at Mount Pleasant, was returning to Crosland Moor where she had started as a pupil teacher in 1872 at a higher-than-usual salary of £12 10s a year. Annie's new salary was to be £105 and it might be supposed this was an increase on her Mount Pleasant salary, even though it was lower than that commanded by Louisa. Was Louisa, like her sister, determined to be paid her worth? It certainly seems that way. Louisa stayed as head at Mount Pleasant Infants' for the remainder of her teaching career – another thirty-two years – and was heavily involved in the implementation of education throughout the borough. On her retirement in July 1919, the local newspaper reported:

> On Wednesday at the Mount Pleasant Infants' a presentation was made to Miss L. Haliday, headmistress, on the occasion of her retirement after 32 years of strenuous and self-sacrificing labour on behalf of the several generations who have passed through her hands.

> During this lengthy period Miss Haliday has endeared herself to both scholars and staff. The latter expressed their regret at the severance of their long and intimate association. The presentation, which took the form of a silver three-tier cake stand supplied by Messrs B. Mallinson and Sons, New Street, Huddersfield, was made by Master Geoffrey Knight one of the top class pupils. Miss Haliday, in her usual happy manner, thanked the scholars and staff for their magnificent present.
>
> *Huddersfield Daily Examiner*, Thursday, 17 July 1919

Not only had Louisa influenced the lives of generations of pupils, she had trained countless female pupil teachers and set them on a worthwhile career.

The Huddersfield School Board, like many others, initially had difficulty recruiting pupil teachers:

> As this Board have experienced considerable difficulty in obtaining suitable candidates for the office of Pupil Teacher, it will be a question for the new Board [elected every three years] to consider whether the present scale of salaries paid to Pupil Teachers is or is not too low. The salaries of the Pupil Teachers employed by the Board are based on the scale adopted by the Government more than twenty years ago [1850s]. Several of the most promising Pupil Teachers in the Board Schools have been withdrawn to enter situations in which they are much better remunerated. The Pupil Teachers in the London Board Schools commence with 6s per week advancing 1s per week each year of their apprenticeship. The commencing salary of the Pupil Teachers in the Huddersfield Board Schools is 4s per week during the first year of their apprenticeship.[1]

With the ever-increasing number of board schools being opened, in 1875 the school board placed an advertisement for male and female pupil teachers over the age of 14 for a number of its new schools. Terms and particulars were not stated in the advertisement, but Huddersfield's schools were open for forty-seven weeks a year and a candidate pupil teacher was generally engaged for £10 a year (just over 4s a week). It is interesting to note that in February 1875, the board recruited fourteen new candidates for pupil teachers: eleven girls and three boys, and in April it was sixteen: thirteen girls and three boys.[2,3] The £10 a year salary remained the same until at least 1880. The number of female pupil teachers in Huddersfield in 1875 – assumed from details of pupil teachers of all years taking needlework exams – was around 125. Clearly, it was an attractive option for bright young women from ordinary backgrounds; there was definite career progression, with many girls moving to other schools within the board, having completed their pupil-teacher apprenticeships.

One example was Carrie Newsome, employed as an ex pupil teacher at Mount Pleasant Infants' in 1887. Born in 1867, Carrie was the daughter of a tailor, and her two sisters Anne and Mary also became teachers, along with her twin, Minnie, who married in 1889 and thus gave up her career. Carrie was clearly a suitable candidate for teacher training; she was presented with certificate of honour as a pupil at Hillhouse School in 1877 and her first job was as a candidate pupil teacher at Beaumont Street Infants in 1880 at the salary of £10. By 1884, she had completed the first stage of her training and her salary as an ex pupil teacher was £35. Continuing her education for certification, she passed the pupil-teachers' class South Kensington Science Examinations in magnetism and electricity, elementary stage, in 1885. Along with several other pupil teachers, she deferred sitting the certification examinations for twelve months in order to attend Huddersfield Technical College in 1888 but their salaries were increased – Carrie's from £45 to £55. The board described these pay rises as 'debts of honour' but recognised it would benefit by the expenditure. Carrie qualified as a certificated assistant and stayed at Mount Pleasant Infants' until 1893, when she was transferred back to her former school at Beaumont Street.[4] By this time, her salary had risen to £65. When she resigned through ill health a year later, the board said it would favour any application once her health was restored. It seems she did not return to teaching; she continued to live with her mother and, later, sister Anne, who, having been appointed head teacher at Berry Brow Infants' in 1892 at a salary of £85, is listed on subsequent censuses as head teacher – Carrie has no occupation. To complete the saga – Anne died in 1927 and Carrie, at the age of 62, finally found love and married Albert Edward Hoyle, 60, a bachelor, in 1929. Perhaps her health never recovered; she died just four years later.

Another of Louisa's protégées was Amelia Hannah Burrans, a first-year pupil teacher at Mount Pleasant Infants' in 1886. Her father, like Louisa's, was a commercial traveller. She worked through the various exams (see Appendix 1) and is noted in 1889 as having passed fairly but needing to pay more attention to geography and needlework, and in 1890 as having passed fairly.[5] After her apprenticeship, the board raised her salary to £35 in December 1890 and she was classified as an ex pupil teacher. Of course, the work towards certification continued. In spring 1891, Louisa recorded in the school logbook that Amelia, 'having passed in the 2nd class at the Queen's Scholarship exam is now considered to have passed fairly. She should be informed she is now qualified under Article 50 but not Article 52.' Article 50 (of the Education Code) specified that, 'Pupil teachers who have passed satisfactorily either the examination for the end of the last year of their engagement or that for admission to a training college may be recognised as assistant teachers in public elementary schools.' It was not the same as being a provisionally certificated teacher, for which Article 52 laid down:

> Pupil teachers who have passed satisfactorily the examination for the end of the last year of their engagement, or obtained a place in the first or second class in the examination for admission to a training college may, if specially recommended by the inspector on the ground of their practical skills as teachers, be recognised as 'provisionally certificated teachers in charge of small schools'.

As was the case for many aspiring young teachers, although Amelia had passed the requisite exam, she required the sanction of the school inspector before she could be considered provisionally certified and apply for the certificate. According to school board appointments and salaries, she was still classified as an ex pupil teacher in 1892, though her salary was increased to £40. Something was eluding her. She studied advanced French in 1891 and passed London University language exams; a year later she passed advanced animal physiology, plus practical, plane and solid geometry, and in 1893 passed advanced hygiene at Huddersfield Technical College. Finally, in 1894, she had passed the certificate and was an assistant teacher at a salary of £55. On 19 December 1895 she left Mount Pleasant to take up a headship at Outlane Board School at a salary of £75. After all that hard work, no doubt encouraged and inspired by Louisa Haliday, Amelia resigned in early 1898, for a 'new sphere of life'. She married Harry Graham on 1 March; the parish register simply has a line under her occupation, as though she had none. However, by 1911, and with three children and a husband, Amelia had returned to teaching and was an assistant mistress at a C of E school. Presumably, she was not going cast aside all that effort to become qualified.

Although Carrie and Amelia were local women given the opportunity to follow worthwhile careers close to home and family, more ambitious women seeking headships perhaps had to travel further, especially in the initial years of the building of elementary schools. The early 1870s saw not only Elizabeth Haliday appointed from Manchester but also Miss Brougham of Longsight, and Miss Mary Hunter of Ardwick Green. Further afield were Miss Annie Egerton from Tarporley, Cheshire; Miss Mary Ann May of Coventry and Mrs A.A. Andrew of King's Lynn. These are just a few examples of the upward mobility a career in elementary school teaching gave to women.

School boards generally provided a secure future for these women. Of course, there were teachers who did not meet the required standards and were dismissed, but those who dedicated their efforts were rewarded with positions in larger schools and enhanced salaries in recognition of increased responsibilities. Still, the school board made economies where it could in reshuffles of headmistresses 'already in service of the board'. Sometimes this resulted in a saving of £100 a year, other times, such as in Huddersfield in 1886, it was just £15. Salary increases were often contested by the men on the school boards, particularly where the headmistress was staying in the same school. In the 1886 review, Miss Hannah Exley Mellor's salary increase from £95 to £100 was opposed. The Reverend R.C. Wilford said she did not warrant an increase as attendance had decreased and, in any case, she had been given a rise only eighteen months previously. It was pointed out there had been outbreaks of both measles and scarlet fever in the district, which had affected attendance (although this was disputed …) and she had raised the standard from good to excellent. Wilford's amendment was voted out and the increase, quite rightly, approved. It seems Berry Brow Girls' School had not been without difficult pupils. A local newspaper reported:

Assault on a Schoolmistress

Elizabeth Brook, a married woman, of Dudmanstane [Deadmanstone], who did not appear, was charged with assaulting Hannah Exley Mellor, of Castle Hill Side. Mr W. Armitage, who appeared for the complainant, said that the defendant was the mother of a girl who attended the Board School at Berry Brow. Miss Mellor, the complainant, was the headmistress of the school, and the girl, Esther Brook, was a somewhat troublesome kind of a girl. On Wednesday, the 5th inst., she was not conducting herself properly in the school, and Miss Mellor ordered her to stand with her face to the wall. This she did for a moment, but on the return of Miss Mellor, who had left the schoolroom for a short time, the girl was again misconducting herself. She was then ordered to stand upon a stool, where she stayed a reasonable time, and was then allowed to resume her place in the class. A little while afterwards the girl's mother (defendant) and another woman went to the schoolroom door and began motioning for her. It appeared that another girl was going home in the afternoon, and this very girl had written a note which had been presented to Miss Mellor to ask her to allow the girl Brook to go home. This was not regarded as satisfactory by the headmistress. The defendant began a disturbance. She used some very bad language to Miss Mellor, but she ultimately went out of the front door, which was fastened after her. She then went round to another door for her little girl, who was preparing to go, and as she was going she struck Miss Mellor in the face two or three times. She also told her daughter that if Miss Mellor told her to stand on a stool again she was to kick her in the face. Her conduct was altogether disgraceful, and he asked that for the sake of the discipline of the school the case should not be passed over lightly. A fine of 10s and 7s expenses was inflicted.

Huddersfield Chronicle, Tuesday, 11 March 1884

Born in 1858, Hannah came from a farming family living on the bleak side of Castle Hill outside Huddersfield. Somehow, she caught the eye of Jonathan Samuel, a man born in Monmouthshire but living in Stockton on Tees, County Durham. They married in 1892. From the census, Jonathan appears to have been a grocer, although his obituary says he had been an iron worker in Teesside before building up a considerable business in Stockton, being the town's mayor, alderman for Durham County Council, and member of the Tees Conservancy Commissioners. In addition to this, he became MP for Stockton 1895–1900 and again from 1910 until his death from a stroke in 1917, aged 64.

Comparing teaching standards

As more and more board schools were built and filled with pupils, it is interesting to note a gulf between funding and standards of education existed and continued to exist, when comparing the voluntary schools (such as St Luke's) with these new schools (such as Moldgreen). Speaking in parliament around quarter of a century after the first board schools had been brought into being, in 1898, John Eldon Gorst (later Sir John), vice president of the Committee on Education, highlighted the differences. Nationally, the managers of the board schools were able to spend £2 11s 8½d per child, while the managers of the voluntary schools were only able to expend £1 18s 10¾d. Standards of teaching were lower too. Although there were 42,000 children in the Manchester board schools and 52,000 in voluntary schools, in terms of Owens' and Manchester Grammar School scholarships by examination, the board school children were granted forty and the voluntary-school children only two. It was similar picture in Liverpool with twice as many children in voluntary schools compared with board schools, and only two children from the voluntary schools gaining scholarships against sixteen from the board schools. Teaching in the voluntary schools was in large schoolrooms, but the purpose-built new board schools had individual classrooms. Pupils experienced 'wonder buildings, sumptuous and palatial beyond belief, brand-new equipment … flush toilets, playgrounds … professionally trained teachers and orderly classrooms', a huge contrast to what was provided elsewhere. In addition, the budgets for voluntary schools necessitated the recruitment of lower-paid, lower-qualified teachers, so the best teachers, i.e. those who had trained in the colleges (ironically, mostly set up by the diocesan boards) were choosing to teach in board schools rather than voluntary. Of the cream of the profession (those with three years' college training) more than 76 per cent of women teachers opted for board schools. There was a lack of teachers too and this was not helped by the fact that more than half of those pupil teachers who had passed the Queen's Scholarship exam, entitling them to a place in a college, 'have to wander about looking for a training college which will take them in'. To alleviate the lack of teachers, a new scheme had been introduced in 1876, referred to by Gorst as 'the Article 68 teacher' (Article 68 being a clause in the Education Code of the time) whereby a young woman, aged 18 and approved by the inspector without any qualification, apart from good health and a vaccination certificate, could enter the teaching profession. Some of these women were what he called 'progressive'. They served as pupil teachers or, after a couple of years, sat the Queen's Scholarship exam. But the majority were non-progressive:

> They are persons who have failed in the Queen's Scholarship examination, or who have never tried to pass it; or they are married women or widows driven by adverse fate to serve for the beggarly wages which many managers are not ashamed to give. I trust that before long some limit will be placed upon the employment of this class. Many of them have been for many years out of the profession, and during that time have been unable to participate in the progress of those years. Speaking generally, their influence upon the standard of teaching must be a lowering one.

The pupil teachers in voluntary schools also received lower-grade training and were overworked as cheap labour. This was particularly so in the countryside, where schools had fewer teachers, so the staff who were employed had little respite from their instruction. 'The life of a pupil teacher is not generally a happy one. They are shockingly overworked.'[6]

Improvements in training are required

One thing all these girls had in common was that they all came from what might be termed working-class or artisan families. There was very little provision for secondary education for girls such as these – other than the courses at pupil-teacher centres, only established in the late nineteenth century for 14-year-olds wishing to continue their education before further training, and training colleges – so most had only an elementary education themselves and that had been imparted by a teacher with only an elementary education herself. Even for those who qualified and wished to attend a training college, places were extremely hard to come by, due to lack of provision. Even as late as 1900, Gorst raised his concerns in parliament about the lack of what he termed 'properly trained teachers'. His speech, on 14 June, illustrated the numbers of men and women sitting the examinations to get into training colleges.[7] It is interesting to note that 2,904 men sat the exams at Christmas 1899 (of which 2,555 were successful to some degree) compared with 10,289 women (of whom 8,645 were successful). Although the ratio of women to men sitting the exam was 3.5:1, the ratio of women to men wanting to take a place at college was

1.4:1 (only 38 per cent of female examinees compared with 97 per cent of male), and of these, only 1,575 women were offered a place at college, whereas 1,042 men were accommodated. It was roughly 40 per cent of all those (female or male) who wanted a place, but lack of accommodation at college was a problem, meaning more than half the would-be teachers were disappointed.

Two types of training college existed: residential and day, and all were full. It was argued that the residential colleges, where students were cooped up with others of the same age and same views on their profession in life might have narrower viewpoints and be deprived of a more liberal education, whereas those attending the day colleges were not sufficiently supervised on moral and character grounds, although neither was mutually exclusive in its influences. Gorst cited the advantages of secondary education for girls, naming a residential ladies' college at Cheltenham (that run by Dorothea Beale):

> where the young ladies who go to be trained are mixed up with the girls of the rest of the school. They are not distinguished from them in any way, and they have the advantage of belonging to a very fine high school, in which there is a very good tone, and which is in every way a desirable place for the education of young women. They do not get that narrowing of opinion which they might got in a place where they were all shut up together.

He also argued the advantages of the day colleges and in particular the ease at which they could be more rapidly expanded to accommodate more teaching students. For some reason, the state had always paid more for teachers trained at residential colleges, but he urged the state should allocate a fixed amount for the training of a teacher and allow the student to choose whether to attend day or residential college.

Campaign to attract more middle-class girls into teaching

As well as schools needing better-trained teachers, some campaigners thought a 'better class' of women ought to be encouraged into the profession. This was not entirely through snobbery; it was seen as a career where middle-class women could gain a degree of independence. A letter from Reverend Morton Shaw in *John Bull* in August 1871 alluded to the pressing question of recruiting teachers for elementary schools (there were forty columns of 'teachers wanted' advertisements in the National Society's *Monthly Packet*), suggesting that 'thousands upon thousands' of educated, unmarried Christian gentlewomen, literally in want of something to do, and 'perpetually feeling overwhelmed with a sense of the uselessness and worthlessness of their lives' might be good candidates. Louisa Hubbard (who devoted her life and means to improving the condition of women of her own class who had to work for their living), in response, wrote:

> Few persons will, I think, question the writer's preliminary statement that we can hardly expect any very large increase of male teachers from the class which has hitherto supplied them, and most will welcome his suggestion that we should rather look for the persons we need among our surplus female population. Our memory supplies us with numerous instances of boys who, after having been educated as pupil teachers, prefer situations as clerks, accountants, &c., to their natural progression into school teachers; and the great difficulty of finding unemployed men to fill any post whatever is a sign that it is not among them that we may expect to find recruits for any fresh demand. All are already occupied in the struggle for dear life which is one of the penalties of our overgrown civilisation, and are supporting not only themselves, but families of women and children dependent on them. It is, therefore, to the female rather than to the male population that we must look in our need, and here the difficulty disappears.
>
> That there is among us a large number of women who ought to be earning their own bread is one of the facts of the present day to which we should no longer turn unwilling, selfish ears. We dislike the fact, but we must face it, and had we done so earlier many lives of struggling destitution which have ended in starvation might have lived on in health and prosperity, earning a blessing to the community and to themselves. We have work which needs women, and we have women who, above all things, need work ... Day by day we hear of narrow incomes and positive destitution among educated women and though we have long since awoke from our first delusion, that work has only to be found and that then a woman is provided for, yet we feel that she has not yet been fairly tried. If it be granted, as by Mr Morton Shaw's admirable showing we may well believe it to be, that women of good principles, moderate education, and some training in the best modes of teaching schools, keeping order, &c., are not only equal to men, but more suitable than they to the charge of elementary schools let us go on and inquire where we shall find the women, and how we shall fit them for their duties. I have long known what it is to believe in the ideal woman of whom Mr Shaw speaks, and of whom he promises us thousands. I grieve to say that a woman of high mould and culture, possessed of versatile talents and unemployed who frets against inaction and is eager for and capable of performing any and every sort of work – the coming woman, in short, of whom we expect so much and on appearance we so confidently depend for the solution of all our feminine problems, is but a figment of our most sanguine fancy. That such

exist I have no doubt; indeed, most of us have the happiness of reckoning several among our friends; but long before the date at which he supposes them to have given up all thought of a worthy marriage, and to bemoaning the uselessness of their lives, they have found or made their work for themselves and are not easily to be removed from the spheres from which they can ill be spared. No – exactly in proportion as they are worth having they are not to be had, and it is better to be disenchanted of our illusions than by clinging to them to prepare for ourselves for further disappointment. I believe there are numbers of young women to whom such a livelihood as the happy, honoured position of a schoolmistress would, indeed, be a providence in the highest sense if, as Mr Morton Shaw says, such an opportunity could be presented to them in a suitable form, and under satisfactory (social) conditions. I refer to the large class of young persons, more or less ladies by birth, the daughters of gentlemen in reduced circumstances, the clergy, etc., who, possessing culture but not accomplishments, form the crowded ranks of applicants for nursery governesses and companions ... I am not pleading for the daughters of tradespeople or farmers who wish to rise, but only for those of gentle birth who desire not to sink ... Let us welcome so legitimate and suitable an opportunity for utilizing the powers of our young Christian gentlewomen, and for providing them with homes in which they may feel that they are performing their duty towards God and man, and earning the sweet reward which ever follows a conscientious and harmonious life.

In essence, she was advocating women who might have previously become governesses in private families to be 'governesses' in elementary schools instead. She was a frequent contributor on the same subject to a number of newspapers, with four consecutive letters (later republished as a pamphlet, 'Work for Ladies in Elementary Schools') in *John Bull* in January 1872. Carefully studying the government regulations, necessary qualifications and training, she translated these into an easily understandable form and brought them to public attention. Her last letter, published 27 January 1872, described the attractive prospects for 'village schoolmistresses':

Being a lady, she must sooner or later be recognised as such by all with whom she comes in contact; and if it be necessary to her circumstances that she should earn her bread by tuition, she may see much to attract her in the modest independence of home of her own, and very possibly will not suffer so much from social isolation as many a governess in private family. Where she has mother or sister, or even both depending upon her, the value of a home, humble though it be, and under the same roof as the village school, will be greatly enhanced. Most schools require least two teachers, either separately for girls and infants, or together as principal and assistant mistresses, and even if not, the presence of a relative, whether professionally engaged or no, will be a great advantage. Trained in college, as we trust ladies may soon be, in the most intimate acquaintance with the duties of domestic economy, and practically experienced in all such details of simple cookery and housework as will fit them to give industrial training to the future wives and mothers of our labouring classes, they will yet require some help in household matters during their attendance in school, to ensure neat apartments and wholesome food in the intervals of labour. Such might be the welcome duties of a mother or young relative, and the quiet lodging near her school, if in town, or a pretty cottage, if in the country, will form a home, which their natural taste may refine into an expression of their social standing, and in which we fancy many fathers would gladly see two of his daughters, preferring for them such life of comfortable independence together, to sending them out separately into ill-paid and perhaps uncongenial situations as dependents. Such situations are not unknown. We hear of one in which two mistresses are each working at a salary of £75 per annum, besides a small house rent free; thus, were these persons sisters, making joint income of £150, and a home not only for themselves, but for their widowed mother. Another infant schoolmistress commanded salary of £80, and might have had sister in the place of assistant mistress £40 or £45 a year.

Louisa Hubbard did not expect these gentlewomen teachers to ever make up more than around 4–5 per cent of the teaching population in board schools, but she was certain they could work happily alongside their 'lower-class colleagues', who 'held out a kindly hand of fellowship to their new comrades, feeling that their profession was worthy of being adopted by persons from any rank of life'. In 1873, Louisa successfully campaigned for the Bishop Otter College (which had been the diocesan training college for elementary schoolmasters and had closed in 1867 through lack of numbers – in contrast to the schoolmistresses' training college) to reopen as a training college for ladies. It remained women-only until 1957.

Eglantyne Jebb, gentlewoman schoolmistress

One of the gentlewomen Louisa Hubbard was advocating for was Eglantyne Jebb who, against her better judgement, was persuaded into teaching.[8] Despite the appeal of the idea of the gentlewoman schoolmistress to Victorian middle-class feminists, veteran school teachers had been expressing doubts about the potential of their new colleagues since the 1870s and these doubts were discussed in the press. One 'certificated mistress' cautioned:

> Our profession is not one in which a lady by birth and education could ever feel at home. The habits and behaviour (especially in low neighbourhoods and some rural districts) would be a constant torture to her, and there is often even more to bear from the parents than from the children.
>
> *The Times (London)*, 16 September 1873

The experience of Hannah Exley Mellor, previously mentioned, which would not have been unique, perhaps bears that caution out.

Eglantyne, born in summer 1876 in Ellesmere, Shropshire, grew up in the world of the English country gentry at the Jebb family estate, The Lyth. Her father, Arthur Trevor Jebb (1839–94), was heir to £3,000 a year and, as well as running his estate, was a school board inspector and organiser of the local debating society. He brought up his six children to understand that 'of those who live in beautiful places, much was required'. His wife, Eglantyne Louisa (1845–1925), started an arts and crafts movement among the local working people. Their four daughters were tutored in German, French and music by an austere governess from Alsatia, Germany, while their mother supervised their drawing and painting lessons. Other subjects were taught to all six children by their rather radical aunt, Louisa Jebb, who lived with the family. Locals referred to her as 'Man Jebb'; she was an ardent campaigner for establishing a cottage hospital in Ellesmere, an ambition to which she eventually succeeded. Her nieces and nephews remembered her as 'the inspirer of dreams, the instigator of many ideas'. She introduced them to practical subjects such as carpentry, wood and metal turning, glass cutting and glazing; and they learnt the art of making and using boomerangs, kites, popguns, bows and arrows, toboggans, stilts, fishing nets, and melting lead over the bedroom fire to cast bullets. Eglantyne was less keen on these occupations, preferring books and storytelling. It was Aunt Louisa who first suggested Eglantyne might take up the calling as a schoolmistress, urging 'that there is a very great need of ladies as National Schoolmistresses because of the good of the children's close contact with them'. That it was fairly low paid made it more desirable for those who did not need money, there being a social stigma to women of her class working for money. Upper-class women who did voluntary social work were generally distinguished from their colleagues by titles prefixed by 'honorary'.

Against her brother's wishes – he thought his four daughters pretty and wealthy enough to make good marriages and that college education would spoil them – Louisa Jebb (who had taken courses at Newnham College, Cambridge) used her private income to send the three youngest to university: Louisa, known as Lill, entered Newnham in 1892; Eglantyne began a three-year history course at Lady Margaret Hall, Oxford in 1895; and Dorothy went to Newnham in 1901 to study economics and moral sciences.

Eglantyne politely turned down the offer from a fellow student to open a school with her. Her plans were uncertain and, up until 1897, she had never stepped inside an elementary school. Her only experience of such places was during a family seaside holiday as a teenager where she gazed down on a school playground and watched the 'little wretches till they went away'. 'The dreadful idea of closer acquaintance had never entered my head,' she wrote to a friend.

Nonetheless, less-than-excellent examination results – she gained second-class in the Oxford final history schools (degrees were not awarded to Oxford's women students until October 1920 and Cambridge waited until 1948 to follow suit) – meant she had to admit that teaching might be a suitable alternative to her longed-for literary career, though she later confided in a cousin that her decision to enrol in teachers' college was 'based on the belief that she was too stupid to do anything else'.

Against advice to 'not waste time at college' because men and women with university qualifications usually headed straight into teaching in fee-paying schools rather than the elementary board schools, Eglantyne was determined to 'get into some college' and was eventually accepted at the B and FSS's College for Women Teachers at Stockwell in south London in September 1898.

Miss Lydia Manley (1847–1911) was the college principal, assisted by eight full-time teachers. According to the nearest census, 1901, there were around 130 young women, aged 19–22, living in, whose occupation is listed as 'future profession teacher'. Eglantyne's mother met with Manley to negotiate the terms of her residency and Eglantyne was admitted as a 'nongovernmental student' under article 115 of the Education Act, which was designed for 'persons who had passed certain University, University Local or equivalent examinations'. It meant she was to consider herself a third-year student 'and pretend to be one', which she understood to mean that while at college, sharing its life, the objects and methods of her training would mainly consist of 'actual teaching'. Only a privileged few could stay on for a third year and of those seven third-year students, four were on placement in France and a fifth was at Ealing College for Teachers of the Deaf. It was a lonely time. Most of the other girls and teachers had already served a five-year pupil teacher apprenticeship in elementary schools before coming to college and were comfortable with the culture and routine of that environment and had excelled in it. They probably regarded Eglantyne as an outsider, but she recognised the strong female subculture at Stockwell, developed under Lydia Manley's leadership. These young women, gathered together and away from home for the first time in their lives, had the sense of being a professional group where long-term friendships were built. The college had its own magazine, a flourishing literary society, and the students organised trips to many places of interest. It must have been an exciting experience for them, full of promise but, sadly, it seems from Eglantyne's letters, she was not extended the 'kindly hand of fellowship' promised by Louisa Hubbard and other advocates of gentlewoman schoolmistresses. She was initially shocked at being snubbed, but became accustomed to it by its repetition. Despite her literary ambitions, she did not join the literary society or help with the college paper. Perhaps having her own room and not sharing the dormitories (described by her as 'gigantic beehives') may have hindered her integration.

Besides her lack of any former experience in elementary schools, Eglantyne, having skipped over the first two years at college to enter as a third-year student, was actually two years behind her fellow students, in both experience and friendship making, but was expected to carry out the same standard of teaching of twenty subjects in an 'authoritative and formal manner'. It was gruelling. She was so nervous she could not eat before lessons. In response, Lydia Manley increased her class size from sixteen to sixty. 'There was no humbug at Stockwell.' Another disadvantage was her lack of knowledge of the domestic subjects women were required to also teach. She was bewildered by it all – her biggest challenge being embroidery, the demanding curriculum subject that so many campaigners sought to modify. By the end of her first term, she was feeling betrayed by the enthusiastic lady mentors who had talked her into a teaching career, yet a determined Eglantyne spent her Christmas holidays practising buttonholes, gussets and gathers. She was tired of receiving pamphlets entitled, 'Elementary Teaching as a Career' and vowed to write one herself: 'Elementary Teaching as a Toil'. When confronted with the natural talent of gifted young women at Stockwell, Eglantyne commented, 'They compel my respect and admiration … I gaze at them with rapt awe …'

She soldiered on, however, and by February 1899 was looking for a teaching position. Rather than take Lydia Manley's suggested opportunity at a London Board School where she could be supervised, Eglantyne set her heart on teaching in a dockland or slum school. It never occurred to her that the London docklands would not welcome her with open arms. Stockwell's staff continued their quest to get her into a school in a safer neighbourhood or even one of the practising schools attached to the college, but she refused. All through early summer she searched, pinning her hopes on a post in a 'poor school' in Waterloo Road: 'I am on tenterhooks to get it, though I suppose I shan't.' Eventually, she realised she was facing discrimination; she was not taken seriously; headmistresses unkindly laughed in her face. Despite a shortage of trained teachers, they did not want to bother with a lady Oxford graduate.

How despondent she must have felt. Fortunately, help was at hand. Her uncle, James Gilmore, a retired housemaster from the prestigious Marlborough College, took her to see some schools, using his influence to get her a position as assistant mistress at St Peter's Elementary School in Marlborough's High Street. Eglantyne took pleasure in her new life. Determined to live on her small salary, she found inexpensive lodgings with a pleasant landlady and a little maid who brought her meals. Throwing herself completely into the role of the 'impoverished schoolmistress' by deliberately cladding herself in 'brown and grey', she ordered only 'one winter dress of cheap fabric and a similar one for the summer, one hat, one pair of gloves and one blouse'.

Eglantyne did not have any trouble with her pupils. In letters to her friend, she described them as steady and simple-minded: 'nine out of ten clean, and eight neat'. As their teacher, her job was to criticise, cajole and correct them, but she could not help observing how grim their lives were and how philosophically they accepted sickness, poverty and even death. However, entries in her diary reveal how much she really detested the work of teaching. She compared it to the treadwheel, blacking shoes and breaking stones. It took her weeks to get used to standing all day. After a year she still complained about 'talking even though your throat is sore, standing even though your back aches, and working extra hours if a headache makes you work slowly'.

One particularly arduous week she wrote:

> Sunday. The prospect of returning to my work tomorrow makes me feel physically ill, my body and heart ache in concert. If I were only going to the dentist tomorrow – but to stand, mutilating scripture to the detriment of inattentive children, I could shed tears over the prospect ...

> Wednesday. I can now recollect nothing of the day which is worth recollecting. ... A day lost ... Was there nothing I might have seen or learnt? ... The children have learnt nothing either. And so it goes: day after day into vacuum ...

> Thursday. Another day has dropped into silence. I have done 10 hours work today and accomplished nothing. Looking back, I cannot remember anything about it, except the faces of the children ...

> Sunday. ... Could I have believed that I should have worked over 6 months and still be afraid – yes, literally afraid of my work – afraid.[9]

It seems her poor preparation for the role of teaching and a lack of peer support contributed to her lack of confidence in the classroom and she convinced herself she had none of the natural qualities of a teacher. She was, however, enchanted by the bold and defiant little pupils such as Fanny and Ann, who, when frightened by a large white dog one November day, executed a defiant 'war dance in the middle of the High Street'. As soon as they noticed 'Miss Jebb' watching them, they 'came tumbling across the street and beamed up in my face all the way home, and I carried a ray of sunshine into my dark little room'.

Eglantyne left teaching after only eighteen months, aged 25, but not because she had given up on the career she had put so much effort into being fit for. In December 1900, her widowed mother, wanting a companion, chose Eglantyne to fulfil the role of daughter-at-home, the dreaded duty of many unmarried girls of her generation. Perhaps her initial fury was tempered by relief, but she had no choice. She continued to contribute to the field of education but in more 'class appropriate' ways, tutoring two young cousins in English and history in 1903; both subsequently attended university and had stellar careers in education. Geraldine Emma May Jebb, the eldest, was a university lecturer at Armstrong College, Newcastle before becoming Principal of Bedford College (see later) from 1930 to 1951, and her younger sister, Eglantyne Mary Jebb was a lecturer in the woman's training department at Birmingham University before she was principal of The Froebel Institute from 1932 to 1955.

Determined not be idle, it was social work that was Eglantyne's real vocation. In the early 1900s she moved, with her mother, to Cambridge. Here she met Margaret Keynes – mother of the economist Maynard Keynes – who employed her at the Cambridge-based Charity Organisation Society (COS), and carried out a survey of the city's social conditions, publishing her findings in a book, *Cambridge: A Social Study*, in 1906. The book was the first of its kind and set out forward-thinking ideas and practical suggestions – laying the ground for Eglantyne's focus on education and continuing development programmes as keys to helping the disadvantaged. Her work at the COS was to pave the way for greater things. Maybe it was her brief experience as a teacher of underprivileged children that sparked her conscience; she was to become one of the outstanding figures in social work at the time.

After the First World War had wreaked its havoc, Eglantyne and her younger sister, Dorothy Frances Buxton (who had effectively been a war correspondent), founded the Fight the Famine Council and the Save the Children Fund (in April 1919) and Eglantyne was appointed one of the assessors. when the Committee for Child Welfare of the League of Nations was formed. Despite persistent poor health, she travelled widely through Europe and accomplished an astonishing amount of work. Her 'frail, almost ethereal figure' was frequently seen 'among the children she loved in far-off lands', and she was much mourned when she died prematurely in December 1928 in a Geneva nursing home.[10]

Chapter 8

Secondary Education for Girls: The Discussions

While the pupil-teacher scheme for training young people to be elementary school teachers worked well and filled the burgeoning vacancies for teachers, it mainly drew from a working-class population, educated to elementary standards only, supplemented by an apprenticeship and some college training (if they were lucky), particularly where girls were concerned, as there was little available secondary education. The campaign to attract more gentlewomen into the profession was not entirely successful and, in any case, many did not have much better education or training than their poorer sisters.

Certain women had been campaigning for decades for better secondary education opportunities for girls, whether that be for the training of governesses or to 'provide for ladies ... a liberal education' at Queen's College and Bedford College. Bedford College had been founded in 1849 by the widowed Elizabeth Jesser Reid (née Sturch) as a women-only higher education institution, the only one at the time providing a liberal and non-sectarian education for female students, encompassing subjects which had previously been thought of as masculine, and therefore not suitable for women, including the sciences, maths and Greek. The North London Collegiate School, launched by Frances Buss in 1850, and Cheltenham Ladies' College, to which Dorothea Beale was appointed principal eight years later, did offer education of an intellectual rigour previously unknown in girls' schools. But it was hardly enough. Of the four colleges, three were in London. Mothers 'of good position' were more likely to send their daughters to a ladies' seminary where they might assimilate, parrot-fashion, a number of sundry facts by a question and answer method through Miss Richmal Mangnall's *Historical and Miscellaneous Questions* or the *Child's Guide to Knowledge*. Miss Mangnall had been educated at Crofton Hall School, Wakefield, progressing to teacher and then headmistress. She died in post in 1820. For decades, her hugely popular book formed the basis of lessons at many schools (including Roe Head, where Charlotte Brontë had studied and taught). Privately published in 1798, it had appeared in eighty-four editions by 1857. Frances Power Cobbe noted that, typically, these finishing schools cost £1,000 for a two-year course at which, 'if the object had been to produce the minimum result at the maximum of cost, nothing could have been better designed for the purpose.' To play the harp or piano, to sing and dance – these accomplishments would make a lady universally admired and lead her into matrimony. It was socially unacceptable for a 'lady' to earn a living (other than maybe as a governess). An unattached woman could make small economies to exist, but not do anything to increase her income and, to add insult to injury, an unmarried woman was seen as a failure.

However, with reformers very well aware of the importance of improving education for girls and the need to train them for the world of work instead of simply expecting them to marry and run homes, female education became one of the issues to be addressed by The National Association for the Promotion of Social Science (Social Science Association for short), founded in 1857 by a group of men led by Lord Brougham. Its purpose was to advise the government in addressing the issues of public health, industrial relations, penal reform and female education. Scottish writer and reformer Isa Knox served as its first secretary. Despite facing much discrimination for her gender and her background (she was the daughter of an Edinburgh hosier and was largely self-taught), Isa tirelessly fought for women's rights for much of the century.

The Association's aims were approved by the *Englishwoman's Journal* when the monthly magazine was launched in March 1858 with Barbara Leigh Smith Bodichon and Bessie Rayner Parkes at its helm. The magazine was to become the official organ of the Social Science Association, reporting on its annual conventions, to which women were encouraged to submit papers; eight of the forty-one papers on Social Economy were submitted by women at the London convention of 1862.

Most of these women contributors were associated with the 'women's movement' – all, unsurprisingly, had something to say about girls' education. In 1860, Barbara Bodichon had been scathing in her critique of middle-class girls' schools, urging that what passed for education in them ought to be investigated and money raised to provide something better and noting 'Magnificent colleges and schools ... costing thousands and thousands of pounds, rich endowments, all over England, have been bestowed by past generations as gifts to the boys of the higher and middle class ...' Jessie Boucherett added evidence, contrasting the endowed school provision for the two sexes, citing Lindsey in Lincolnshire, which had ten endowed grammar schools for boys and not one for girls. She believed all future endowments should be directed for the education of girls; many needed to be self-supporting and were suffering distress through their 'unfitness for any occupation requiring intelligence'.

This was not followed up; meanwhile, the Association had its attention diverted to the problem of providing some kind of external criteria on which to judge girls' education. At the 1862 convention, Frances Power Cobbe presented a paper on university degrees for women, but it was Emily Davies who conducted a successful campaign to allow girls admission to the University Local Examinations (the Oxford and Cambridge Locals, sometimes known as the Middle-Class Examinations, had been introduced in 1857–8 to provide a useful external standard for (boys') secondary schools)) and in 1863 the Cambridge Syndicate was persuaded to hold a girls' examination as a trial. Following the examination's success, memoranda were sent to influential bodies and a leaflet was produced, supporting the initiative and encouraging other girls to come forward for the exam. Emily Davies ordered 'a large supply for distribution', starting in Cambridge itself.

The Social Science Association decided an investigation into the state of middle-class schools was required and in June 1864, Lord Lyttelton, together with a small deputation of colleagues from the society, persuaded the prime minister, Viscount Palmerston, to set up a Royal Commission.

The Schools Inquiry Commission

Of the three government commissions on education between 1858 and 1864, this, the Schools Inquiry Commission (the Taunton Commission), was the last. Chaired by Lord Taunton, hence its name, its aim was to scrutinise the condition of post-elementary education in the country, mainly through schools provided for the middle classes: the endowed schools (820), proprietary schools (109) and private schools. It defined endowed schools as those 'maintained wholly or partly by means of a permanent charitable endowment'; private schools were those that were the property of the master or mistress who conducted them; and proprietary schools were 'neither maintained wholly or partially by any permanent charitable endowment, nor the property of the masters or mistresses'. A very wide range of schools indeed.

Various men contributed to the questions that would need to be raised, but again it was Emily Davies who forcefully urged that girls' educational needs were addressed. She wrote to Lyttelton in October 1864, asking whether it was intended to embrace girls' schools in the investigations of the Royal Commission:

> I presume there can be no objections to including these schools, but we are anxious that they should not slip through by inadvertence and in some similar cases it has been found that the whole question has turned upon a doubt as to whether certain pronouns are to be interpreted as masculine or common. We are very desirous, therefore, that the Instructions should be framed as expressly to include girls, and we should be greatly obliged if you would have the goodness to bring the matter before Lord Granville ... I venture to trouble you on the subject as we understand that you are about to act as one of the Commissioners.[1]

She reminded him of the admission of girls to the Cambridge Locals exams, in which he had been 'actively concerned', and he replied to assure her that girls' education would indeed be included in the inquiry. Hearing nothing further, Emily lobbied others on the same subject, eventually sending a memorandum directly to the newly appointed Commissioners urging 'that the Education of Girls and the means of improving it are within the scope of your inquiry'. It is likely that, up until then, this had never occurred to the Commissioners, but their reply via the secretary, Henry Roby, assured her they would 'endeavour to embrace in their inquiry the education of both sexes alike' and 'he himself will be glad to aid the inquiry in any way he can'. He was good to his word and kept Emily well informed on all matters he felt could concern her, including a confidential list of the (all-male) assistant commissioners and their instructions, and invited her to put forward names of witnesses who 'would be best able to speak and able to speak best' about the state of girls' schools. He also asked her for advice on the questions to be posed in regard to girls' schools.

Various people of influence were called upon to give evidence at the inquiry; the first person to be interviewed at any length about girls' education, on 1 November 1865, was W.B. Hodgson LLB, a man with thirty years' experience in education, who had been secretary, then principal, of the Liverpool Institute, establishing a separate school for 300 girls in 1843. But the Commissioners asked him 183 questions around boys' education before finally asking, 'What is your opinion of the general state of the education of the young women of the middle classes of this country?' and following his answer (that it was not good and the benefits of endowments should be more fairly distributed) with just a further five questions.[2] Nonetheless, when Emily Davies was sent a transcript of that evidence, she was heartened that the Commissioners were better disposed than she had imagined. She furnished Roby with further suggestions on what could be asked and, knowing she was better placed to put forward the points of importance, he encouraged her to 'draw up some list of heads under which your evidence could best fall, [as] it will contribute much to the good order of the Examination'. It was these initiatives that set the stage for the questioning of the ladies who were subsequently invited to give their evidence.

Between 30 November 1865 and 19 April 1866, nine women attended the inquiry: Emily Davies; Frances Mary Buss; Mary Eliza Porter; Miss Frances Martin (superintendent at Bedford College school); Miss Eleanor Elizabeth Smith (noted as being a visiting lady to Bedford College school); Miss Susan Kyberd (mistress of Chantry School, Frome, Somerset); Miss Gertrude King (secretary to the Society for the Employment of Women); Dorothea Beale; and Miss Elizabeth Clarke Wolstenholme (later Wolstenholme-Elmy) (proprietor of a small girls' school in Manchester). Even though the Commissioners were good-natured and encouraging, being questioned by seven men was an ordeal for some. Even the forthright Emily Davies found the prospect alarming; she was frightened of acquitting herself poorly and had to conceal her nervousness. Frances Buss was petrified, worried she might say or imply something that might do more harm than good to the cause. She was almost speechless in front of Her Majesty's Commissioners and one of them hurried into Henry Roby's office, to ask Emily, now being 'regaled with claret and biscuits',

Plaque commemorating Ellen Rigg in Cartmel Priory, Cumbria. (Author's own image)

> Ellen dedicated thirty-three years to the teaching of children in Cartmel Sunday School.

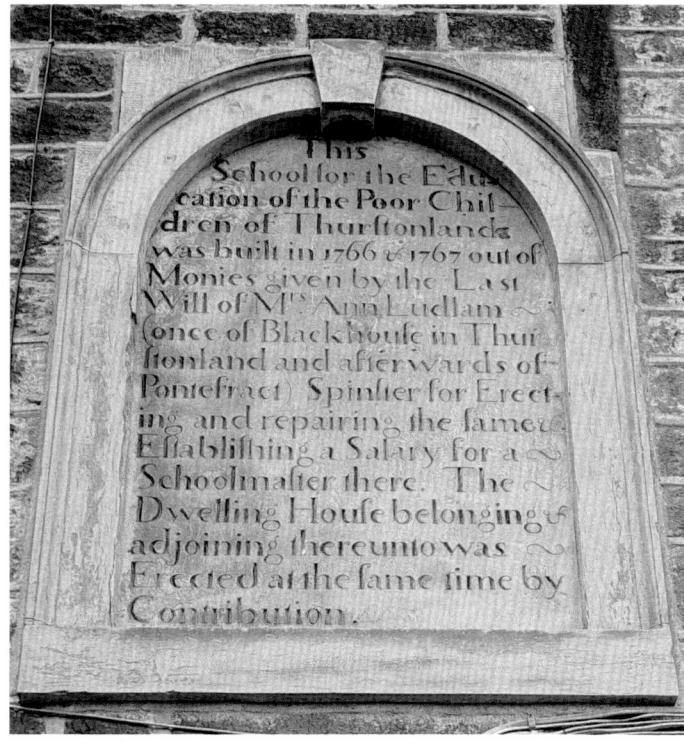

Stone plaque on Thurstonland School, near Holmfirth, West Yorkshire. (Author's own image)

> The plaque notes the school's foundation at the bequest of Ann Ludlam of Black House, Thurstonland, who set up a trust for the erection and maintenance of a school, plus the salary of a schoolmaster, for the 'education of the poor of the township' in 1763. The trust still exists.

Helen Taylor (with J.S. Mill). (Public Domain)

Member of the London School Board, outspoken and forthright, some men dubbed Helen 'the acid maiden'. She campaigned vigorously for the rights of working-class children and their families.

Above left: Florence Fenwick Miller. (Public Domain)

Florence studied for a medical degree before becoming a member of the London School Board; she later supported herself through journalism.

Above right: Frances Mary Buss. (Courtesy of NLCS)

Founder of North London Collegiate School for Ladies in 1850; the school became the model for future girls' secondary schools. Frances presided over the school, even as her health deteriorated, until her death in 1894.

Miss Buss and her Staff. (Courtesy of NLCS)

This photograph was taken in 1890 when Frances Buss (centre) was 63. Her failing health shows.

Above left: Dorothea Beale 1859. (Public Domain)

Headmistress of Cheltenham Ladies' College from 1858 until her death in 1906, Dorothea left the school to face an operation from which she never recovered.

Above right: Mary Eliza Porter. (Courtesy of BGGS)

The first headmistress of the first endowed girls' school, the first Girls' Public Day School Company school, Bradford Girls' Grammar School and Bedford Girls' Modern School and founder member of the Headmistresses Association.

Uppingham Headmistresses' Conference 11 June 1887. (Courtesy of Uppingham School Archives)

Fifty-nine headmistresses attended the 1887 Association of Headmistresses Conference held at Uppingham School at the invitation of Reverend Edward Thring (centre of photograph).

Bradford Girls' Grammar School, Hallfield Road. (Courtesy of BGGS)

The Bradford Ladies' Educational Association campaigned hard to raise £5,000 to buy this property in 1875.

Above left and above right: Elizabeth Day (left in 1888, right in 1898). (Photographs reproduced courtesy of the governors of Manchester High School for Girls)

Elizabeth Day was the first headmistress of Manchester Girls' High School from 1874 to 1898, when she retired.

Above left: Sophie Bryant. (Courtesy of NLCS)

The first woman in the UK to be awarded DSc, Sophie Bryant succeeded Frances Buss as head of NLCS in 1894 and remained there till her retirement in 1918, aged 68.

Above right: Maria Grey. (Public Domain)

Founder of the Women's Education Union, the Girls' Public Day School Company and the Teachers' Training & Registration Society College (later named the Maria Grey Training College).

Henrietta, Baroness Stanley of Alderley. (Public Domain)

Lady Stanley's campaigning work for women's education had many strands, including the founding of the Girls' Public Day School Company and Girton College.

Miss Stocker and teachers. (Courtesy of BGGS)

Mary Ida Stocker took over the headship at Bradford Girls' Grammar after a scandal. Her steady leadership saw the number of pupils doubling in a decade.

Above left: Emily Davies. (Portrait of Emily Davies by Rudolf Lehmann, 1880)

Emily published The Higher Education of Women *highlighting the differences between boys' and girls' education, making a case for women's access to university education in order to allow them to fulfil their potential and qualify for professional employment.*

Above right: Margaret Eleanor Pillow 1892. (Courtesy of Paul Clarke)

Teacher, lecturer, headmistress and contributor to the Bryce Commission of 1894/5, she changed career in 1892 to become England's first female sanitary inspector.

Above left: Louisa Hubbard. (Public Domain)

Louisa devoted her life and means to improving the condition of women of her own class who had to work for their living, including encouraging gentlewomen to train as teachers.

Above right: Eglantyne Jebb. (Public Domain)

Determined to become a 'gentlewoman teacher', Eglantyne eventually found her true calling and, with her sister, founded the Save the Children Fund.

Elizabeth Jesser Reid. (Public Domain)

Founder of Bedford College, a women-only training college, later part of London University.

to come back to support Frances. Despite their fear of failure, their evidence was compelling and, with the others' contributions, was to help form future policy on the secondary education of girls – how, what and where they should be taught – and how this might be funded.

All nine women were asked similar questions, those prompted by the 'list of heads' sent by Emily Davies to Henry Roby:

What should you say was the present state of the education of girls of that class in this country?

It was generally felt middle-class girls were poorly educated and extremely ignorant. They seldom knew any arithmetic – 'a large number of girls of 13, 14, or 15 come to us who can scarcely do the simplest sum in arithmetic' – which meant they could not be taught mathematics. They attributed this to defective teaching in the schools they had previously attended and by a lack of standards in home teaching. Parents of these girls also came in for some criticism in that they were rather fond of the showy accomplishments (being able to speak French and play the piano, for example) they had been taught in the private schools, instead of being anxious that their daughters receive a well-grounded education and learn to exercise their faculties.

In contrast, lower-class girls who had been taught in the National Schools were far superior. Eleanor Smith expanded on the 'great defect in the education of girls' and its superficial character:

> In this [lower] class the girls are often endeavouring to rise above their previous station by means of their education. Many of them intend to become teachers and to take a position a little better than that of their parents; whereas the girls who come to Bedford Square do so for the most part to obtain the education which belongs to their station; they are not attempting to rise.
>
> I only wish further to insist once more on the great evil of girls spending 10 important years of life, 7 to 17, in learning *not* to understand French and *not* to play the piano; and then when a habit of labouring without result and of looking for none of the rewards of industry is formed, the world wonders why women are idle and frivolous, and why those who have learnt nothing cannot teach.[3]

Should the education of a girl differ essentially from the education of a boy in the same rank of life, with regard to the subjects which are to be taught, and is the education of girls very much neglected?

Parental indifference and the opinion of the country in general meant raising the standard of girls' education was not at the forefront of anyone's mind. Inevitably, parents attached more importance to the education of sons, since they had to go out into the world and earn a living, and therefore spent their money accordingly. And it followed that those benefactors and business people who financed schools tended to lend their support to boys' schools rather than girls'. Not only that, many girls, it seemed, were not that interested in studying – partly, perhaps, because of the way lessons were taught. In consequence, the education of girls was much neglected.

Directing their inquiry to what was to be done, the Commissioners asked:

Have you turned your attention to the state of endowments with reference to the schools for girls and should a portion of the endowments be secured for the better education of girls?

With only a few proprietary solely girls' secondary schools and little public support for more of this type, it was clear from all the women respondents that it was very important to devise some means by which good girls' schools should be established throughout the country in the same way that good boys' schools were being, and had been, established. The endowments by which these boys' schools were financed were, according to their original purpose, in many cases intended for both sexes – for 'the children of the parish' or the 'children of a (certain) district', and had become applied solely to boys. That a portion of these endowments should be diverted to the education of girls was obvious. The money could be spent on buildings and perhaps, scholarships and exhibitions, and thence forward they would be self-supporting. Economies of scale would help keep the costs down; the current girls' schools, being so small, were very expensive.

Of course, this would mean recruiting good teachers for the new girls' secondary schools and this raised another question.

As far as you have been able to judge, do you think that the class of schoolmistresses is as good as it ought to be and can you suggest any means by which that defect which seems to be very much at the root of the want of good schoolmistresses generally can be remedied?

By the 1860s it seems, there was no lack of schoolmistresses, in fact Emily Davies suggested there were too many, although only a few were well qualified. The inferior teachers competed with the good ones and, with only little means of determining which was which, they brought each other down and depressed wages (and this discouraged more competent women from entering the profession).

Eleanor Smith noted that, 'in order to have good teachers you must give opportunities of learning to those who are to be teachers. There are hardly any good and cheap schools now, and women who wish to be well taught cannot get what they ask.'[4]

Frances Buss had generally been successful in obtaining mistresses who had trained at the Home and Colonial College– the girls coming up through her school were too young at 20 to be entrusted with the charge and moral training of a large class. However, she still had difficulty recruiting sufficient well-educated mistresses and her belief was 'we should do better with certificated mistresses, trained in the National Schools' – the girls mainly from the lower classes. Unfortunately for Frances Buss, the government would not allow her to employ certificated mistresses, although she had engaged several who had been trained but had 'fallen short of the certificate', or who from change of circumstances had resigned a government school (although not 'state schools', the National Schools had been under government inspection since 1833 and the pupil-teacher training scheme was a formal government initiative from 1846). 'I do not think there is any better teaching than is given by the Government-trained mistresses, and that if we can secure one of those mistresses she is perfectly capable of making the teaching interesting, discarding text books almost entirely, and making the teaching oral.'[5] She had one caveat though: they were 'very deficient in accomplishments'. This is rather at odds with other respondents who denounced the focus on such instruction.

It was clear that to improve standards of girls' education, there needed to be an improvement in training and certification of schoolmistresses. That would come.

***

Outside London, the only secondary girls' school of any size or note (with 131 regular students, all day pupils) was Cheltenham Ladies' College, a proprietary school, presided over by Dorothea Beale. Her experience, and therefore her view, was to be respected over all others. She had been in post for six years when she came to give her evidence to the Commission. But, like other contributors, she was probably nervous. Reserved and shy, Dorothea was not a socialite; her small talk had been described as 'the kind to freeze conversation'.[6] The penultimate woman to be invited, perhaps well aware by now of the line of questioning and her shortfalls regarding conversation, she came prepared with written evidence, supplying the gentlemen with numerous papers, including statistics from examinations, the prospectus and the nomination form (a form of entrance; only the daughters of independent gentlemen or professional men were admitted – the same criteria as for the boys at Cheltenham College where many of the girls' brothers were being educated). She noted that all girls were tested on a broad range of subjects on entry and many were found lacking, and she showed the Commissioners the full details. The pupils were taught by both mistresses and visiting masters, but she considered it 'essential to the right moral training of girls that much of the actual teaching (especially that of the Bible), and certainly the whole internal discipline of the school, should be in the hands of a lady' and that women were far more patient in going over matters 'again and again' and therefore more successful with young children. Only the higher class of gentlemen teachers were chosen to teach the girls: 'those whom we consider men of first-rate ability and who do not despise their work'.[7]

But how did girls respond to being educated in good day schools instead of at home under a governess. Was it favourable to the healthy development of a girl's mind?

Dorothea Beale was very clear:

> I think unquestionably at a day school, because they can then compare themselves with one another, and are less likely to be indolent or conceited. Home teaching often fails to interest, because the teacher herself finds the work monotonous. Again, suppose there are three or four or five, as there may be, then a governess cannot give proper attention to the elder ones and not neglect the younger ones, and vice versa; and children learn more happily together, and also they see others obedient, and they become obedient too. There is less danger of ill temper and obstinacy; they do not like to make themselves remarkable by insubordination.

Answering the question on whether interaction and conversation with others in a public establishment was better for girls than home education, she replied:

> We have very strict regulations as to the pupils' talking with one another. I do not think it would be good to bring 130 girls together, and give them unlimited leave to talk to one another and play together. I do not think that would be so good for them; but if they join in the lessons, and then go home, and are kept in good order at school, and are not allowed to talk indiscriminately together, then I think you get the benefit of home training and school training without the dangers.[8]

There seemed to be some concern that girls' health might be injured by their eagerness in study. Thomas Dyke Acland MP, an educational reformer and one of the Commissioners, asked Dorothea for her opinion on this. Unsurprisingly, she refuted this ridiculous idea:

> I think [study] improves their health very much, and I am sure great harm is often done by a hasty recommendation to throw aside all study, when a temperate and wisely regulated mental diet is really required. They will not do nothing – you cannot say to the human mind that it shall absolutely rest; but if they have not wholesome and proper and unexciting occupations, they will spend their time on sensational novels and things much more injurious to their health. When I have heard complaints about health being injured by study, they have proceeded from those who have done least work at college. Indeed I do not know of any case of a pupil who has really worked, and whose

> health has been injured; we have had complaints in a few cases where the girls have been decidedly not industrious.
>
> For one girl in the higher middle classes who suffers from over-work, there are, I believe, hundreds whose health suffers from the feverish love of excitement, from the irritability produced by idleness, and frivolity, and discontent. I am persuaded, and my opinion has been confirmed by experienced doctors, that the want of wholesome occupation lies at the root of much of the languid debility of which we hear so much after girls have left school.[9]

Eleanor Smith concurred. A lack of education showed most miserably later; it diminished a woman's happiness and usefulness. A lack of discipline made women restless and unreasonable, and their waste of time was a loss to themselves and those around them. It was the want of the habit of employment and the want of serious tastes which made them 'frivolous and dependent on excitement for passing their time'.

Another bonus, apparently, of giving girls an education was it had a good influence on their brothers and their young friends. The question, 'Do you think, in point of fact, that the want of appreciation of female cultivation by young men is due partly to their not expecting to find it, and thus to their trifling with young women, in a way which they would not if they had more respect for them?' implies that men's poor behaviour towards women was because women were not properly educated.

From the women's point of view, the evidence-giving had gone very well. Emily Davies wrote to Barbara Bodichon, saying she felt very hopeful about things in general:

> We had a gathering last week to meet some of the Commission people. We put Dr Hodgson in the Chair and he conducted very nicely. To my surprise, several of the schoolmistresses spoke, and did it very well. The best speech was from Mr Roby, Secretary to the Commission. He said he thought there was a great ferment going on about the education of women, and he hoped it would go further and be helped by the investigations of the Commission. ... with scarcely an exception the Assistant Commissioners 'go in for the girls'.[10]

As well as the questioning of various people, the assistant commissioners investigated girls' (and boys') schools throughout England and Wales. They spoke with teachers and pupils, listened to lessons, examined buildings, discussed the number of staff and their experience. They sent out eight-page questionnaires to schools; many of them resisted what the heads saw as an intrusion. The headmistresses of Clifton and Bath had banded together; no one had a right to come between them and the parents of their pupils, since teachers and parents should be 'the sole judges of what was the proper course of education ...' and there was no law of the land that 'obliges me to accede to it [submitting their private plan to public scrutiny]'.

Classifying girls' schools was also a problem. Although London had a myriad of girls' schools, how could they be classified? Where did secondary education end and where did superior education begin? One Commissioner noted there seemed to be no regular system of education for girls (as there was not, this was no great revelation). Another noted how small the girls' schools were in comparison to the boys', and how much more expensive.

The report's conclusion

After its extensive investigations, in 1868 the Taunton Commission published its twenty-volume report. Within the first volume was a chapter dedicated to the Commission's findings on girls' schools. In its introduction, it noted the antipathy towards girls' education:

> We have had much evidence, showing the general indifference of parents to girls' education, both in itself and as compared to that of boys. It leads to a less immediate and tangible pecuniary result; there is a long-established and inveterate prejudice, though it may not often be distinctly expressed, that girls are less capable of mental cultivation, and less in need of it, than boys; that accomplishments, and what is showy and superficially attractive, are what is really essential for them; and in particular, that as regards their relations to the other sex and the probabilities of marriage, more solid attainments are actually disadvantageous rather than the reverse.

And in tones of a Jane Austen novel:

> Parents who have daughters will always look to their being provided for in marriage, will always believe that the gentler graces and winning qualities of character will be their best passports to marriage, and will always expect their husbands to take on themselves the intellectual toil and the active exertions needed for the support of the family. 'The ideal presented to a young girl,' says an able writer, Miss Davies, 'is to be amiable, inoffensive, always ready to give pleasure and to be pleased.'

Some hope for better education for girls was on the horizon though:

> The far-sighted and enlightened views about the education of girls, expressed by the many able and experienced ladies and other authorities whom we have consulted, we have no doubt, will meet with ever-increasing acceptance in

this country; but we believe their advocates must be content to expect, even ultimately, a proportion of failures somewhat larger than must be reckoned on in most such attempts, and distinctly more than is probable in the corresponding work of the education of boys.

And it would make them better wives:

> We cannot, however, say this without pointing out, though it may almost appear a truism, that the popular feeling to which we have referred, on one most important subject, that of the married life of women, is founded on a grave and radical misconception – a misconception especially, though by no means only, injurious to the Middle Class, and increasingly so in these days. The most material service may be rendered to the husband, in the conduct of his business and the most serious branches of his domestic affairs, by a wife trained and habituated to a life altogether different from that of mere gentleness and amiability of which we have spoken; a life of no slight intellectual proficiency, and capacity for many functions too commonly thought to be reserved for the male sex.

Even Dorothea Beale, who demanded education for women 'in the fullest sense of the word' and agreed a woman's mind was just as worth cultivating as a man's and that woman's brain was no way inferior to a man's, believed that, 'woman has been endowed with mental and moral capacities, and ... that it was intended these should be cultivated and improved for the glory of the Creator and the relief of man's estate.' Her view was that a girl's education should be different from a boy's in order to perform her subordinate part in the world. She was pretty much in a minority among the advocates of higher education for women.

Before going into the details of their findings, the report summarised the condition of girls' education. It was not good:

> The general deficiency in girls' education is stated with the utmost confidence, and with entire agreement, with whatever difference of words, by many witnesses of authority. Want of thoroughness and foundation; want of system; slovenliness and showy superficiality; inattention to rudiments; undue time given to accomplishments, and those not taught intelligently or in any scientific manner; want of organisation – these may sufficiently indicate the character of the complaints we have received, in their most general aspect. It is needless to observe that the same complaints apply to a great extent to boys' education. But on the whole the evidence is clear that, not as they might be but as they are, the Girls' Schools are inferior in this view to the Boys' Schools.

In essence, the inquiry confirmed that provision of secondary education was poor; from a population of 4 million young people aged 10–20, only 36,874 scholars were receiving secondary education, outside the nine public schools, and schools were unevenly distributed. The endowments, many for tiny schools set up centuries earlier (the oldest having been originally established in Carlisle by St Cuthbert in 686), were being misused – of the 800-plus endowed schools, just 14 were girls' secondary schools (one being the clergymen's daughters' school at Casterton), and there were fewer than twenty other secondary schools solely for the estimated 2 million girls aged 10–20 in the whole of England and Wales.[11] This, of course, did not include the many previously mentioned small (and unclassified) private girls' schools for young ladies, and there were others that had been omitted. Little wonder then that the Commissioners recommended the establishment of a national system of secondary education based on existing endowed schools. The Endowed Schools Act 1869: 'An Act to amend the Law relating to Endowed Schools and other Educational Endowments in England, and otherwise to provide for the Advancement of Education', received Royal Assent on 2 August 1869.

In its first draft, the Endowed Schools Bill made no provision for girls other than empowering the Commissioners to do what was necessary 'to render any educational endowment most conducive to the advancement of the education of boys and girls or either of them'. Henry Winterbotham, a young Liberal MP, sought to have this amended to 'provision shall be made, so far as conveniently may be, for extending the benefits of endowments equally to boys and girls', 'equally' being the key word. It was voted down, but Winterbotham did not give up and Lyttelton also fought for the word in the Lords. By now, the efforts of the committee had come to the attention of the women's movement, namely the North of England Council for Promoting the Higher Education of Women, founded in 1867 (following the expansion of the Liverpool Ladies' Educational Society) by Anne Jemima Clough and Josephine Butler. Winterbotham urged them to write a memorandum supporting the word equally, but Josephine, president of the Council, advised caution: 'A word too much ... may be in danger of damaging our cause.'

Backwards and forwards went the clause. W.E. Forster, who was also wrestling with the Elementary Education Act and its ultimate compromises, said he was bound to consider how they could get the measure carried out. A good deal of the enormous endowments possessed were already appropriated and for the most part by boys. Prising that money from them was not going to be easy. Fresh funds would be a different matter and could be divided between girls and boys.

In the end, Section 12 'Schemes to Extend Benefits to Girls' simply read: 'In framing schemes under this Act, provision shall be made so far as conveniently may be for extending to girls the benefits of endowments.'

Chapter 9

Secondary Education for Girls: The Struggle Begins

'So far as conveniently may be' ... There was everything to hope for now the men were bound by the Act and their own convictions to do what they could to get endowments for girls. On 3 August 1869, the day after the Act was given Royal Assent, three Endowed Schools Commissioners – Lord Lyttelton, Arthur Hobhouse and Canon H.G. Robinson – and a secretary, Henry Roby, who was treated as an equal, were appointed.

But where to begin? Without the means to address the whole country, they decided to concentrate on just two districts in the early months of 1870: the West Riding of Yorkshire, and Somerset and Dorset, simply because the Commissioners knew the areas. Canon Robinson, who was rector of Bolton Abbey in the county (until 1874) had charge of the West Riding. They set to work systematically, but the implementation of Section 12 was not the only aspect of the task; the purpose was to reorganise the endowed schools' provision and, to that end, girls were not the only consideration.

The West Riding had around sixty endowments, but half of these were very small – between £6 and £80 per year – Sheffield had £282 for a population of 185,000; Huddersfield with 35,000 inhabitants had nothing at all. Leeds (population 207,165), by contrast had gross income from the charity of £2,609 and Rishworth, a parish near Halifax, £3,120 for a population of 1,244. Rishworth, the wealthiest in Yorkshire, provided secondary education for fifty-five boys and just fifteen girls, all boarders.[1]

It was decided to divide the county into seven districts: Bradford; Dewsbury and Wakefield; Doncaster; Halifax and Huddersfield; Leeds and Ripon; Sedbergh and Giggleswick; and Sheffield. Bradford was the first to receive attention. 'What does Bradford want?' Canon Robinson asked himself, concluding that, 'It wants and can well afford to pay for high education but it must be adapted.' His assistant, Mr D.R. Fearon, was sent into the fray where he found, quite curiously, 'for a District teeming with modern industries ... full of the life of the present age,' the governors at Bradford Grammar School insisted Greek be taught and that scholars receive a classical education to fit them for university. The Commissioners thought Bradford would be better served by a school of the modern scientific type where Greek and Latin were not taught and therefore did not dominate the curriculum. Bradford refused and a public inquiry ('not to elicit opinion but to ascertain facts'), was held on 10 January 1871. Witnesses from all walks of life – manufacturers, merchants, clergy, justices of the peace, medical men, retired colonels – all came forward and gave what were, essentially, their opinions. As may be expected, these men were all in favour of keeping Greek as part of the curriculum. But what was probably most surprising was the opinion of Joseph Edward Jenkinson, a warehouseman, who agreed that boys intended for commercial life did not need to learn Greek but ought to have it available to them should they, through their education, decide on a professional career or university. He cited that other fathers in his [less affluent] position would wish for their sons to have the opportunity for such advancement and they would allow any of them to be placed in the upper school.[2] Such were the ambitions of Bradford's working men.

All very well, but what about the girls? As predicted, the proposals for a (second-grade only) girls' school 'of somewhat elastic type' met with protest once the subject of money came up. A draft scheme requiring £250 per year to be set aside for girls, with another £50 to be added at a later point, was objected to by the governors of the boys' school: 'The principle of Girls' education is approved of but the Governors consider it of much more importance to have a first-rate boys' school and until that is established would prefer not to cripple the funds ...'. They counter-offered £200 but only then once funds were available, insisting the foundation of a girls' school was 'dangerous to the success of a really efficient Boys' school ... they therefore request your Honorable Board to postpone the claims upon the endowment for the education of Girls until the Boys' School shall have become firmly established.' The Commissioners capitulated; the girls' school was deferred for three years (and was actually opened four years later, in 1875) and the teaching of Greek to the boys was conceded.

The Commissioners' scheme adopted for the management of Bradford's endowed schools included the following clauses:

30. This foundation shall consist of two branches, one for the education of boys, the other for the education of girls.

31. From and after the date of this scheme, or within three years from such date, the governors shall appropriate the annual sum of £200, and on the determination or failure of the pension hereafter contemplated for the present schoolmaster or that assigned to the late usher, the further annual sum of £50 for the establishment and maintenance of a girls' school, and

such school shall be organised, supported, and managed in accordance with directions to be hereafter set forth in a supplementary scheme.

The 'supplementary scheme' was drafted by the committee of the Bradford Ladies' Educational Association (BLEA) 'with very much care, and in accordance with the best advice they could obtain'. It was no easy task; there were opposing requirements from various interested parties: the Commissioners; the governors of the boys' school; and the local supporters of the BLEA, which involved many difficulties and much delay. It was also felt the sum allocated to the girls was insufficient for the establishment of a good first-grade school at a moderate scale of fees. The ladies of the BLEA were not going to let things lie and set about ensuring the endowment was supplemented by enough money to buy suitable premises for a school to be housed. It would take time.

Meanwhile, in neighbouring Keighley, where the existing endowment was a third of that of Bradford's and the school was achieving very little, a new Mechanics' Institute was nearing completion. This would offer a trade school, well equipped for teaching of science, in direct competition to the failing endowed school. With the ambitions of Keighley's fathers perhaps not aspiring to have their sons learn Greek, the new trade school was high in their esteem. Fearon seized on the idea of using the existing grammar school for the girls and supporting the new boys' trade school with some of the endowment. And so, in 1871, the first new endowed girls' grammar school was established; supported by the Drake and Tonson Foundation, it was known as Drake and Tonson's Girls' Grammar School. And its first headmistress? None other than Mary Eliza Porter. Some thought it a 'hazardous experiment', but within two years it was providing secondary education for fifty-six girls whose parents paid £4–£8 a year. The endowment income from various sources, including Drake and Tonson, was £300 and it had been originally proposed that £200 of this should be allocated to the girls' school. For reasons unknown, Fearon reduced this to £150; the trade school trustees asked that it be further reduced to £100 and this was agreed to. The girls lost out again.

Bradford Ladies' Educational Association

The BLEA had been established in April 1868 after Anne Clough of the North of England Council for promoting the Higher Education of Women had addressed a meeting at St George's Hall in Bradford. Anne was campaigning throughout the north of England, persuading local influential ladies to organise a series of lectures for ladies on a wide range of topics, from natural sciences to history. Ladies who had attended the lectures were given the option of sitting an examination at the end of the series and if they 'reached the standard expected of them' they received statements attesting to their achievement. The influential ladies in Bradford included Jane Forster, the wife of W.E. Forster MP; Catherine Salt, the daughter-in-law of Sir Titus Salt; Mary Schlesinger, German wife of one of the many German merchants in the town; 'and others'. When it was suggested the lectures might also be available to men, Reverend S.G. Green, thinking they had better keep to the specific purpose of the institute, moved 'That a society be formed, to be titled the Bradford Ladies' Educational Association, for the purpose of instituting lectures on literary and scientific subjects'. All concurred and a committee of fourteen ladies was formed at the suggestion of Louis Compton Miall, a professor of biology, who also disapproved of allowing men to attend the lectures, and added:

> appropriate remarks on a scheme of study which he recommended as taking hold of young ladies just at the period when the preparatory education ceased. He expressed a hope that the time would come when it would cease to be a received opinion that women might be allowed to remain in calm ignorance of all the laws of the universe, and of all the results of human thought, and when a wide sympathy with every kind of intellectual activity and a sound judgment on all truly important subjects would be considered as the end of all education, whether of man or woman.
>
> *Leeds Mercury*, Friday, 17 April 1868

It seems getting the course of lectures off the ground was no easy task, since the *Bradford Observer* of 7 December 1868 thought:

> A friendly word may encourage those ladies of Bradford who are labouring in the face of many obstacles to establish a course of more advanced instruction for the young persons of their own sex. We beg to assure them that their efforts are recognised as needful and difficult work by all who are truly interested in educational movements.

There were difficulties in raising funds; there was neglect and indifference. Some complained about the cost of the lectures (eminent professors who gave the lectures expected to be paid), but the newspaper urged:

> Two of the lectures on English literature and physical geography have been already delivered, and the attendance has been hitherto fairly remunerative. ... the young ladies of the Bradford Ladies' Educational Association are the elite of their class in this town, the most intelligent and the best informed, those to whom we shall look by and by for tone of higher culture in Bradford society. We may hope that before long the ladies' classes of Bradford will

be as successful and securely established as those of Liverpool, Manchester and Leeds. It is of the nature of all educational work to grow, and although for a time the supply may exceed the demand, perseverance will ultimately produce the desired result.

It is interesting to note this support for women's education from the *Bradford Observer*. The newspaper's proprietors were William Byles and his son William Pollard Byles, husband of Sarah Ann Byles, one of the key ladies of BLEA (and later elected to Bradford's School Board, in 1888, where she, unsurprisingly, sat on the education and school attendance committees). William Pollard's much younger half-sister Harriett Byles was one of the young ladies who benefited from the lectures, going on to teach at Salt Girls' High School in Shipley in 1876 and becoming its headmistress from 1886–1920.

Although the foundation of the endowment scheme created a nucleus for the establishment of girls' secondary schools, it did not completely solve the problem of girls' education. Other funding was necessary and, in Bradford, with the end of three years' girls' school deferral and the promised endowment in sight, the following notice was published in the *Bradford Observer* on 1 January 1874:

BRADFORD LADIES' EDUCATIONAL ASSOCIATION.

LIST OF SUBSCIBERS to the Fund for Establishing a PUBLIC GIRLS' SCHOOL in BRADFORD. Amount to be raised £6,000.

By the Trust of the Bradford Grammar School the sum of £200 a year (to be increased when certain pensions lapse to £250) is to be devoted to the Education of Girls, in accordance with a scheme to be hereafter approved by Her Majesty's Endowed School Commissioners. The Bradford Ladies' Educational Association are raising this fund to purchase and furnish suitable premises to supplement the endowment referred to and thus to bring within the reach of girls the same educational advantages as those now enjoyed by boys.
    Further Subscriptions will be gladly received by the Hon Secretaries to the Fund. Miss LAMBERT, Ashton House. Mrs W. POLLARD BYLES, St Mary's Road. Bradford, December 31, 1873.

The list of subscribers read like a 'who's who' of Bradford. Sir Titus Salt, Henry Brown and Isaac Holden topped the list with £500 each, followed by the Rt Hon. W.E Forster MP at £250 and Samuel Cunliffe Lister at £150. Other wealthy industrialists put their hands in their pockets; the German merchants contributed, including Julius Delius, father of composer Frederick. Total to date from the 103 subscribers (including 3 women) was £4,628 15s.

An amusing editorial appeared on 19 November 1874. The writer cited the bumptious Mr Brooke, a character in George Eliot's *Middlemarch*, whose opinion it was that women ought to occupy themselves solely with needlework, crochet 'and that sort of thing, you know', and added that such men still existed who gloried in the trifling character of their daughters' accomplishments:

> Many an old gentleman would assume a purple and apoplectic appearance if he had any suspicion his daughter could read Virgil, or had worked through two or three books of Euclid ... Of course, the girls' schools conformed to the ideas of the parents. It was very much less trouble to teach the pupils a few slight accomplishments than to give them a sound educational training; and as the parents preferred the easier method, the mistresses naturally adopted it. Hence it has come to pass that the education of girls has almost always been the merest sham. As long as it was very expensive, and the girls were taught nothing worth knowing, the parents were quite satisfied; and the teachers were not likely to quarrel with such an arrangement.

But 'a great change is in progress'. The nation, having altered its ideas about education, was promoting the idea of girls' education and the paper had very great pleasure in drawing attention to how these ideas were being carried out practically in Bradford, in particular by the BLEA, to which the people of Bradford were indebted. Difficulties had been overcome; prejudices had been argued against. Most of the money had been raised, most suitable premises (a former boys' school on Hallfield Road) had been purchased and the scheme was nearing completion. All that was now needed was a good mistress.

Fortunately, others had done similar work elsewhere – mainly in London – so precedents had been set. Bradford's was only the second girls' secondary school in Yorkshire to be established since the Endowed Schools Act. Wakefield Girls' High School was to follow three years later; Leeds, with its boys' grammar school with a £2,500 annual income, had a protracted wrangling over funds, and did not receive any endowment for a school for girls until 1901. With vested interests preventing Leeds Grammar sharing its funds, it was up to the women to do something about creating a girls' secondary school in this flourishing borough. It was Frances Elizabeth Lupton (née Greenhow) who was the main driving force behind the Leeds Ladies' Educational Association and the Leeds School of Cookery (opened in July 1875 by Baroness Angela Burdett Coutts) and it was she who, when no endowment was forthcoming, led a meeting to establish a joint-stock company, The Leeds Girls' High School Company Ltd, in order they might create the necessary school.

Leeds Girls' High School opened in September 1876, with Mrs Lupton as its vice president and Miss Catherine Lucy Kennedy its headmistress.

While Leeds was wrangling for its girls' school, Bradford got on with appointing its first headmistress. There were thirty candidates for the post of headmistress for Bradford Girls' Grammar School and they selected the very best:

> the choice fell unanimously on Miss [Mary Eliza] Porter, of London. Miss Porter has for many years occupied a most distinguished position among teachers. For six years she presided over the Bolham Training School for Teachers, in Devonshire. Many of her pupils now fill important posts. The evidence which she gave before the Schools Inquiry Commission led to her being selected, in 1872, to organise the first Girls' Endowed School in the country – that at Keighley. After having been there for a year, her services were so urgently required in London by the Girls' Public Day School Company, that she was induced to leave Keighley and go to Chelsea, to organise there the first school opened by the company. She worked there with remarkable success for more than two years, but feeling that the schemes of the Endowed Schools Commissioners gave her a wider scope of usefulness, she applied for the headmistress-ship of the Bradford School. The Council of the Chelsea School keenly regret her loss, and they furnish brilliant testimonials, not only of Miss Porter's enthusiasm in the work of education, but of the rare tact and ability which direct her labours. There are at present but few ladies who, however zealous in educational matters they may be, are qualified to undertake the heavy responsibilities involved in organising such a school as this in Bradford; and we feel that the Governors and the public of Bradford are alike to be congratulated in having been fortunate enough to secure the services of so distinguished a lady as Miss Porter.
>
> *Bradford Observer*, Wednesday, 11 August 1875

On Monday, 27 September 1875, Bradford Girls' Grammar School (BGGS) opened with 'a large roll of pupils and abundant promise of usefulness' to 'begin a new era in the educational history of the town'. The school was already oversubscribed with 112 pupils, 'the largest number with which any public girls' school of the first grade in the country has begun, and it abundantly proves that the school supplies a want which was felt in the community' and there would be no further admissions until after Christmas. This was to spare the teaching staff, who would be 'fully taxed' in their labours – they had expected around 60 girls to enrol – but would eventually accommodate 200 – and by July 1876 the roll had increased to 198. Tuition fees reflected the high grade of the school at 4 guineas a term; 5 guineas if girls entered over the age of 12 (the maximum fees allowed by the Commission was £20 per year);

hours were 9 a.m. to 1 p.m. Monday to Friday; and subjects taught were: reading and writing; arithmetic; book-keeping and mathematics; English grammar, composition and literature; history and geography; Latin, French and German; natural science; political economy; domestic economy and the laws of health; needlework; drawing; and vocal music and callisthenics.

Although a respected architect, Richard Mawson, who – with his brother – had designed most of Bradford's prestigious buildings, had given his time freely to oversee the alterations to the building, which had turned out to be in much need of repair, a further sum of £2,000 had been required to adapt and furnish the building. The school now boasted a large assembly hall, seven good classrooms, an art room, a dining room, large lavatories, dressing rooms, and a gymnasium (as yet unfinished), as well as 'dwelling rooms for the head mistress'. Outside was a 'capital playground (concrete)'.

The formal opening of the school by Lady Frederick Cavendish took place on Wednesday, 29 September, with a 'fashionable assemblage' of those who had been instrumental in bringing the school to fruition, and was followed, that evening, by a public meeting in St George's Hall.

Among the numerous speeches at the school's opening, Mary Porter's was the one that set the tone for the teaching and behaviour of her girls; an ethos that was to prevail at the school for the next 100 years and beyond! Her aim was to lay a good foundation; what they professed to teach should be thoroughly well learnt by the girls so they could build on it in later life. She was against cramming in too many subjects – after all, 'what comes in at high pressure will almost certainly go out at high pressure,' and hoped her girls would not later say, on hearing subjects of interest being talked about, 'Oh yes, I learnt all about that when I was at school, but I have forgotten it entirely since I left.'

Mary Porter also appealed to parents to ensure their daughters went to bed in good time, that their homework was completed at an early hour (no dawdling about) and not used as an excuse to stay up late, and to not go out 'visiting' on a school night.

Sir Mathew Wilson MP, a long-term 'zealous and sanguine supporter of the improvement of female education' who 'had not prepared any speech' for the gathering at St George's Hall, spoke wisely and eloquently about the influence and education of women. Telling the audience that if they looked back at history:

> they would find that there was hardly an eminent man who had not owed a great part of his intellectual ability to the high acquirements and ability of his mother and that the happiness of a man and his success in life depended more on his wife than on any other person ... could there be a subject more sacred, more interesting, to the advancement and prosperity of individuals, and, consequently, of the nation, than the education of women?

These new day schools, he went on, combined the advantages of a public education with those of home instruction: 'the competition and rivalry of a large body of pupils with all the amenities and teachings of home life'. Another highly gratifying feature of the school was that it brought together a variety of classes:

> One of the greatest defects of the society of this country was the broad line of demarcation that separated the different classes (applause). He knew no means better calculated to remove that crying evil so effectively than education (hear, hear). When they brought a number of pupils together, some of them could not fail to acquire an affection and regard for each other that would more or less continue to the end of their lives. Many of them might fill very different positions in after life in society, but they would retain for each other a sincere regard and even affection which would confer unspeakable advantages on both parties.

Echoing the sentiments of Edward Miall, who had given a similar speech about the importance of women on the same stage seven years earlier, he noted every year gave more and more political power to men who were largely influenced by their wives. The education of women, therefore, would 'do more to promote wise and successful decisions in political matters than any other means that could possibly be taken'. What an erudite man he was.

The opening of BGGS was reported outside of the borough too:

> A novelty in grammar schools has this week been inaugurated at Bradford in Yorkshire, in the shape of a grammar school for girls. The foundation of the Bradford Boys' Grammar School dates back to the time of King Charles II, and this institution was the first of the old trusts that were dealt with by the Commissioners under the Endowed Schools Act of Mr Forster. This girls' grammar school is the outcome of the Commissioners' scheme, and it is the first of the kind that has been established in Great Britain. ... The school will supply an unacknowledged and long-felt want, and it is an example worthy of imitation by most other large towns.
>
> *Stalybridge Reporter*, Saturday, 2 October 1875

That the people of Bradford were so keen to see their daughters educated in a first-rate school is quite telling. Where, previously, girls' education beyond elementary had been the privilege of the upper middle classes – 'the ladies' – now the middle classes, with their wealth wrought through industry rather than inheritance, recognised the advantages of a good education and had the wherewithal to fund it.

A few other industrial towns were successful in prising endowments from established boys' schools in order to build schools for girls. Birmingham used its King Edward VI foundation to create five girls' schools, the first being the King Edward VI High School for Girls which opened its classrooms in 1881, though one master of the boys' school was none too pleased at being squeezed into closer quarters, declaring he 'wished that all the girls of Birmingham had but one neck, and that had a rope around it'.

In 1874, a change of government saw the abolition of the Endowed Schools Commission and its powers transferred to the Charity Commission by the end of that year. One of the reasons for its disbanding appears to have been through the unpopularity of the Commissioners, partly because 'they had the audacity to convert superfluous schools for boys into much-needed schools for girls.' Perhaps, some said, the Endowed Schools Act was ahead of its time. It had not been an easy task for the Commissioners to establish girls' schools and it would not be any easier for their successors. Now there were only two Commissioners instead of three and they had no extra powers. In the years between 1875 and 1902, when the Secondary Education Act was introduced, the number of endowments secured for girls under the Charity Commissioners barely exceeded the those in the five years to 1875 (see Appendix 4 for full list of girls-only endowed secondary schools).

The struggles for funding

When the Endowed Schools Act was first brought into law, it may have seemed to those already running girls' schools that, at last, their mission to bring girls' education to the fore had been endorsed. Of course, they may not have envisaged the struggles that lay ahead. Frances Buss had been impressed by the Endowed Schools' Commission and began to think about her own school's future. To ensure its permanence, she set up a trust and moved the school to 'better and more commodious premises in the Camden Road'. A board of management, with several ladies and gentlemen, a constitution and the trust were all in place by 1870. 'We are now, therefore legally, a public grammar school for girls,' she wrote. The school was renamed the North London Collegiate School for Girls (instead of Ladies) and she became a salaried employee instead of the school's proprietor and profit-taker. At more or less the same time, she established an inexpensive school for the middle classes, The Camden School, which took over the vacated premises of the old school. Frances Buss remained superintendent, but the school had its own headmistress, Miss Marion Elford. The fees were deliberately low, the education simple but sound, and there was the opportunity for scholarships to the North London for promising pupils. With costs for rebuilding, equipment and teaching outstripping income from fees, Frances Buss, with bright optimism, drew up a scheme to raise money to support the school. As with Bradford, she needed to raise £5,000–£6,000 and thought this would be fairly straightforward since £60,000 had been raised 'with ease' for a new boys' school for the middle classes in Cowper Street in the City of London. All she was asking was for a tenth of that amount to be given for girls from similar backgrounds and she was happy to beg and cajole to raise the money. She had plenty of helpers, and some detractors. Supporters wrote letters to *The Times*; she approached philanthropists; appeals were made to City companies; the lord mayor spoke at the Camden prizegiving, but to little avail. It took three years to raise £700.

Eventually, there was a glimmer of hope. In late May 1871, Maria Grey presented a paper at a meeting of the Society of Arts on the topic of secondary education for girls, the difficulty of securing funding for it and the inequalities in the distribution of endowments. At that meeting was Reverend William Rogers, the man who had collected the £60,000 for the Cowper Street School – and had also collected £5,000 for a similar girls' school in the City, which was yet to be established. Maria Grey supposed this money could be given to the Camden School instead. Although Frances Buss's school met all the criteria, it was 3 miles from the City and it was decided that the money be used to found a school in that location. But when it was discovered there was other money available for that girls' school, the £5,000 (raised explicitly for a girls' school) was handed over to the Cowper Street boys' school so it could have a new hall. It was no wonder the women were at a very low ebb.

All seemed lost, though the ladies did not give up. Firstly, there was some cheer when a letter arrived from Sandringham, dated 15 November 1871, stating that HRH the Princess of Wales (later Queen Alexandra) fully recognised 'the importance and great need of improvement in the education of girls of the poorer middle classes' and had much pleasure in acceding to the request that these schools be put under her patronage. A cheque for 50 guineas was enclosed. Maybe it was the desire to be associated with a school with royal patronage that spurred on others to contribute; the previously fruitless appeal to the City companies began to show some yields in 1872 when £1,000 was donated by one of the governors, Miss Ewart, granddaughter of politician William Ewart. Henry Roby also stepped in, with a successful appeal to the Brewers' Company – it controlled the Platt charity – and the donation went towards new buildings for both schools. More was to come, from the Clothworkers' Company, who paid for scholarships for girls going on to further studies from the North London Collegiate. On 13 May 1875, the scheme to administer Camden and North Collegiate schools as endowed schools was signed by Queen Victoria. Their future was secure.

As for authority in these new endowed schools, the headmistress was queen. The scheme made her responsible for the 'whole internal organisation, management and discipline of the school' and (except in schools of the lowest grade) she was to appoint and dismiss her assistants. The headmistress, however, could not be dismissed unless two-thirds of the governors concurred. Financially, she was more certain of her position; the scheme laid down a fixed stipend plus a capitation fee – payment per pupil – both of which were based on the leaving age of girls and the grade of schools and fell within a range to be negotiated with the individual school's governors. Of course, this was lower than a headmaster's pay, but the scheme did open up employment prospects of a totally new order for women. With £100 stipend and £3 capitation, Frances Buss, with her 200 pupils at North London, would earn a very respectable salary of £700. 'We women owe a deep debt to the Endowed Schools' Commission,' she declared.

More money was to flow into the North London Collegiate's coffers from the Clothworkers' Company, resulting in the opening of a new assembly hall to be shared by both schools (known as the Clothworkers' Hall) in 1879. The event was combined with the annual prizegiving and the Princess of Wales, the school's patron, had been called upon to distribute prizes, accompanied by her husband, whom Frances Buss observed was 'perhaps unusually stout and bald for so young a man, and his neck is short, which makes him look stouter still', in contrast to his 'tall, slender wife with a very long throat'. Amusingly, the prince was noted for his predilection for attractive women. First, he shook hands rather vigorously (and 'quite unnecessarily') with the wife of the vice chairman of the Brewers' Company 'a most elegant and charming woman', then was observed by pupils 'coming to life' when certain attractive girls came up to receive their prizes. The Prince of Wales, called upon to reply to a vote of thanks on behalf of his wife, noted that he looked upon Frances Buss's school as the mother school of all those girls' schools that were 'cropping up in the country' and were sure to do good. Frances was equally enamoured with the prince when he sought out two Norwegian ladies to whom he had been introduced, that they might be engaged in conversation with the princess (who, of course, was Danish). 'The man of the highest rank in the country recognised womanhood as superior to his own rank,' she gushed.

That summer was probably the high spot of Frances Buss's career. She had been headmistress for almost thirty years in a school she had founded and her decision to put the school on a secure footing by making it a trust had been wise, as had her founding of a second, more affordable school. Both were overflowing with girls. Now she had the satisfaction of knowing her schools were being used as a model for the countless other girls' secondary schools being established nationwide.

The Girls' Public Day School Company

Soon after the publication of the Report of the Schools' Inquiry Commission, Maria Grey, perhaps sensing the wheels of girls' education would continue to grind slowly despite its recommendations, acted to expedite the process.

In the Education Department at the Social Science Congress held at Leeds Mechanics' Institution in October 1871, the question was posed, 'What are the special requirements for the improvement of the education of girls?' Two papers were presented, one by Maria, the other by Mary Gurney, with Maria reading her own paper and advocating the plan proposed by Emily Davies and Anne Clough that the establishment throughout the country of large day schools for girls would be the way forward and:

> that girls should have an object life to work for, and not look to marriage as their only career. Girls should be taught from childhood that they, like their brothers, must take their share of the work of life, and must be educated to do it well. They should not only be allowed but induced to work for their own maintenance where their parents could not make independent provision for them, or, if they were provided for, they should hold themselves bound to help and train themselves to help efficiently in doing the unpaid work of the world.

Mary's paper, 'Middle Class Schools for Girls', was read by Reverend B. Lambert. It was a thorough analysis of girls' education with comparisons of what was happening in Prussia, Germany, Switzerland, Scandinavia and the USA and citing The Camden School as a great example of a school for middle-class girls. She voiced her hope that the Endowed Schools' Commission would create schools for middle-class girls.

Both noted that to have sufficient self-control, self-dependence, self-reliance, and discrimination, judgment, and determination, women must be educated. ... Not only were better schools and better teachers wanted but more of them; they also urged that female teachers should be more systematically trained.

Of course, there were detractors in the ensuing debate. Reverend Dr H. Smythe, who really should have known better, opined that the present influence of women would be reduced if women 'were allowed to jostle among men in the occupations and struggles of life'. Not only that, he feared that transferring the education of girls to large schools, and then drafting them into universities, would not elevate their character and indeed would change their nature. 'In the rough competition of public schools, and the still rougher competition of universities afterwards, there would be changed that part of woman which men engaged in the battle of life most admired and were most influenced by.'[3] Fortunately, his views were very much in the minority.

On the same day, 9 October 1871, Maria took the opportunity to present her proposal for the founding of the National Union for the Improvement of Education for Women of all Classes (later known, more simply, as the Women's Education Union) to a meeting in the board room of the Leeds Board of Guardians. Its purpose was to pull together all the different efforts being made throughout the country to promote the same objective (sometimes in ignorance of each other's work) and to create good communication between the various councils to give them greater powers of influence in publicising the dire state of girls' education in the country and the importance of improving it. The union would 'collect and disseminate information' in respect of the advantages of home or school education, large or small schools, and the influence of endowments. The local associations would continue their work, but corresponding with the union, plus there would be a general meeting annually to which they would each send a representative. Any woman or man could join for the subscription of 5 shillings a year; corporate organisations might be affiliated for not less than £1 annually.

With its key objectives of establishing good and cheap schools for girls of every class above those attending the elementary schools; advocating the training and registration of teachers; and providing means for training female teachers, the union was launched. Its committee included Maria Grey, as temporary president (Princess Louise (Queen Victoria's daughter) succeeded her shortly afterwards)), Emily Davies and Miss Alice le Geyt as well as the gentlemen supporters.

Within eight months, they had drawn up plans to form a limited liability company, the Girls' Public Day School Company, 'for the purpose of establishing good and cheap day schools for the secondary education of girls', which they presented at the Royal Albert Hall on 7 June 1872:

> We wish to draw your attention to the great need of really good Schools that can be attended at a moderate cost, for the better education of Girls and Young Women. This want was shown to exist by the reports of the Schools Enquiry Commission. The Union for Improving the Education of Women proposes to meet this want, and as the necessary funds are too large to be provided out of private means, and the hope of help from endowments is remote, the experiment is to be tried of raising them by a Limited Liability Company, which will begin by founding a public Day School for Girls in South-west London.
>
> *Courier and West-End Advertiser*, Saturday, 15 June 1872

These schools would be public schools, in the sense of being not exclusive either as to class or creed. They were to be day schools and cheap schools – boarding schools being seen as breaking up the home influences that were so essential 'to fit girls for the after duties of life' – and large in order to keep costs down so they could pay the right salaries to attract efficient teachers. It was also proposed they should be training schools.[4]

The first school was to be established in a central position adjacent to Chelsea, Brompton and South Kensington, and based on the proven successful model at the North London Collegiate and Camden Street schools. The school year was to be divided into three terms, with fees from £2 2s each term in the preparatory department, to £8 8s in the higher classes of the senior department (incidentally, twice the fees of Bradford Girls' Grammar) which would include the use of maps and books of reference, and all expenses for writing and drawing materials. Besides the usual elementary studies, lessons would be given in ancient and modern languages, mathematics, the elements of moral science, logic, physical science (especially physiology as applied to health), social and domestic economy, music, etc. Instrumental music, solo singing, and dancing (what might be called 'accomplishments') were extra according the level of teaching required. To raise the requisite capital, shares of £5 each were issued and by 15 June a total of 340 shares had been purchased, amounting to £1,700. Why this was so much more successful than the appeal by Frances Buss is a mystery.

As well as Maria Grey, the women behind this enterprise were her sister Emily Shirreff, Mary Gurney and Lady Henrietta Stanley of Alderley. If this first school was a success, they promised similar schools would be founded in places where they were needed, with a proviso that 400 shares were subscribed to. The school opened on 21 January 1873 at Durham House, Chelsea, with just twenty or so girls and its headmistress was, of course, none other than Mary Eliza Porter, who having been the first headmistress of the first endowed girls' secondary school (Keighley), now became the first headmistress for the Girls' Public Day School Company (GPDSC). The school moved to new premises on Cromwell Road, South Kensington in September 1880 and the name was changed to Kensington High School. It was here that Emily Wilding Davison, forever remembered as the suffragette who met her tragic death at Epsom in June 1913, received her secondary education from 12–18 between 1885 and 1891 before enrolling at Royal Holloway College on 14 January 1892, where she studied for just two years, before her father's death meant there was no further funding for her education, though she was able to spend a further term at St Hugh's Oxford. She was later a governess for a family at Spratton Grange, Northamptonshire[5] before turning to the suffrage cause.

The second school opened by the GPDSC was Notting Hill and Bayswater, in 1873, followed by another in Croydon the following year. By July 1875, a further five had been founded: Clapham, Hackney, Bath, Norwich and Nottingham, taking the work outside the London sphere.

The GPDSC proved successful, not only in opening secondary schools for girls throughout England but also in its educational standards and secure finances. By 1883, there were twenty-seven schools operating a system of education that was thoroughly sound, cheap, and good; it was advancing the standard of female education through the employment of 'some of the ablest mistresses who had ever managed schools in this country'. 'So admirably had the affairs of the company been conducted', that since 1878 it had been able to pay a dividend of 5 per cent to the investors. This dividend could have been larger, but it was felt to be the first duty of the organisation to spend the money on educational purposes to the highest advantage rather than be governed by ordinary commercial principles. This view was agreed at a shareholders' meeting.

At a prizegiving for the ten London schools on 16 March 1883 at the Royal Albert Hall, the location of the company's founding, it was noted that in its ten short years, the company had done so much for its founders to be rightfully proud of. At the close of the distribution of prizes by the Princess of Wales, the Marquis of Lansdowne made the following remarks:

> The work upon which they were engaged was one of the highest national importance. The policy of the Council was to afford a sound education for English girls, and although in this they had, perhaps, acted in advance of public opinion, public opinion was now steadily moving to the standpoint they had taken up. He did not believe that the gift of education would ever make a woman the less gentle or graceful, and why they attached great importance to the education of women was because women were the great educators of the people, owing to the position which they occupied as the centre of English homes. Heretofore girls had had to rest content with a spurious education, and the first systematic attempt to alter that state of things had been made by the Council of the Girls' Public Day School Company. The usefulness of the Company was not to be measured by the number of pupils educated, or the number of schools only, but also by the effect which it had had in raising the standard of female education throughout the country.
>
> *Bath Chronicle and Weekly Gazette*, Thursday, 22 March 1883

He added that the schools had bridged class divisions, through daughters of ministers of the Crown mixing with girls who were there on school board exhibitions and all feeling an equal pride in belonging to a High School for Girls. The Prince of Wales, also in attendance and speaking on behalf of his wife, echoed the sentiments, and in closing, 'I wish you all, young ladies, success in the life which is before you, and I trust you will continue as working successfully you have hitherto done, and then you will win other prizes in life, in addition to those which you have won today.'

By 1894, there were thirty-five GPDSC schools with the title 'High School for Girls', plus a middle school at Clapham and a standalone preparatory school in Newcastle upon Tyne, as well as twenty-three attached preparatory schools.

Twenty-one of the high schools were outside London – stretching across the country from Carlisle to Gateshead; Liverpool to York; Newton Abbot to Ipswich; and Weymouth to Brighton (for full list see Appendix 5).

A report from 1904 states there were 7,113 pupils in 34 schools as well as girls who came into schools for specific lessons. With a reorganisation in secondary education, following the 1902 Secondary Education Act, in October 1905 the GPDSC council recommended the company be converted into a trust. This was to take advantage of any available funding to maintain girls' secondary schools. Although the company had given the first great impetus to the education of girls, progress of events meant that as a private income-bearing company, it would probably be overlooked by the state (the Board of Education) and the county councils in the organisation of secondary education, and might lose grants it had formerly been in receipt of. The GPDSC council proposed it continue to administer the schools but gradually cease to be a trading company, repaying the entire capital to the shareholders within certain periods. In the meantime, it would pay them interest at 4 per cent per annum, and set about creating a permanent educational trust. The shareholders would lose nothing, and their schools would gradually become trust schools with the status of endowed schools. This way, they would be on a level with the other public schools in the country in terms of receiving grants on the same scale as those given to schools under public management. This was all agreed and the company became a trust shortly afterwards.

***

Where the women led, the men followed. Seeing the success of the GPDSC, which was non-denominational in its teaching of religion, leading churchmen sought to establish a limited company, with the specific aim of founding day high schools for girls in accordance with the teachings of the Church of England. A provisional committee, including sixteen bishops and four Cambridge University college heads, was formed and the Church Schools Company's inaugural meeting was held in April 1883, chaired by the Archbishop of Canterbury, Edward Benson. Of course, since the company's primary mission was to provide high schools for middle-class girls, it could not really function without women experienced in such matters. Recruited onto the committee were Dorothea Beale, who would have been respected for her strong Christian faith, followed by Frances Buss, Helen Gladstone (who had studied at Newnham, Cambridge and later became vice principal of the college) and Laura Soames, an expert in phonetics. The valuable contribution these talented, educated women could make to the cause of girls' education was fully embraced and their service on the education committee ensured the right headmistresses were selected for the new schools.

The first school opened in early 1884 in Surbiton with Miss Mary Amelia Bennett, one of the first women to graduate from Girton College, Cambridge – where she had read classics – as headmistress. The company had rapidly raised £37,865 in £5 shares and new girls' high schools followed swiftly: Bury St Edmunds, Sunderland, Durham, Newcastle upon Tyne, Dewsbury, Tottenham, Brighton, Richmond, Reigate, Guildford, Leicester, Kendal, Woolwich – all in the first five years. A handful of boys' schools were also established. By 1902, it had 25 schools in total and 2,109 pupils on its books, so the schools were much smaller than those run by the GPDSC.

Other smaller limited (or joint-stock) companies were formed around the same time; some seem to have been to create just one girls' high school in a particular location (as with Leeds in 1876), others perhaps a few. The High Schools Company for Girls opened its first girls' secondary school at Wallasey on the Wirral in September 1883 under the headmistress-ship of Miss Laura G. Eaton, formerly of the Ladies' College, Guernsey. Another school followed at Birkenhead in 1884 under Miss Grace Frost. There was competition too, with individual schools being established in Tranmere and Oxton nearby. There were allegations of some being favoured by the council and creating a monopoly, but it was pointed out that:

> Education is no monopoly; the High School for Girls, like other scholastic enterprises, merely seeks to supply a demand which is believed to exist, and it can hope for success only in proportion as it meets the needs and wishes of the public. It is founded in no spirit of hostility to private schools, of which there are really not enough in this neighbourhood, hundreds of new families having settled here during the past few years. … Surely a 'Father' has no ground for complaint in that capacity that increased facilities should be offered for the education of girls; high schools have been opened with success in London, Manchester, Exeter, Liverpool, Oxford, Leamington, Loughborough, Chester, and more towns than I can name. Birkenhead, with its large residential population, is rather late in only now supplying itself with so usual and valuable an institution.
>
> *Birkenhead News, Wednesday, 22 October 1884*

Secondary education for girls was now, well and truly, accepted and appreciated.

Chapter 10

Opportunities for Headmistresses

The opening of the new girls' secondary schools not only broadened the opportunity for middle-class girls to have a higher education but also increased the number of satisfying well-paid posts for women. Naturally, they were not paid at the same rate as men but, since they tended to be single women without a family to support, it could be argued that they did not require as much money as men to have a very comfortable living.

However, the position of headmistress could be an isolated one and, particularly in the early days, there had been no real precedent set for how a headmistress should run a school. How should they appoint and dismiss staff? Which books should they use and what were the best methods for teaching lessons? Where would they find and train the minimum number of teachers? And how would they deal with governors? In September 1874, Frances Buss wrote to a friend saying it was time to form an 'Association of Headmistresses and hold occasional conferences in order to know what we ought to assert and what surrender' and by 22 December that year the Association of Head Mistresses of Endowed and Proprietary Schools had been formed. Nine women met at Frances's home in Primrose Hill: Frances; Dorothea; Elizabeth Day, Manchester High School; Selina Hadland, Milton Mount College, Gravesend; Elsie Day, Grey Coat Hospital, Westminster; Harriet Morant Jones, Notting Hill High School; Marion Elford, The Camden School; Caroline C. Derrick, St Martin's Middle-Class School, London; and Mary Eliza Porter, Chelsea High School.

As an example of the scope of their activities, a report from the annual conference in March 1878, held at Bradford Girls' Grammar School where Mary Porter was by then head, notes the seventeen headmistresses in attendance (Dorothea was absent from the list) and the object of these conferences being 'to promote a feeling of sympathy and cooperation among the members and to give them opportunities of comparing their experiences on various important points'.[1] The main topics for discussion were the course of study for girls; the difficulties connected with the arrangement of homework for girls in higher forms; the arrangement of the curriculum so as to secure width and thoroughness without overwork; the Rt Hon W.E. Forster's scheme of inspection; suggestions for the examination of teachers by the universities; and some questions on health. An intense but productive meeting. Three years later, the conference was held at North London Collegiate with 41 in attendance, representing 7,300 pupils. Numbers attending continued to grow – more girls' schools meant more headmistresses – and in June 1887 the association took the unusual step of holding the conference at a boys' public school as the invited guests of Reverend Edward Thring of Uppingham School. Thring was determined to foster cooperation between the great schools with their ancient traditions that hindered them and the new girls' high schools that were becoming a power in the land. He had already addressed girls at Leamington Spa and Worcester high schools when he issued his invitation to the association. In preparation for the conference, Frances Buss visited Uppingham in November 1886, where she confessed to Reverend Thring that the committee had been rendered 'silent and speechless, so much were they struck by the public recognition'. The fifty-nine headmistresses were well looked after and entertained by boys, masters and their wives; Thring described them as, 'a delightful company, entirely free from all nonsense: not a trace of "women's rights" amongst them, but the most sensible, sober-minded workers and thinkers ... a very remarkable set of able and interesting women they were'.

This giving of the right hand of fellowship on the part of a representative of boys' education to the teachers of their sisters was hailed by the association as an event of happy augury for the cause of women's education.[2] Reverend Thring, addressing the conference, also attended by Uppingham masters, noted that the room in which the first headmasters' conference had taken place in 1869 was now 'witnessing a reunion significant of new beginning in the partnership of women with men' and he dwelt on the characteristic office of women teachers, maintaining they were 'the best fitted to correct the evils of modern competition and to give in educational systems the rightful predominance to character over intellect'. If new thinking and necessary reforms were to be introduced in education, it would be by women:

> the fine and delicate life-power, with its influence on life, is done by the women ... you are fresh and enthusiastic, and comparatively untrammelled whilst we are weighed down by tradition, cast like iron in the rigid moulds of the past ... the hope of teaching lies in you. Yours is the power.[3]

Afterwards, Frances Buss wrote to Reverend Thring on the association's behalf, asking him to accept a few books for the school library in remembrance of the visit. It was an 'event in educational history of no small significance', she wrote. She was right; these pioneering headmistresses created the foundation for girls to have a good secondary education and to be empowered to be independent and pursue worthwhile careers. Sadly, Edward Thring died only a few months later, on 22 October 1887, the day after his greatest wish that a high school for girls be created in Uppingham had been advertised as coming to fruition and was to open under the headmistress-ship of Miss Mary Beisiegel, late of Newnham College. Although his own three daughters had been educated at home by governesses, Thring had strongly advised Mary and her sister Lillie, daughters of one of the masters – who had been sent to board at Handsworth Ladies' College – to open the school and had pledged his powerful support and assistance. The school was never large, with a maximum of around twenty-five girls, and after the Beisiegel sisters ceased their connection with the school in early 1892 (Lillie to marry and Mary to be a missionary) and a new principal, Florence Wilde, was appointed, the numbers fell into decline. By January 1895, the whole 'household' was for sale on account of Florence's leaving. There are a number of possibilities for the failure of the school, not least that Florence had only taught at elementary level prior to taking up the post and that since 1894 girls had been able to travel by railway from Uppingham to the well-regarded high school for girls at Stamford.[4]

***

For some time to come, teaching remained the main profession open to women. It is interesting to note how these headmistresses progressed their careers. Some stayed many years at the same school; Frances Buss and Dorothea Beale put their lives' work into their respective schools, Mary Eliza Porter, on the other hand, seemed to move from one opportunity to another around the country. From Tiverton to Gateshead, Keighley to Chelsea, Bradford to the Isle of Man and thence to Bedford Modern School for Girls.

In 1880, there was much conjecture in the Bradford newspapers surrounding the reason for Mary Porter's resignation from Bradford Girls' Grammar after only five years in the post. In what was the social media of the day, various correspondents put forward their theories, but that she was respected and revered for her work by her pupils and their parents is evident in a letter signed by more than sixty people wishing her well and the presentation by her girls of a 'beautiful kettle-drum service in silver' as she bade them farewell just before Christmas 1880 and left for a new position on the Isle of Man. Into her place stepped Miss Agnes Y. Lee, formerly headmistress of Allsopp's Endowed Girls' School, Burton on Trent, where for two years she had worked up the school from a state of 'comparative inefficiency to one of great utility and success. Previously she had two years' training at Miss Bussey's [*sic*] well-known collegiate schools, in the north of London; and these facts, together with other strong recommendations, induced the unanimous vote referred to.'

It was not until there had been a scandal at BGGS that the reason for Mary Porter's departure became known – almost twelve months after her 'resignation'. Again, the social media of the day worked its wonders. It became known in

September that Agnes Lee had resigned her post after only nine months, and it seems the resulting decline in the reputation of the school prompted Mary Porter to lay bare all she had been subjected to, in a letter to the *Bradford Daily Telegraph*, published 3 October 1881. The full letter is below, as it highlights the difficulties a headmistress in charge had in dealing with the school governors – one of the topics of discussion within the Association of Headmistresses. Considering she had been so well regarded in her qualifications, experience and ability 'to undertake the heavy responsibilities involved in organising such a school as this in Bradford' it is shocking that she was turned on by the school governors who, presumably, thought they knew better:

> THE BRADFORD GIRLS' GRAMMAR SCHOOL. To the Editor of the Bradford Daily Telegraph. Sir – Everyone will admit that the Girls' Grammar School ought unquestionably to be governed as a public trust for the benefit of the town of Bradford. I think the facts which I wish to bring under the notice of the public of Bradford will go far to show that one or two governors who have had great influence in directing the policy of the council have allowed themselves to be swayed by personal motives. The first and only cause of the sudden change from friendship to enmity in the relations of these particular governors with myself was that I was firm in refusing to let a certain form of uncleanliness in hair be tolerated in the school. In the very few cases which it occurred I required the parents to keep their daughters at home till it was set right, that there might be risk of infection to others. Unfortunately for myself the same measures were not adopted at the Saltaire Girls' Schools, and those governors were offended that I should set up a higher standard in this respect than was thought necessary in the other schools of which they were also governors. The few parents who were offended by the regulations soon came round, but the governors in question from that time became enemies, and began a system of petty persecutions, which after three years ended in my being driven from my post. There is a scheme drawn up by the Endowed Schools Commission on which the government of this school should be based. By the provisions of this scheme it is enacted that the headmistress shall be free to carry out all the internal duties of school management without interference on the part of the governors. For some time before I resigned this arrangement was completely ignored, and I was harassed by perpetual interference with the smallest details of my work. The fact too that these governors instituted the plan of having a secret minute book in which all the entries were made by one of these governors speaks for itself. When they told me that certain parents had made some complaints I naturally asked for their names that I might take the matter in dispute in a friendly manner.

They refused to give their names, and the chairman added that 'they could not trust me to see the parents'. It is certainly unfortunate for the Bradford Girls' Grammar School that some of its governors are also on the council of the Salt Schools, for one or two of these governors have been known to urge parents to take away their children from the Bradford Girls' School and send them to the Saltaire Girls' School. They also tried to win teachers from their allegiance to myself. Those who know how unbroken was the harmony which subsisted between myself and my large staff of teachers all the five years I remained at Bradford will know how signally this attempt failed. On return to Bradford after the summer holidays last year, I was requested at an ordinary meeting of the governors to make certain alterations in the timetables which I knew would not be to the advantage of the pupils or the convenience of their parents. They would not listen to my objections, and at last I gave way under protest, only pleading that the governors would at least agree among themselves as to the alterations to be made, as some proposed one thing and some another. A few days after I was confined to my bed by severe attack of illness brought on entirely by mental worry. The governors hastily called a special meeting, and without the slightest warning of their intentions sent me a request, which they said was unanimous, that I would resign. No reason was given for this action, but they mentioned an early date when they would meet to receive my resignation. In this letter, in which they said that they had accepted it, they informed me that they had voted me the sum of £50 as a token of their goodwill. I need hardly say that the gift was not accepted. I think it right to add that one or two of the Bradford governors seem not only to have deliberately formed the plan of driving me away by persistent persecution, but also have taken steps to prevent my obtaining remunerative and honourable employment elsewhere. In more than one good appointment, where my testimonials and the character of the work I had done would have secured election, I was rejected, in one case at the last moment, solely through influence used against me from Bradford, which I am informed took the form of vague statements which could not be taken hold of or refuted, though care was taken that they should be injurious enough to secure my rejection. I was recommended privately to my present post, but the experiment of trying to raise a high school here has not succeeded, because the population is too small to support such a school. I shall therefore leave at Christmas, with no security that the same unworthy influence may not again be used to prevent my obtaining another post. Some of these facts are getting known, and when the governors advertise for a headmistress to fill the vacant post at Bradford, as they are bound to under the scheme, it is hardly likely any really good candidate will apply, few good experienced teachers would like the risk of working under governors who have thus requited the labours of their first headmistress. The governors at Bradford have stated that I could not get on with the governing bodies of the other schools where I have been; this is quite untrue. If the Bradford governors had treated me as well I was treated by the governors at Keighley (my first public school) I should have nothing complain of. I left that school to become the headmistress of the first school opened by the Public Day School Company. From the members of that council I received much kindness and consideration. At one time some members of that council differed from myself in respect to the conduct of a teacher, but those members who had had more practical acquaintance with education supported my view of the case. When I left that school for Bradford the various members of the council expressed their keen regret at the loss of my services and their kind personal feeling towards myself both in the testimonials which they gave and in many private letters which I have by me. I have not met with the slightest difficulty in working with the governors of this school, who have treated me with uniform kindness. I think it only due to myself that should now place these facts before the public of Bradford. I remain, yours, &c,, Mary E. Porter, The High School, Castletown, Isle of Man, September 26th, 1881.

Bradford Daily Telegraph, Monday, 3 October 1881

This created a flurry of correspondence from which can be gleaned that Mary Porter was pushed out so the governors could appoint 'a much more complaisant and charming schoolmistress', but despite Agnes Lee's 'strong recommendations' (and there was some doubt cast as to just who had made them) the governors discovered their new protégée 'scandalously disgraced them, and gave such a shock to the reputation of the school that it will be viewed with suspicion'. What Agnes Lee did is not clear; perhaps it was so scandalous it was kept out of the newspapers in case of litigation. There were calls for the resignation of the governors; a fund was set up to help the now unemployed Mary Porter. The school appointed Miss Mary Ida Stocker, recorded as a private governess to a Leeds physician in 1871 and who had joined BGGS in 1878, aged 33, and was already a head of department, as a *pro tem* headmistress. With 'a great sense of duty and loyalty to the school and the cause of education', she remained in post until 1894, doing an excellent job and doubling the number of pupils. Her resignation, along with that of her second-in-command, was in order to 'acquire a private school', an unusual course of action, perhaps, although it appears to have been a girls' boarding school in affluent Harrogate. Happily, Mary Porter soon found a new position and was principal at the Bedford Modern School for Girls from its opening in May 1882 until she retired in 1894. Bedford Modern was one of two schools for girls opened by the Harpur Trust in May 1882; the other was Bedford High School for Girls. The 'Modern' (fees £4 a year) was for girls aged 7–17 who, after completing their course, could gain exhibitions for transfer to the 'High' (fees £7 a year), which took girls up to the age of 20.

Standards continue to rise

As better education and training became available for girls, many were inspired by their mistresses to take up secondary school teaching as a career. As a result, better-qualified teachers meant better-taught girls, which continued to raise the standard of girls' education.

Miss Buss, Miss Beale and Miss Porter born 1827, 1831 and 1835 respectively, could only avail themselves of courses at Queen's College to train for their vocation, there being no day schools for girls – apart from those for daughters of the poor. Selina Hadland, born in 1838, appointed principal at Milton Mount College in 1871, only had her own previous teaching experience to draw on when following the college's purpose of not only teaching girls but also aspiring to make them teachers. Many other secondary schoolmistresses were woefully under-qualified in the 1860s, but thanks to Emily Davies's successful campaign to allow girls to sit the 'Cambridge Locals' and her pioneering work with Barbara Bodichon and Lady Stanley in establishing Girton College, the foundations on which others could progress girls' education were set.

More training; better opportunities

Within a fairly short time span, the campaigning and work of the earlier women meant girls born from the beginning of the next decade had much better opportunities to study. It was helped by the succession of women's colleges, created from 1869, and the new developments that also took place the universities. A 'College for Women' was opened on 16 October 1869 at Benslow House, Hitchin, with a goal to create a permanent institution and eventually secure full membership of Cambridge University. With student numbers growing and the house's lease ending, the college moved nearer to Cambridge – to a new-built ladies' college at Girton. Swiftly following was Newnham, founded in 1871 and presided over by Anne Jemima Clough; it too moved to larger premises in Cambridge, in 1875. Women's colleges Somerville and Lady Margaret Hall at Oxford were both founded in 1879. Neither university allowed women to be awarded degrees (although they qualified at degree level and women were permitted to sit Tripos examinations at Cambridge from 1881) until the twentieth century – Oxford in 1920 and Cambridge in 1948. London University was more accommodating, with women being allowed to study for degrees from 1878; both Bedford College (established

1849) and Royal Holloway (1886) were women-only institutions associated with London. In Ireland, women were admitted to all degrees at Royal University of Ireland and Trinity College, Dublin from 1880, and in the north of England the colleges of Victoria University (in Manchester (1880) Liverpool (1881) and Leeds (1887)) were, from the first, open to women as well as men. St Hugh's College, Oxford (founded by Elizabeth Wordsworth, great-niece of the poet) opened in 1886, expressly to provide opportunities to poorer women. Training colleges specifically for secondary schoolmistresses also opened, the first being the Teachers' Training & Registration Society College in 1878 (later named Maria Grey Training College after its founder) and in 1885, the Cambridge Training College for Women Teachers, later named Hughes Hall after its first principal, Elizabeth Phillips Hughes, who had studied at Cheltenham Ladies and at Newnham.[5] The Cambridge Training College, founded by Frances Buss and Sophie Bryant, was intended for training graduates to teach, as many were neglecting the professional training they required (either because they could not afford it or despised it and could get a job without it), but the intentions had to be relaxed to allow a sufficient number of students to secure economic viability. The residential college provided a year's professional training for secondary school teachers and prepared women for the Cambridge Teachers' Certificate (Theory and Practice) and for the Teachers' Diploma of the London University. Students attended Cambridge University lectures on teaching, as well as those given by resident and visiting lecturers to the college and were given ample opportunity to practice their teaching skills in science, languages, mathematics, and other subjects in various schools in the city. Women were determined to embrace these better opportunities and, through their own hard work, they ensured the success of their endeavours, as these examples show.

Ellen Allen

Ellen Allen, the first headmistress at Wakefield Girls' High School in 1878, seems to have come to her post via a rather circuitous route. The daughter of a Norfolk currier and leatherworker, she was born in spring 1839. When she was appointed to Wakefield's headship, it was declared she was a certificated Cambridge student, and a Clothworker's Scholar, Newnham Hall. Her birth year meant she faced a similar paucity of educational opportunities as Misses Buss, Beale, Porter and Hadland, but it seems she trained as a governess and is listed on the 1871 census, aged 33, as a 'servant' within the large household of William J. Legh MP (later Baron Newton) at Lyme Park, Cheshire (probably best known as Pemberley in the BBC series of *Pride and Prejudice*). How she came to be in such a glorious place may be through Legh's wife's family as her father was the archdeacon of Norwich and there is clearly a Norfolk connection. Her charges included Thomas Wodehouse Legh, who became a diplomat (and later a lord) and Gilbert Legh who became a major in the Grenadier Guards, as well as their sisters, Dulcibella and Mabel Maude, who became a gentlewoman and wife of a hereditary peer respectively. Ellen possibly found herself in that no-woman's land between the well-to-do family (they also had a London house in Belgrave Square) and the servants and decided to study when the opportunity to go to Newnham arose after its foundation in 1871. Perhaps her employer, recognising her abilities, paid for her to study, but the Clothworkers' scholarship will also have helped. It was noted (on her leaving the school in 1894) that she had been known to one of governors for some time before her appointment and her several excellent testimonials had made selecting her from the numerous candidates 'a pleasure'. Clearly, she had made a good impression where it counted. Her salary at Wakefield was £100 plus £2 per girl; provision had been made to accommodate 100 girls, so her earnings would have been £300 a year (half that of the headmaster at Queen Elizabeth's Grammar School for Boys at £200 and £4 per boy).

Elizabeth Day

Described as 'quick-witted and nimble-minded', Elizabeth Day, born in 1844, was Manchester Girls' High School's first headmistress. Educated at a day school in South Molton St, London from the age of 10 to 14 and then for a short time at a 'very peculiar boarding school' in Rugby, she initially went to Queen's College to study German (only) in 1861 (where her sisters were already studying full-time) and worked as a governess. In 1866, Elizabeth seized the opportunity to be a pupil teacher at Queen's attached practising school. Becoming deeply aware of her ignorance, she attended all the lectures available to her and studied in the college library, covering her own expenses from her savings. In need of remunerative work, she returned to private teaching in 1867, but still attended classes at Queen's. Three days a week, she worked or studied 8 a.m. till 7 p.m., two days 8 a.m. to 6 p.m., and on Saturdays she stopped at 3 p.m. Even after all this, she was not allowed to sit the Queen's College General Certificate because she had not fulfilled the conditions of taking the full course for two years. In April 1871, determined to measure herself in some way, she opted to enter for the women's examination in Cambridge. More study ensued; she joined classes in arithmetic and English literature at Rugby School, followed by divinity and English history, and, having passed the exams, was offered a small scholarship to go to Cambridge the next year to join the classes just being started. Not able to afford this, she contented herself with joining several correspondence classes both at Cambridge and Rugby, in preparation for the Language and Moral Science groups, which she intended to take in 1872. Added to this were classes in political economy, Latin, Greek, French, logic, essays and more English literature. It was too much alongside her regular teaching work, so she dropped the classes in logic! Passing well, she was awarded Professor Mayor's prize for languages and was given £30 for buying books and further £5 gratuity. In 1873, she entered the examinations again, this time gaining a first class in languages, with distinctions in Italian and English literature. These achievements brought her to the notice of Manchester, where the new girls' public school was to be opened. Would she be interested in applying for the headmistress's post, they wondered. After various consultations with friends, she eventually decided to find out more. Coming highly recommended by the men who had tutored her, she was warmly welcomed by the Manchester committee and hospitably accommodated. Thus, in July 1873 her determined efforts to train as an excellent schoolmistress came to fruition and she was appointed headmistress of the new school for girls in the burgeoning borough. It opened on 21 January 1874 with sixty girls.[6] Elizabeth stayed at the school until her retirement in 1898 and was succeeded by Miss Sara Annie Burstall (b. 1859). Sara had attended Frances Buss's Camden School and gained a scholarship to North London Collegiate in 1875, where she became an outstanding scholar, winning prize after prize in a wide range of subjects, and was awarded a Clothworkers' scholarship to Girton in 1878. She returned to Frances Buss to teach at North London Collegiate in 1882, where she undertook further studies, including a teachers' diploma in London in 1894, and rose to chief assistant mistress, before moving to Manchester in 1898, where she was later also appointed lecturer on education at Owen's College.

Sophie Bryant

One woman to grasp the opportunity of a university education was the aforementioned Sophie Bryant (née Willcock), born 1850, who succeeded Frances Buss as head at North London Collegiate. Sophie had been largely educated at home by her father, a tutor and fellow of Trinity College, Dublin until the family moved to London when he took up a professorship at London University. In 1866, Sophie obtained the Arnott Scholarship to study at Bedford College. While there, she passed the Senior Cambridge Examination with first-class honours and distinction in English and mathematics, the first girl to obtain a distinction in mathematics. She married a doctor in 1869 but was widowed the next year. In 1875, Sophie was invited by Frances Buss to join the staff of North London Collegiate and there she taught mathematics. While working as a teacher, Sophie continued to study, passing the Cambridge Higher Local Examinations in English, mathematics, political economy, and logic, obtaining first class in each group, and special distinctions in English composition and logic in 1875. She entered London University in 1878, as soon as it opened its degree courses to women, and was one of the first two women to graduate, in 1881, with a first-class honours BSc in mental and moral sciences and a second-class honours in mathematics. This was not enough; in 1884, she earned the degree of DSc, which required 'a "thorough practical knowledge" of psychology, logic, and ethics, and "general acquaintance" with the physiology of the nervous system and organs of sense in man and other animals; with the history of philosophy, political philosophy, and political economy', from the same university, the first woman in the UK to do so. Her teaching of mathematics at North London Collegiate helped break down the widely held beliefs that girls' brains could not cope with the subject and she inspired many of her pupils to enrol at Girton College.

Other new secondary schools for girls, opened from the 1870s, were also headed by mistresses with good qualifications.

Catherine Lucy Kennedy

Catherine Kennedy, born in Preston, Lancashire in 1851, was the daughter of a clergyman school inspector and niece of the head of Shrewsbury School (who was also a professor of Greek at Cambridge), who, it was noted on her appointment at Leeds Girls' High in 1876, had 'passed the Cambridge Higher Local Examination with first-class honours, distinguished in religious knowledge, arithmetic, Latin, French, and German'. Catherine joined Dorothea Beale as an assistant mistress at Cheltenham in 1874, where she taught classics and mathematics for two years before progressing her career in Yorkshire. In late 1891, she resigned to look after her widowed mother who was in poor health and the position was advertised at a salary of £250 plus capitation fees and board and lodging. After her mother's death, in 1896 she took up a headmistress's post at St Elphin's School for Clergymen's Daughters in Warrington. The school expanded to take other girls and moved to Darley Dale in Derbyshire in 1904. There she remained until her early death from septic pneumonia in 1910.

Helena Langhorne Powell

Helena succeeded Catherine at Leeds Girls' High in 1892. Born eleven years after her predecessor, in September 1862, she had attended one of the early GPDSC high schools at Clapham and then Newnham College, where she gained a first-class mark in history in 1884. Her first teaching post was as assistant mistress at Oxford High School, another of the GPDSC schools, from 1885 to 1892, before she was appointed headmistress at Leeds. There she remained for a decade, until taking the position of principal at the Cambridge Training College for Women Teachers in 1903. Helena, in what appears to be almost a job swap, became principal of St Mary's College, Lancaster Gate, London in 1908; her successor at Cambridge, Miss Mary Hay Wood, had been the vice principal at St Mary's. Mary's education had been at North London Collegiate, and she had taken the classical Tripos at Girton in 1889, later returning to North London to teach classics before taking up her post to train secondary schoolmistresses at St Mary's in 1904. Both well-educated and well-respected ladies remained in their respective posts until retirement twenty-five years later.

Gertrude McCroben

Born in March 1863, Gertrude was the daughter of a Bradford draper and, with her two older sisters, was one of the first girls to study at Bradford Girls' Grammar under Mary Porter. Probably inspired into the teaching profession by Mary Porter, Gertrude gained one of the scholarships funded by Bradford worthies (in her case, Titus Salt) to study mathematics at Newnham in 1880 and, having gained triple honours in the subject, became a mathematics teacher at Manchester Girls' High under the headship of Elizabeth Day. In 1894, she succeeded Ellen Allen as headmistress at Wakefield Girls' High, a position, according to the *Bradford Daily Telegraph*, that carried with it considerable honour and emolument. Her work at Wakefield saw her placing emphasis on science, sport, art and music. Although she retired in 1921, she maintained a keen interest in teaching, becoming an occasional inspector for the board of education.

***

Looking back to Bradford Girls' Grammar and its fourth headmistress (or third if the second is discounted for her short and scandalous tenure), it is interesting to note the range of experience and qualifications of the teaching staff of 1895 and that the head still had control over whom she selected.

Miss Margaret Elizabeth Roberts (born in 1861), the longest-serving headmistress the school ever had, entered the position in September 1894. Her own education and experience was impressive: she had attended Norwich and Oxford Girls' high schools (both early GPDSC establishments), and was one of the first girls to study at Somerville College, Oxford before (according to newspapers, though she is not on the list of students 1879–1911) training to be a teacher at the new Teachers' Training and Registration Society College. In May 1882, she joined the staff of the newly opened Bedford Girls' High School – the same time as Mary Porter became head at Bedford Girls' Modern School (both founded by the Harpur Trust). They must have become well acquainted with each other; the two schools were on the same site and under the same board of management, though of course, Margaret was not head of her school and would not have been party to any Association of Headmistresses' discussions about how to deal with governors. She rose to become senior mistress at Bedford and was awarded one of the eight travelling scholarships by the Royal Commission on Education in 1893.

Had Mary Porter forewarned her about the BGGS governors? It cannot ever be determined, of course, but Margaret was not long into her tenure before controversy started.

In late November 1894, just a few months after taking the headship at BGGS, Margaret Roberts had reason to dismiss a Miss Taylor. Dissatisfied with the new head's actions, eight other mistresses resigned in support of their colleague and seemingly gave exaggerated and unfair stories to the governors about Miss Roberts' conduct as their reason for their action. The governors, inquiring very thoroughly into the matter, concluded that Miss Roberts had been right to dismiss Miss Taylor and that the other mistresses had acted rather hastily, perhaps out of a sense of mistaken honour and in the hope that Miss Taylor would be reinstated and Miss Roberts condemned. Not all the governors agreed; Sarah Byles sided with the ex-mistresses. Clearly, Miss Roberts did not want the rebellious mistresses back and rapidly filled the nine vacancies (approximately half the staff number) with highly qualified mistresses. A list of 'ladies of undoubted efficiency and high university qualifications, and many with large experience' appeared in the *Bradford Daily Telegraph* on 19 January 1895. The new mistresses, as detailed, were:

1. Miss [Charlotte Stanley] Banks: Royal Holloway College, Oxford Honours in Modern Languages
2. Miss [Agnes Gertrude] Clement: Royal Holloway College, BA London [1892], Oxford Final Honours in English
3. Miss [Caroline Sarah] Falding: Newnham College, Cambridge; London Inter-Arts Exam; Cambridge Classical Tripos; Formerly Second Mistress at Carlisle High School
4. Miss [Edith] Horsfall: The Ladies College, Cheltenham and of Oxford [St Hilda's], BA Hons London University [1894]
5. Miss M.M. Jones: Victoria College, Belfast; BA Royal University of Ireland
6. Miss Lawrence: University College, Bristol and the Training College, Cambridge, Distinguished in Political Economy and Literature. For several years senior assistant mistress at Sheffield Girls' High School
7. Mrs McKillop: Somerville Hall, Oxford, BSc Oxford, Final Honours School of Natural Science; recently lecturer on Natural Science at Royal Holloway College
8. Miss K. Miall: Newnham College, Cambridge, Junior Optime Mathematical Tripos
9. Miss [Alice Townley] Scott: Aberystwyth College; BA London

That these women had seized the educational opportunities now available to them is clear. Further research reveals that Charlotte Banks had attended Higher Tranmere Girls' High at Birkenhead and had entered Royal Holloway College in October 1890, aged 20. At school, she passed the Oxford Junior Locals and the Cambridge Higher Locals, then at RHC, the Oxford Final Honours in Languages with First class in French and German. Agnes Clement, who had entered Royal Holloway College, aged 19, at the same time as her new colleague, had been a pupil at Manchester Girls' High where she had passed the Cambridge Senior Locals and the London Matriculation exams to gain entry to the university. She studied for her BA from London in 1892 and gained Oxford Final Honours in English. The third London University graduate joining the school staff in 1895 was Alice Scott. Born in Preston in 1872 and educated at its and Bedford's girls' high schools, she had matriculated in 1888, studied at University College, Aberystwyth, gaining her BA (in Spanish) from London in 1890 and gaining a double first teachers' diploma at Cambridge University.[7] Prior to coming to Bradford, Alice had been assistant mistress at Reigate High School, one of the Church Schools Company schools. She did not stay long at BGGS, taking up a post as headmistress at Bury St Edmund's High School (another of Church Schools Company Schools) in 1899. Four years later, she was selected, out of eighty-five candidates, as the headmistress for Bingley Girls' Grammar. There she remained for thirty-four years until retirement in 1937, after which she moved back to the family home of 145 Todmorden Road, Burnley, living with her spinster sisters, Julia Penketh and Marion Whiteford Scott (retired secondary and elementary school teachers respectively).

Chapter 11

Educated Women Exert Their Influence

The Endowed Schools Act certainly made an impact on secondary education for girls; by the mid-1890s there were around 80 endowed girls' schools giving secondary education to 4,860 girls. Even more were attending the proprietary schools founded by bodies such as the GPDSC (7,111 girls attending 36 schools), the Church Schools Company (around 2,000 girls at 24 schools), and others.[1] In addition to this (and as a result of higher aspirations for educated women), five new women-only colleges had been established: Girton (first at Hitchin and later near Cambridge) in 1869, Newnham (at Cambridge) in 1871, Somerville (at Oxford) in 1879, Lady Margaret Hall (at Oxford) in 1879, and Holloway (near Egham, in Surrey) in 1886. Bedford College, London (established in 1849) had also now attained a similar rank. And, of course, women were studying for degrees alongside men at some universities. By 1895, all British universities had opened their degrees to women except Oxford and Cambridge. Secondary and further education for middle-class girls had made considerable strides.

It was time to take stock again and in 1894, twenty-five years after the publication of the Taunton Report which had set all this in motion, the Royal Commission on Secondary Education – the Bryce Commission after its chair, Liberal politician James Bryce – was appointed. This time, women would be very much involved.

The Commissioners

There were three female Commissioners who sat alongside fourteen men to pose questions to and hear evidence from the witnesses: 'Our trusty and well-beloved Lucy Caroline Cavendish (commonly called Lady Frederick Cavendish), Widow; Our trusty and well-beloved Sophie Bryant, Doctor of Science Widow; Our trusty and well-beloved Eleanor Mildred Sidgwick, wife of Henry Sidgwick, Esquire, Doctor in Letters, Professor of Moral Philosophy in Our University of Cambridge'. It is curious that Eleanor Sidgwick's husband's accomplishments are listed rather than her own. Eleanor (née Balfour and sister of Alice Blanche, a notable pioneer in the study of genetics, and Arthur James, who would later become prime minister), as well as being the wife of Henry, was one of the first students at Newnham, where she assisted and co-authored papers with Lord Rayleigh in their research of electricity. She was an ardent campaigner for women's education and taught mathematics at Newnham, and by the time of the Bryce Commission in 1894, she was principal at Newnham. Lucy Cavendish (daughter of Lord Lyttelton) was indeed a widow (her husband having been assassinated by Irish republicans, the Irish Invincibles, in Dublin, the day after he took office as Chief Secretary for Ireland in May 1882), but she was also very active in campaigning for girls' and women's education, using her wealth to support the GPDSC and being long-time president of the Yorkshire Ladies' Council of Education (see later) from 1885 to 1912. Sophie Bryant needs no further introduction.

The Lady Assistant Commissioners

In addition to these three women were several Lady Assistant Commissioners appointed alongside men to investigate some of the selected districts: Mrs Ella S. Armitage on Devonshire; Mrs Frances A. Kitchener on the Hundreds of Salford and West Derby, in the County Palatinate of Lancaster; Mrs Eleanor Lee Warner on Norfolk; Mrs Dilys Glynne Jones on Warwickshire; and Miss Catherine Lucy Kennedy on the West Riding of Yorkshire.

Their remit noted:

> It is thought desirable to supplement the inquiries to be made by Assistant Commissioners in the selected districts by some further inquiry on the part of a Lady Commissioner, directed to leading points of difference that may exist in the educational organisation required for girls as compared with that required for boys.

Special attention was drawn to various points, including: the extent and character of the demand for secondary education for girls; how far the defects in the education of girls pointed out by the previous Schools Enquiry Commission had been remedied; what deficiencies still existed in the present supply of secondary schools for girls of all classes; and how a system of technical education for girls should be organised with regard to the varying wants of the different social strata in both urban and rural districts. They were also required to investigate the provision of scholarships for girls, the relationship between secondary education and careers for girls, and how to address the difficulties which arose from the fact that parents often still wavered between the three views of the object of a girl's education: marriage; preparation for some employment or profession; or the turning out of a cultivated mind and formed character. Tied in with the latter was how much parents were prepared to pay for their daughters' education compared with that of their sons, how much local authorities would contribute in the way of grants for either sex, and the lower pay of assistant mistresses. Their written reports were submitted to the Commission and published in its report in 1895.

Ella Armitage, admitting her report was rather lengthy, complained that a 'caste' system operated in Devonshire, dominated by landowners and navy and military personnel whose view about girls' education 'is that it should be as far as possible claustral [cloistered], that girls should be kept from any contamination with people who drop their Hs or earn their salt. It is thought that careful seclusion is absolutely necessary for the development of that refinement which should characterise a lady.' Thus, the prevailing tone of Devonshire society meant there were only six high schools teaching 500 girls in the whole of the county.

Parents of all classes were not taking their daughters' education seriously:

> Almost all the answers I received ... were practically unanimous in asserting that parents do not regard the mental training of girls as a matter of serious importance. Day pupils are kept from school for the most trifling pretexts, for example, that a relation has come to visit them. Many teachers expressed a wish for a compulsory attendance regulation for secondary schools. In some of the more stagnant country towns, I was assured that parents who have good means, and could well afford to keep their girls at school till 18, will often take them away at 12 years old, and allow them to grow up in idleness.

Her hopes for improvement in the dire situation were pinned on the women of the county:

> I was much interested to find that in almost every place I visited some one person, very often a lady, was fighting the battle of education in one way or another ... ladies especially should be enlisted as leaders in any new educational movement which may be the outcome of this Commission. It is to be regretted that they are not to be found on all the governing bodies which have to do with the education of girls. ... It is from them that we may chiefly expect the personal influence which alone can overcome the difficulties prevented by the caste problem. And many Devonshire ladies have already shown that they can bring both ability and devotion to the service of the cause of education.

In contrast to the more rural Devon, the Hundreds of Salford and West Derby, in the County Palatine of Lancaster, were densely populated with distinctive towns each with a separate identity and requirements. Believing she did not have sufficient time (only three months) in which to fully investigate and report on the area, Frances Kitchener focused on Manchester, Liverpool, Rochdale, Bury and Bolton and from these centres visited nearly all the places where girls' schools of any importance existed (St Helen's, Warrington, Wigan, Upholland, Stockport, Southport, Oldham). This included all the girls' endowed and proprietary schools, a large number of private schools, both expensive and cheap, and, apart from two, all the higher-grade board schools in which ex-standard classes, or organised science schools, existed, as well as several higher-grade voluntary schools. It was no mean task! One of her conclusions was that there was an urgent need of some educational authority:

> which should provide secondary schools for girls in the vast areas in which their education is left to chance, in the shape of private adventure schools, which may or may not be sufficient to the need; and which should organise existing girls' schools, giving to each its due place and limit in one consistent system of education.

That said, there was a need to be mindful of the different requirements of individual districts:

> I have also been profoundly impressed with the individual character possessed by every town which I learnt to know; with its inexplicable differences from other towns, even those similar in size and external features, and with the importance of keeping this individuality in view, in any educational legislation, and leaving each place free within defined limits, to adapt the principles laid down by any educational authority to its own needs.

Frances noted with 'unmixed and thankful satisfaction' that girls' education had vastly improved since the melancholy accounts from the last Commission that told of girls in schools across the country:

> spending their days, and the minds of their pupils, in handing on to yet another generation, the frivolous and mischievous traditions of the last ... of enlightened headmistresses being obliged to see the children waste nine hours a week on music, regardless of whether they had sufficient musical ability to give themselves or their friends the faintest pleasure as the result; when it was seriously doubted whether a girl's brains were able to grapple with the difficulties of vulgar fractions, and when it was generally considered that her physical and moral delicacy was so frail, that both would be injured by a written examination to be looked over by a strange man.

Most of those schools were gone; public examinations had long been open to girls, and this healthy competition with boys' work, with the attendant assimilation of the curriculum of boys' schools had done much to raise the tone of the work in girls' schools, from the lowest classes to the top. Better educational opportunities for women had raised the standards of teaching too:

> The whole race of assistant mistresses is so changed that it is difficult to believe that many are sisters and daughters of the ignorant and oppressed women on whom so much slightly contemptuous pity was bestowed less than 30 years ago ... The main improvement in female teachers is to be laid in the improvement of the schools in which they are themselves educated, and this becomes a part, and a most important part, of the general question before us ... This improvement in Education has taken place and has done all, and indeed more than all, which the Commissioners hoped. The benefit, too, is an ever-increasing one, gathering strength in each teaching generation, which receives all that the last has achieved, and when it passes by in turn, sets the new generation on its way on a higher platform than the one from which it started.

One bugbear remained: their daughters' learning to play the piano well was still a parental ambition for many, but as instrumental music had been removed from the regular course of education and some girls were spending too many hours practising the piano at home, many headmistresses, worried about their pupils' overwork, had devised schemes of homework to ensure they did not spend too long hours over their preparation. Of course, there was always the possibility of this care being made useless by long hours of music practice – exacted by independent music teachers and allowed by unwise parents. This, concluded Frances, was 'a danger affecting few, while the gain of checking unmusical music is universal. The ladies to whom I pointed out this risk recognised it as one, but said, "After all, one must leave some things to the common sense of the parents."'

On the subject of technical education for less-academic girls for whom a career in teaching was not a prospect but who would need to earn a living, Frances had some recommendations. It was easy to train boys for a career as all the industries in the country were open to them and they essentially had to choose which path to follow according to the industries of their particular locality. But for girls, first they had to find out what means of earning an income were available to them – after all, there was little point in learning the intricacies of a trade only to find there was no job opportunity at the end. She categorised girls into three types: those who stayed home to help their mothers, perhaps eventually going into service; those who could begin to earn at once, in shops, as milliners or dressmakers, or a few of the best in the post office (the types of jobs that would be generally available nationwide) or in factories (depending on the location – there were some well-paid posts open to women in Bury for example, but elsewhere the work was rough and poorly paid and probably only the resort of the really poor); and, most importantly, those who would train as pupil teachers and eventually, elementary mistresses. Her proposal was that the Elementary Education Department should come to the aid of the older children, and instead of their education stopping once they had passed the sixth standard at the age of 11 or 12, children not able to go to secondary school for whatever reason, could stay on for a seventh, eighth and ninth grades before starting work. With a swell of feeling against the employment of young children in factories, more were spending idle time at home (where the Devil might make work for their hands …) until old enough to work. Keeping them in education would have more than one benefit. Still, demand for girls' education would never be equal to that for boys until there was equivalent demand for skilled and highly paid woman's labour. It was a 'chicken and egg' situation: a higher average of girls' education might lead to openings for their employment, but nobody knew what that might be and it was not the nature of 'the British parent to spend money on this kind of preparation for the repayment of which he must wait in faith'. For some intelligent girls who showed too much interest in their lessons or wanted to pursue a professional career, mothers could still be a stumbling block. 'Blueness' was a fear: Frances reported that one headmistress had received notice that a star pupil was being removed; another at the same school was not being allowed to proceed to Newnham as she desired. Both mothers had independently explained that 'young men nowadays do not seem to like girls to "be blue"'. Another mother, congratulated on her daughter's exceptional ability at mathematics, complained she was a tiresome child, and 'I can't get her to care for music or French, or something that's some use.' The battle for better education for girls was an uphill one, strewn with many obstacles.

While there were many of the same issues in Norfolk and parents were still economising on their daughters' education, it does seem there was slightly better news in some quarters. The report, submitted jointly by Mr and Mrs Lee Warner, was briefer than others, their being restricted to carrying out the research during the school holidays 'when they had sufficient leisure time'. Nonetheless, they were able to report that it was gratifying to see that high schools (there were three main ones: Norwich Girls' School of the GPDSC; Lynn Girls' School, another proprietary school; and Thetford Grammar School for Girls, started in 1887 by the Charity Commissioners) were recognised as raising the standard of education demanded by parents; and the examination lists of the universities and of the College of Preceptors revealed an increasing number of Norfolk girls who were being encouraged by their teachers – and allowed by their parents – to test their knowledge. This attitude was helping to increase attendance and punctuality and reduce the instances of girls being kept at home for the slightest of reasons. Parents in Norfolk were starting to appreciate the effectiveness of a good provincial school and county councils were being persuaded to see the value of paying the examination fees for girls who passed. It seemed, also, that as men became better educated they were insisting on better education for their wives and daughters – even the Norfolk farmers were starting to understand that education was a good thing. Demand at Lynn had been created by the supply of the girls' school; the rather genteel Thetford was having more of a fight, but improvement was coming.

To address the questions on technical schools, the Lee Warners had enlisted the help of Mrs Pillow, who was described as 'the wife of the technical education secretary, a member of the Norwich School Board, writer of a book on domestic economy, formerly headmistress of elementary or higher-grade schools'. Margaret Eleanor Pillow (née Scott) was all of those things and more. Born in Norwich in 1857, Margaret was one of those girls for whom education proved a huge benefit. Her father, James Scott Gulfillan (known as James Scott) was a travelling cutler, and Margaret, clearly a bright girl, was apprenticed as a pupil teacher from 1872 to 1876 at St Paul's City Trust School in Norwich.[2] At the end of her apprenticeship, she was awarded a first-class Queen's Scholarship and studied at Norwich Training College for a further two years before going to Cambridge for five years where she focused on sociology, physiology and history. She taught at schools in Norwich in the early 1880s before moving to London to take up a headmistress post at All Souls' Schools, South Hampstead, where she also lectured on physiology, hygiene, and domestic economy at the Marylebone Central Classes for Training Pupil Teachers and the Wordsworth Training College. During the 1890s, Margaret was a member of the National Health Society, giving lectures for the benefit of teachers on Personal and School Hygiene at such places as the Duke Street Higher-Grade Schools, where 'she had much to say that was likely to prove suggestive and valuable to her hearers'.[3] She went on to co-write 'a work which ought to find a place in the library of every intelligent householder', *Domestic Economy: Comprising the Laws of Health in their Application to Home Life and Work*, with Arthur Newsholme, first published in 1891, the same year she was:

> unanimously elected by the Marylebone Branch of the National Union of Teachers to be Parliamentary Secretary for the Borough of Hampstead upon matters connected with the Education Code. This honour conferred upon Miss Scott is a well-deserved one, and there is no doubt her duties in this respect will be carried out with the same thoroughness and efficiency which has characterised all past efforts in similar directions.
>
> *Hampstead News*, Thursday, 10 December 1891

Shortly after this, she retired from her headship at All Souls' to take up a new career as a sanitary inspector. Her testimonials were glowing; it was remarked that her good common sense was almost unique and, added to her knowledge, made her a genius. She had carved out a new profession for women and was to be the first recognised qualified lady sanitary inspector. On 20 July 1892, aged 33, she married Edward Pillow, Organising Secretary for Technical Education, Norfolk County Council. Her occupation is not stated on the church record. Moving back to Norfolk, she served on the committee of the Norwich Sanitary Aid Commission and had two sons (born 1894 and 1895, the same time as she contributed to the Bryce Commission). After she was widowed in 1910, Margaret turned her hand to being an examiner on domestic subjects and by 1921 she was doing this alongside being the proprietor of the Princes Tea and Luncheon Rooms on Castle St, Norwich, where she advertised as selling fancy and ornamented cakes of all kinds and special dishes for invalids. What a woman! Little wonder then that her report championed the cause for girls to be taught the sciences of hygiene, physiology, cookery, domestic economy, cutting out and needlework, recommending that the scientific side, together with the practice of the arts, should be taught, and should include some knowledge of chemistry. She noted that changes in society had shifted so the majority of girls were beginning to think of getting some employment, although they were leaving the decision towards the end of their school career, and suggested they should be guided at an earlier stage so they could pursue the right course of study, be it practical or academic. Doubtless, her own experience was in mind when she reported:

> Those who are educated with a view to becoming workers, and who, after receiving a good education, proceed to further training, become teachers in schools of various kinds from the elementary to the highest, civil servants, nurses, governesses in families (high class), doctors, dispensers, lecturers in science, nursing, and the domestic arts, art teachers, journalists, and lately a few sanitary and factory inspectors, shorthand, and type-writers.

Catherine Lucy Kennedy, former headmistress at Leeds Girls' High and, at the time, taking a career break to care for her ailing mother, was the Lady Assistant Commissioner charged with investigating girls' education in the West Riding of Yorkshire, where the first girls' endowed school had been created. In a district where women were known for their work ethic and independence, she noted, somewhat curiously, that:

> The inhabitants of the West Riding have been proverbially accredited with a distinctive independence of spirit, and I think it is the love of independence which often in the case of their daughters' life career takes the form of a strong

repugnance to allowing them to become the recipients of salaries or wages, because this would, they think, place them in the position of paid dependents.

It did not mean the women did no work:

> I was told in some towns of the West Riding that residents who were in well-to-do or even in wealthy circumstances felt no reluctance about allowing the women of the family either to discharge all domestic tasks without the aid of a servant, or, at any rate, to assist very largely in the fulfilment of such duties, where servants were employed in addition. Baking and laundry-work seem to be carried on at home much more extensively in Yorkshire than in the South of England, and many of the girls attending secondary schools in the West Riding are proficient in cooking from the practical experience gained in their own homes.

Considering the oversubscription at schools such as Bradford Girls' Grammar, it is odd that she noted: 'I fear that on the whole there is a widespread apathy throughout the West Riding with regard to the intellectual education of girls.' The girls themselves appear to have thought differently though and clearly had influence over their parents:

> There is one other element to be taken into consideration as influencing the system of education in West Riding schools, and this is an element which, unlike the one I have last mentioned, generally has a favourable effect. I refer to the liberality with which parents often allow their daughters considerable freedom of choice in their studies, and in the length of time during which they are permitted to remain at school. In one town where I understood that the custom of expecting girls to devote themselves to domestic duties prevailed very strongly, I expressed some astonishment on learning that many of those girls nevertheless remained at school until 18 or 19 years of age. I was told that this was a concession to the personal inclinations of the girls themselves.
>
> It is much to be hoped that the opportunities for study afforded to West Riding girls may continue to increase in value and frequency, as the results already attained sufficiently prove that they are fully entitled by their earnestness and their ability to every kind of encouragement in intellectual pursuits. Without attempting to give any detailed list I may mention in illustration of their success that girls from West Riding [secondary] schools have gained Gilchrist, Winkworth, and Russell Gurney scholarships, and have won First Classes in the Classical, Mathematical, Modern and Mediaeval Languages, Natural Sciences, Moral Sciences, and Historical Triposes.

There was healthy competition for entrance scholarships from elementary to secondary school too. Girls were seeing the opportunities for careers as elementary teachers under the school boards and the need to have a secondary education before training as a pupil teacher. These scholarships enabled girls from less well-off families to climb the career ladder.

Funding was always an issue; some girls could not fulfil their dreams of becoming a teacher if there was no money to pay for their studies. Sometimes, the only assistance provided was by the headmistresses themselves who instigated student mistress-ships for deserving and promising pupils – an opportunity to continue their studies that they might otherwise not have had. Catherine noted: 'The fact that this system in places of secondary education is frequently characteristic of girls' schools indicates the special need felt in them with regard to this point.'

It was a good system though:

> I learnt from the headmistress of the Leeds Girls' High School that when she was applied to recently by a neighbouring school, in a case of sudden emergency, to spare an assistant mistress, as she was unable to spare one of her regular staff, she sent a student-teacher, who gave such satisfaction, that a permanent salaried appointment was offered her at the school directly a vacancy occurred.

On the third type of scholarship, that to a place of higher education, she noted that Bradford Girls' Grammar School occupied a unique position as being the only town in the West Riding (possibly the whole of England), in which the opportunity for study at university was secured for its deserving pupils 'by the munificence of private persons'. The headmistress (Miss Stocker) spoke of these scholarships being 'the making of the school', not only on account of the advantages which they afforded to individual girls, but also on account of their influence in raising the tone of work in the upper forms generally. These scholarships were funded by Sir Titus Salt (who had founded another girls' school in Shipley, where the second headmistress, Harriett Byles, sister-in-law of Sarah Byles, the great fundraiser for BGGS, presided for thirty-four years) and Henry Brown, a wealthy department store owner (who also funded one of two entrance scholarships, for which there were forty-five candidates). In addition, W.E. Forster MP funded a scholarship of £50 a year for three years, every year.

Various girls had benefited from these scholarships, enabling them to study at Newnham, Girton, Somerville and other colleges of their choice. Early recipients included Jessie Amelia Sallitt, a worsted spinner's daughter, born August 1860, the first to gain a Forster Scholarship to Newnham, in 1878, who became a headmistress of a girls' high school in Yarmouth, Norfolk (a Church Schools Company School).

Jessie's sisters, Ada and Katherine, both joined the teaching staff at BGGS in its early days. Marion Greenwood, who gained a Brown's scholarship to study at Newnham in 1879, went on to lecture in science; Gertrude McCroben was a Salt's scholar and became headmistress at Wakefield Girls' High, and another champion of teaching science to girls; and Mary Anna Byles (sister of the aforementioned Harriett) was the 1882 Salt's scholar, also to Newnham, and the first girl in the school to gain a first class in the Cambridge Locals.[4] She too became a high school teacher before marriage and emigration to the US.

As for technical training for girls, this was largely provided by the Yorkshire Ladies' Council of Education (YLCE) which, through the zeal and ability of local ladies, had established a well-equipped school of training in cookery, laundry work, domestic economy, dressmaking and needlework at its central office in Leeds. Other local committees had formed branches in Wakefield and Sheffield, and had established similar schools under local management.

The origins of the YLCE date back to 1866 when a ladies' committee was set up on the board of education to supervise and support women and girls taking Oxford and Cambridge Local examinations. In 1875, the committee became independent of the board of education and established itself as the Yorkshire Ladies' Council of Education. This group of prominent women, recognising the needs of women living in poor conditions in the industrial areas and the value of education in helping to improve their lives, turned its attention to bettering the educational opportunities for girls. In 1892, it set up the Yorkshire Loan Training Fund to help women meet the expenses incurred in establishing a career. It still works to support women in education.[5]

Over the previous two decades, its work had created a growing interest in these more domestic subjects, especially among secondary school girls not intending to go to university at the end of their school career. Even girls who did not necessarily intend to pursue a career in one of these trades found the courses a useful preparation for the duties of home life. Girls over 18 were admitted to the courses, which included woodcarving, millinery, dressmaking, training for teachers of dressmaking, laundry work, training for teachers of laundry work, cookery and training for teachers of cookery.

The YLCE's work was far reaching. By working with the relevant local councils, the women had been able to deliver instruction in various locations: they trained elementary teachers in cookery; gave courses of cookery and laundry work to Girls' Friendly Societies; cookery and dressmaking at Friendless Girls' Homes; cookery instructions in public elementary schools (both board and voluntary) to 1,385 girls; and 60 public cookery demonstrations at the Leeds Cookery School had been attended by a total of 912 women and girls. Two hundred and seventy peripatetic courses of instruction in cookery, laundry work, dressmaking, plain sewing, woodcarving, or health lectures had been given in the East and West Ridings of Yorkshire and in Leeds to 21,982 pupils from every social class and occupation – millhands, married working women, servants and governesses included. They even supplied staff to teach women and girls in Cornwall, Derby, Durham, Nottingham, Oxford and West Sussex. The list went on.

The success of this education could be measured in the subsequent careers of the students. Appointments had been secured all over England, including permanent appointments under the school boards of Leeds, Birmingham, Nottingham, Hartlepool, Plymouth, Luton, Tottenham, Exeter and London, and temporary appointments under the county councils for Northumberland, Lancashire, Durham, Suffolk and London. Others were teaching at centres in Hastings, Manchester and Pontefract.

In addition to the great work of the YLCE, technical courses for girls had been attached to institutes in many of the West Riding towns and girls from all social classes were happily mixing and availing themselves of the opportunity to learn practical, as well as the more domestic, subjects. Their progress was measured through examinations by institutions such as the City and Guilds of London Institute, the National Union for the Technical Education of Women, the Science and Art Department and the Society of Arts. Women of all social classes could now prove their worth to employers.

The evidence givers

Ten women (out of a total of eighty-five witnesses) were called to give evidence to the Commission over the forty-five days it sat between 24 April 1894 and 26 March 1895. These were: Mary Gurney, member of the council of the GPDSC since its foundation; Miss M.M. Blackmore, headmistress of the Roan School for Girls, Greenwich; Miss Elizabeth Phillips Hughes, Principal of Cambridge Training College for Women Teachers; Dorothea Beale; Miss S. Allen Olney, member of the governing body of the Private Schools Association; Miss Alice Augusta Woods, formerly headmistress at Chiswick High and for last two years principal of the Maria Grey Training College; Miss Harriet Morant Jones, headmistress at Notting Hill High School and Miss Elizabeth Day, Manchester High School, both representing the Association of Headmistresses; and Miss Amy Lumby, principal of St Hilda's College, Cheltenham, lecturer at Cheltenham Ladies' and president of the Association of Assistant Mistresses. Also representing the Association of Assistant Mistresses was Mrs Marion Withiel BA, second mistress at Notting Hill High School.

With a wide experience of teaching staff (the GPDSC had thirty-six schools across the country), Mary Gurney was well placed to answer questions on staff recruitment, retention, career progression and pay. Much of the recruitment was at the discretion of the appointed headmistress and it was clear that over the passage of time there was an increasing pool of better-trained teachers to choose from, that most of the headmistresses had qualifications from Cambridge or Oxford and that training and certification resulted in salaries above the usual rate being paid. It is interesting to note that at the time of the evidence-collecting there were very few schools where the dismissal of ineffective assistant teachers rested solely on the headmistress. Alice Woods noted on 2 October 1894 that there should be a right of appeal to the governing body in all cases, but she knew of no acknowledged case of friction that had warranted such a measure. Such a situation was just around the corner at Bradford Girls' Grammar (see Chapter 10).

Better teaching, of course, meant better examination results and once a GPDSC school was established, girls were encouraged to sit examinations in various subjects under the Oxford and Cambridge Board. Mary Gurney added:

> I should like also to say with regard to the Joint Board examination that we took the highest place of the girls' schools in the country last year; 15 girls from Sheffield and 10 from Wimbledon and 10 from Oxford took higher certificates. We reckon practically that we take the same position in the country as Cheltenham Ladies' College and the North London Collegiate School for Girls.

From incomplete statistics obtained by Mary Gurney, almost 600 girls had gone on to college, and nearly 300 had gained external scholarships. With a further 245 taking degrees and 141 going to training colleges, she was rightly proud of what the GPDSC had achieved in the cause of girls' education.[6]

Miss Blackmore told the Commission that some of the poor girls who had won scholarships from elementary schools (so paid reduced fees at secondary school) had become pupil teachers or bookkeepers in large shops locally. Interestingly, some of the middle-class families who had no need of the reduced fees of scholarships were sending their children to elementary schools in order to gain them (thus depriving the less well-off) and she believed there ought to be a 'poverty test' to prevent this. Dorothea Beale, in her evidence, also raised concerns on what she termed the unsatisfactory system of scholarships, saying it encouraged mercenary motives, robbed poorer schools of their pupils and was injurious to younger children. Her solution was for headmistresses and headmasters to select promising children to sit scholarship examinations, instead of it being a competitive free-for-all. She too thought 'a statement of circumstances' was necessary. The Association of Headmistresses (via Elizabeth Day and Harriet Morant Jones) was of the opinion that too many scholarships were being awarded to girls of only average ability whose future career was not improved by their educational advantages, although the elementary school scholars going to Manchester Girls' High were girls of exceptional ability and had all done well.

Elizabeth Hughes was able to expand on the type of teacher training provided at the Cambridge Training College, where she believed secondary school teachers ought to be trained at no cost. Currently the cost was £70 for a girl occupying a single room, though there was one scholarship of £25 available for a university graduate. The course comprised thirty weeks' instruction in the theory and practice of teaching, and could not be shortened if it was to remain efficient. Students were also sent out to local schools for teaching practice, including boys' schools. The subjects of instruction were based on what the young women planned to teach, as only a few students had the real gift of teaching and could teach well in any subject they knew. She also claimed (being Welsh perhaps!) that those of Celtic origin made the best teachers. The students devoted six to seven hours a day to their work, providing they were strong enough, and some had already been headmistresses or taught in schools and were taking courses to further their careers. Some students accepted posts in elementary schools and left; others were at high schools. She suggested similar colleges could be established throughout country, or perhaps a large central training college could be created.

Miss Blackmore thought fully qualified secondary school teachers, because of the cost of their training, should receive a minimum £100 salary and that more scholarships to fund training should be available, something Dorothea Beale also noted and Elizabeth Day and Harriet Morant Jones agreed with. However, Elizabeth Day also though that once training was more universally recognised, many parents would foot the bill for their daughters' training – although poverty qualifications ought always to be attached to training scholarships and not cover whole cost like the Queen's Scholarships did. The two representatives from the Assistant Headmistresses Association reported that the salaries of assistant teachers (at (£35–£60) were frequently too low for them to be able to maintain themselves in efficiency or provide for old age and were in favour of setting minimum salary of £80.

Alice Woods reported that students at Maria Grey Training College were prepared for the examination of the Cambridge Teachers' Training Syndicate; the course was for a year but she thought a two-year course would be better and during that second year, students could learn more handicraft and drawing. The college had two departments, one for kindergarten and the other for high schoolmistresses, and the courses were still in the experimental stages (after sixteen years), possibly as demands in education kept changing and a variety of systems was tried. As with Cambridge Training College, theory and practice were carried out simultaneously (the college was attached to Kilburn and Brondesbury High School and students also taught at Netherwood Boys' Board School – the teaching of boys at elementary school class developed the disciplinary powers of the student), but as a day college, the fees were lower at £24 a year in lower and £30 in upper division. The new building, opened in 1892, had room for seventy-five students and needed fifty to be self-supporting. Twelve scholarships were available, plus a principal's loan fund; even so the college was struggling for numbers, there being just forty-eight at the time. Considering there were more girls wanting to be secondary school teachers than there were places at the training colleges (Cambridge, and departments at Bedford College, Cheltenham Ladies' and the Mary Datchelor School), this seems odd. Demand for training was increasing, as it was recognised that training facilitated getting work and better salaries (although this was not found to be the case in Elizabeth Day's evidence) in an increasingly competitive market; some schools would not employ teachers who had not been at a training college. Certainly, the Association of Headmistresses was firmly in favour, although training was still in an 'experimental' stage.

As teaching had now become more professionally organised and accredited, there were calls for a compulsory register of teachers to be created, undertaken by an educational council rather than a government department and that no person with an unsatisfactory character should be on that register. The Commission's report summed up the evidence:

> The formation of such a register has long been desired by a large number of the members of the teaching profession, and the evidence, which we have received during the course of our enquiry, shows that the need for some official test and standard of professional efficiency has now become a matter of general agreement. It is clear that, since the publication of the Report of the Schools Enquiry Commission, there has been a steady and even rapid improvement in the qualifications of the teaching staff in the great majority of schools, whether public, proprietary or private. This advance in efficiency seems to have strengthened the demand for registration, because those who perceive the advantage which Secondary Education has already derived from the improved training and preparation of its teachers desire the establishment of a register in order to stimulate others, who still linger in the doubtful borderland between competence and inefficiency, to obtain higher qualifications for the practice of their profession.

Amy Lumby and Marion Withiel from the Association of Assistant Mistresses felt the register should include the year of registration; knowledge; qualifications; and teaching experience or certificate of training, and that fees should be as low as possible – perhaps 2 guineas a year. All on the register should be over 20 years old.

The Private Schools Association, represented at the inquiry by Miss S. Allen Olney who was on its governing board, had been discussing concerns over potential legislation to bring secondary schooling under state control that might be the outcome of the ongoing Commission; that the PSA did not have a representative sitting on that Commission to defend the efficient private secondary schools was 'a glaring injustice'. There were fears that the Commission's eventual report would 'strike a deadly blow at some of the members'.[7] It did agree with registration though.

The PSA had formed in 1882 and represented 584 schools, including many preparatory schools and 'girls' schools with a curriculum suited to a life of leisure'. Miss Allen Olney claimed the association had led the way in many educational reforms, but its schools possessed greater elasticity and could adapt themselves to wishes of parents without disturbing the curriculum. Perhaps influenced by the men who essentially ran the PSA, the views on secondary education were in contrast to other evidence givers. She reported that the PSA believed there was no deficiency in the provision of secondary education, except in thinly populated rural districts and that all parents who required secondary education were able to pay for it; it was merely a question of supply and demand and any deficiency could only be estimated by house-to-house visitation to ascertain the number of parents who could afford it. She also stated that children could not pass satisfactorily from elementary to secondary education under the present system of elementary education and that the higher-grade elementary schools, which kept children to 16, were a mistake and should be abolished. There was no need for scholarships and they were currently frequently gained by children with only average ability. So much for widening opportunities for the lower classes.

The questionnaire responses

Various memoranda were sent out to numerous bodies worldwide, seeking opinions (for information and guidance of the Commission) on a vast range of topics relating to secondary education.

Many of the opinions reflected the evidence already given by witnesses and Assistant Commissioners, but it is interesting to note there were a number of influential women who responded to the memorandum sent to members of the universities of Oxford, Cambridge, Durham and Victoria with regard to the universities' role in the training of teachers for secondary education. These ladies were: Mrs Bertha Jane Johnson (née Todd) lately Honorary Secretary for the Association of the Education of Women in Oxford (she had resigned in a dispute over the appointment of tutors at Somerville); Miss Marion Grace Kennedy, Executive Secretary of the Association for Promoting the Higher Education of Women in Cambridge; Miss Mary Elizabeth Hargood, Honorary Secretary of the Cambridge

University Local Lectures Association; Miss Agnes Catherine Maitland, Principal of Somerville College, Oxford; and Miss Annie Mary Anne Henley Rogers, tutor in classics to the Association of the Education of Women in Oxford (and had succeeded Bertha Johnson as Honorary Secretary).

Bertha Johnson noted that over half the students who had been on the books of the Association for the Education of Women in Oxford were at the time teaching, or had taught, or were intending to teach in secondary schools.

Proportions were similar at Cambridge – and Marion Kennedy was able to expand further on this from an analysis of the educational posts held by former students of Newnham College. The total number of students having left the college between October 1871 and June 1893 was 720. Of that number, 667 remained and by 1894, there were 374 in the teaching profession, either as headmistresses, assistant mistresses or lecturers

Table showing Educational Posts held by Students of Newnham College

Institution	Head Mistresses	Assistant Mistresses
Schools of the Public Day Schools Company	6	36
Endowed schools	14	23
Proprietary and other high schools	29	66
Private schools	24	32
Elementary schools and training colleges	2	13
Total	75	170
Lecturers at Newnham College	12	
Lecturers elsewhere	10	
Principal of the Cambridge Training College	1	
Visiting teachers	23	
Teachers under county or borough councils	4	
Teachers in the Colonies and in America	27	
Private governesses	23	
Teachers taking an interval of rest or study	14	
Teachers looking for posts	7	
Teachers from whom no return has been lately received	8	
Total		374

She noted that, with the exception of the North London Collegiate School and Cheltenham College (both founded much earlier), the public schools for girls had grown up side by side with the colleges for women; an increasing proportion of the women students had been drawn from them, and in turn the students had gone to them as teachers, leading to an interchange of communication as to common aims and mutual needs. Agnes Maitland also observed that the number of women who had received a college education and were teaching in secondary schools both of the lower and the higher grades, was increasing daily, with the increase being greatest among high schools. The work that women had done meant things would only get better in terms of education for women.

Another wide-ranging 'paper of queries' had been issued to certain individuals:

> The Commissioners have prepared these questions with a view to obtain information from a great variety of persons, and request you to favour them with answers to those questions only with regard to which you have special knowledge or experience, or in which you are specially interested. They will be obliged if you will give reasons or illustrations in support of your opinion on each point on which you give an answer, but as concisely as the subject may permit.

It is apparent from some of the questioning, that there was a plan to bring secondary education under state control:

Section VIII – District Authorities for Secondary Education

1. What should be the area of a district authority (e.g. a county or a group of counties)?

2. Should this authority be an existing one (e.g. the county council) or one created ad hoc, by legislation or otherwise? And if so, how chosen?

3. What should be the borough authority (a) in county borough, (b) in smaller boroughs? Should it be an existing one (e.g. the town council or school board) or created ad hoc? And if so, how chosen?

4. How should the respective jurisdictions of the district and borough authorities be adjusted (e.g. should the district authority have any and what powers over (a) county boroughs, (b) other boroughs)?

5. What elements ought to be represented on district or other authorities for Secondary Education (e.g. universities, local university colleges, teachers)?

6. Should a district or borough authority have any and what powers in respect of:

Elementary education.
Control over governing bodies of secondary schools.
The creation of new secondary schools.
Rating.
The re-arrangement of endowments.
Examination or inspection.

Of the women who responded to this question, Miss Anna Beatrice Anderton BA, who had graduated from London University in 1890, gave the most comprehensive and clearest opinions to some of the questions posed, as follows:

1. I am of opinion that the district authority should have as large an area as is consistent with efficient work – not less than a county, unless a high population demands otherwise.

2. This district authority should be created ad hoc, by legislation. I should not give the control of the education of a district to county councils or local board, because I fear it would be impossible to avoid difficulties, arising from:

a. The presence of men on the board unskilled in the subject.
b. The presence of local petty feelings and of party spirit.
c. The tendency of the county council to narrow down education to scientific and technical instruction.

The authority must be as broadly representative as possible, and I do not believe that it is possible, from past experience, to get this broad representation by allowing the county council to co-opt experts. As far as I can see, it will be necessary to have a duly elected council entirely independent of county councils and other local powers.

5. The composition of such an authority might be, perhaps –
One fourth county council members.

One fourth school board members.
One fourth university men and members of local educational bodies.
One fourth actual teachers.

6. a. While the school board is in existence I think it would cause needless friction for the district authority to interfere at all in the management of elementary education.

b. (i). Where the district authority decides that a new school is needed, and has obtained permission from the central authority to found that school, I suppose that it will necessarily control the governing body of that school.

(ii). Where it grants money to a secondary school already existing, justice will demand that it shall have representation on the governing body, in proportion to the amount of aid given.

(iii). Otherwise I should strongly deprecate its interference with secondary schools.

(iii a.) The functions of the district authority should be simply the creation of new schools and supervision of these; this creation to be done only after proof that the existing provision is insufficient, or after the central authority has been satisfied by inspection that the teaching in the existing schools is not good, or is unsuited to the particular needs of the district.

(iii b.) I would give it no authority for examination or inspection in any schools but those founded by itself. All inspection (State-examination I do not favour, as shown above) should in my opinion be carried on by the central authority.

Despite her seeming misgivings, ten years later, Anna became the first headmistress of the Reigate County School for Girls when it was housed in the Redhill Technical Institute, a building never intended to be a school. 'Her strong personality. high cultural attainments, steadfast striving for high ideals, and a deep affection for the girls entrusted to her care, enabled her to overcome the difficulties of environment ...'[8] There she stayed until 1922, by which time the school's numbers had grown to 300. On leaving the school, she went to South America, where, for some years, she undertook scholastic work of a missionary nature, and was head of a flourishing school. The South American Missionary Society remained one of her great interests after her return to the UK.

Frances Buss was issued with the memorandum and had much to say about the progression of girls' education and cited her own experience with her two schools, noting that (if they did not simply go home to a domestic life) girls from the Camden (lower-grade) School went to jobs in the Civil Service or similar, while the girls from the NLCS (higher-grade) went to higher education. She added that the two schools were adapted respectively to these different ends. Many bright girls had no difficulty in working their way up from either elementary or through neighbouring second-grade schools into the higher school and on to university. That education was finally providing opportunities for girls to progress must be in no doubt.

On the question of the expansion, by the state, of secondary schools, she had less to say, and only addressed the question (5) on who ought to be represented on boards for secondary education: 'Universities, university colleges and teachers, should certainly all be represented on these authorities ... The representation should be large enough to secure balance and not throw too much work, or responsibility on one or two. Women teachers should be represented as well as men.'

Perhaps her deteriorating health meant she had little capacity to look into a future where the state might be responsible for secondary education. By the time her views were published, Frances Buss was dead. She had been fighting kidney disease since the late 1880s and she looked twenty years older than her 60 years. Life had become a daily struggle, but it was brightened by the invitation to be part of the Bryce Commission; had her health been better, she might have been one of the three women Commissioners. Her last visit to her school was 7 November 1894 and she died, aged 67, on Christmas Eve. More than 2,000 mourners filled Holy Trinity Church, Kentish Town on New Year's Eve and Canon Brown later spoke of her pioneering achievements: she had made thousands of girls happier and enabled hundreds of women to do good and congenial work. A former pupil wrote of her gratitude and pride that she was one of 'Miss Buss's girls', while Dorothea Beale wrote of her friend's desire to help young headmistresses by advising them on the dangers and opportunities of their responsible position.

The only other woman to comment on the question of state-run secondary education was Miss Edith Elizabeth Maria Creak BA – one of the first five students at Newnham and one of the first women graduates of London University – who had stellar experience, first as an assistant mistress for a year at a company-owned girls' high school in Plymouth, then with the GPDSC as headmistress of Brighton High School (June 1876–July 1883) and subsequently of the Girls' High School on King Edward VI's Foundation in Birmingham, where she remained until her retirement in 1910.

She was concerned that putting secondary schools under the control of the school boards, might 'be fatal to the interests of education'. Her fears were that English prejudices might mean that parents considered rate-aided secondary schools to be only a form of elementary schools and if that was their impression, they would have nothing to do with them – 'to the great injury of the schools as well as of the children thus kept away'. Social class was very much an issue:

> It must always be remembered that a school depends on the material available in the way of pupils, as well as on to teaching, and that the presence of children from cultivated homes is of the greatest help to a school. Take a school of children from such homes, and introduce a small proportion of children from homes a little lower in the scale, and the levelling up will be most satisfactory; introduce too large a proportion of the less cultivated element, or draw from too low a stratum, and the children we want to raise will miss much of the gain we desire for them.

In many ways, her ideas on secondary education continue to this day: a largely comprehensive system, supplemented by a range of other schools:

> If rate-aided secondary schools are to be established, I think that in common justice arrangements must be made for compensating existing private schools. I think that proprietary schools should be taken over by the State, either by central or local authority, and that in the case of private schools three courses should be followed, (a) those heads who like to follow the course suggested in the answer to the first question of this section, or to carry on their schools entirely at their own risk, should be allowed to do so; (b) suitable teachers who wished it should be appointed to public schools; (c) those who did not wish to go or to come under Government control in any way should be compensated. Higher-grade elementary schools should be closed.

Chapter 12

The Next Steps

Among its findings, the Bryce Report of 1895 identified there were defects in the organisation of secondary education and these could be classified under three heads:

1. The powers of authorities, and their relations to each other;
2. The relations between schools;
3. The internal organisation of schools.

The three main authorities were: the Charity Commission; the Department of Science and Art; and the Education Department. Each had an independent sphere of authority and no real connection to one other, although the departments might consult on particular common affairs and make joint arrangements for a specific purpose. For example, a grammar school, although working under a scheme framed and administered by the Charity Commissioners, might be earning grants, or also include an organised science school (which would be subject to the regulations laid down by the Department of Science and Art) and might be receiving scholars from elementary schools, 'whose earlier training has followed lines prescribed by the Education Department'.

There were issues with overlapping of education provision, and this was hardly surprising, as within the same town or district, local power over secondary education could be shared:

> between a county or borough council, a school board, various governing bodies, managing committees of proprietary schools, local committees under the Science and Art Department, and managers of voluntary schools. ... It is not surprising that, under such conditions, ability, energy, and a cordial desire for co-operation have not always availed to prevent waste of power, or one-sided developments of educational forces.

In summary, the Commission noted that the first problems to be solved were those of organisation, for the harmonising of the agencies which exercised them and for greater unity of control. It recommended the creation of local authorities to be responsible for all secondary (including technical) education within their respective areas, plus a central authority to oversee the provision of secondary education throughout England. As with elementary education, use would be made of the existing schools, and where provision of secondary education was deficient, funds under the control of local authorities – and currently allocated for technical education – would be made available for secondary education in general. Parents would still have to pay, so more second- and third-grade schools would be created with fees within the reach of those of limited means.

With Britain lagging behind the US and Europe in its provision of secondary education, and therefore losing ground on industrial and trade developments, pressure for state-supported education was growing. The rector of the University of St Andrews stated, 'It is not too much to say that commercial and trade decay lies before us unless we can pull ourselves together on this matter. Where our competitors are spending thousands of pounds, we spend half a dozen pence.' Others observed that people were demanding education reform from a sense of shame of having the 'worst-instructed instructed peasantry in Western Europe' and the industrial population's fear of being unable to meet commercial competition. 'School power' and well as 'sea power' would sustain the British Empire.

Provision of education was far more than providing buildings and infrastructure; better teachers were needed too. Regarding the internal organisation of schools, the Commission reported the 'foremost need is that secondary teachers should be systematically trained in the methods and practice of education'. Although this had long been the case for elementary teachers, the same rules did not apply 'to schools of a higher grade'. This seems to have evolved from the masculine world of the public school where:

> the English ideal of a secondary teacher has been the assistant master in a great public school, usually a graduate in honours of Oxford or Cambridge, who comes from the university to the school without any previous experience in teaching. In a great boarding school, a master's influence over the boys depends so hugely, indeed so predominantly, on his moral and social qualifications that, if only he is a respectable scholar, the general estimate formed of him – in other words, his reputed success as a schoolmaster – will not be greatly affected by the fact that he is an indifferent teacher. Secondly, men untrained, except by their own experience, have proved good teachers; and it is also true that in the case of great teachers the gifts which make greatness cannot be taught: whence there arises a popular impression that a teacher is born, not made.

It is a long-held notion that a woman has to work far harder and be better qualified than a man to attain the same level of appreciation in the workplace and, to this end, women were leading the way in becoming properly trained; the Bryce report acknowledged this:

> The attempts to provide systematically trained secondary teachers have not hitherto been encouraged by any appreciable demand for them in boys' schools. But there is a considerable demand in girls' secondary schools. In 1879 the University of Cambridge established the 'Teachers' Training Syndicate', under which examinations in the theory, history, and practice of teaching are held at various centres in the United Kingdom. Certificates of two kinds are given, viz., (1) of theoretical knowledge, and (2) of practical efficiency: the first can be obtained separately; the second cannot be obtained without the first, or without a year's work in teaching at a recognised school. The candidates thus far have been chiefly women.

Was it male arrogance that meant the one established secondary training college for men had only a brief existence? The reason for its failure was given as the lack of support from the headmasters of public schools. Women, on the other hand, encouraged each other to train at the colleges they had established. The report recognised these as:

1. Colleges which offer a year's course of professional training, and possess a suitable practising school under their own direction; as Maria Grey College, London, and St. George's College, Edinburgh.
2. Colleges which offer a year's course of professional training, and are permitted to use for practising some suitable public school or schools; as the Cambridge Training College, and Bedford College, London.
3. Schools which employ student teachers and prepare them, and a few outside students, to pass the professional examination for the certificate of the University of Cambridge, or for that of the University of London (open only to BAs of London); as the Cheltenham Ladies' College and Datchelor Girls' School, Camberwell.
4. Colleges and schools which train governesses, either for private families or for schools, but do not require any public standard of knowledge that would suffice for teachers of secondary schools, nor present their students for any public certificate or diploma. There are various societies of this type.
5. Colleges which give certificates to their own candidates (Home and Colonial Society).

It noted that 'The training of secondary teachers should be systematic and thorough. At present the absence of such training is one of the causes which injuriously affect secondary education.'

The move towards state-controlled education

The first step was more legislation in the form of the Board of Education Act 1899, which came into force on 1 April 1900. Its purpose was to establish a 'Board of Education charged with the superintendence of matters relating to education in England and Wales', which would replace the Education Department, including the Department of Science and Art. This was followed, in December 1902, by the Education Act 1902: 'An Act to make further provision with respect to Education in England and Wales'. In short, the new legislation abolished all 2,568 school boards and handed over their duties to local borough or county councils. As well as developing the existing system of elementary schools, the 328 new Local Education Authorities (LEAs) had powers to establish new secondary and technical schools and were encouraged, though not compelled, to subsidise the existing grammar schools and to provide free places for working-class children. They could also create new secondary 'grammar' schools.

Balfour's Education Act had endured fifty-three days of debate in parliament and, outside those hallowed walls, the Association of Headmistresses discussed its provisions at committee meetings and conference. What would become of the status and prestige, even the existence, of the schools they had fought to establish? Would their cherished individuality be threatened? Would the teaching profession play any further part in guiding the course of education?

In the 1901 conference, the headmistresses took some comfort in learning that the 'proposed authorities should have regard to existing schools', and in the following year the conference registered general approval, although strongly criticised the failure of the legislation to provide for the inclusion of women on the proposed education committees. They were not barred from doing so, but the committees tended to be comprised of existing councillors, and since women could not be elected onto these councils, the only way they could be involved was through co-option onto technical education committees. New girls' schools would be established without the involvement of any women. Addressing a prizegiving at Bath High School in December 1901, Agnes Maitland of Somerville College said it seemed to her that they were at the parting of the ways. They knew there was further legislation coming regarding secondary schools and there was a danger that women who had done so much for the secondary education of the girls were likely to be ousted from having a fair, right and proper share in saying what the education of girls should be for the future. But for the efforts of women, that better education of girls could never have come to pass, and it would very sad result for the whole nation if the women had no voice in saying what lines should be followed in the secondary education of girls in the future.[1]

Debates and amendments continued for almost another year before a last-minute adjustment was made to the Act in mid-November 1902. A fortnight earlier, Balfour had made written protest to the newspapers that the statement that women could not sit on education committees was not only untrue, but untrue to very exaggerated degree, adding, 'Not only can women sit on the committees, but it is hard to see how a committee can be properly constituted, under words of the Bill, from which women will be excluded.' But to ensure there was no ambiguity, Henry Hobhouse MP moved an amendment to provide for the inclusion of women on education committees. All accepted and it was specified in the legislation.

However, it was still a backward step for women. Florence Fenwick Miller, as ever with her eye on the detail, wrote:

> PASSING THE EDUCATION ACT. Now that the chances of improving the Education Bill are ended, and the worst is known, it is time to observe how much suffrage we women have lost at the hands of our *soi-disant* friend, the present Prime Minister. Mr Balfour is supposed to be a friend of long standing to women's suffrage. But when we glance over the record of his exercise of his influence, first as Leader of the House of Commons, and then, as Prime Minister, we are reminded of the cynical old saying: 'Save me from my friends.' ... And now comes the Education Act, which has taken away from women the most important citizen's right and power of public service which had up to the present been secured for them.

She went on to cite the great (unpaid) work done for both girls' and boys' education by the women who had been elected time after time by their constituents over the preceding thirty years, but noted that although women, married or single, might be members on the new education committees as well of the boards of management for the separate schools, and every committee of education must include at least one (co-opted) woman member, much had been lost. This was because women could vote for county council members but could not be councillors themselves – so women would not be able to choose other women to sit on the education committees, as previously they had in electing school boards. Women were thus deprived of the opportunity of showing 'a lady could pass through a hotly contested election without derogating from her personal dignity and grace, and also of proving that numbers of men electors will vote for women representatives'. These opportunities, so important in their proving of women's fitness for public life, were now closed.

Florence believed that the women who might be chosen by the county councillors would not be of the same calibre as those who had campaigned to be elected and re-elected; they would not be subjected to the rigours of questioning and showing their understanding and knowledge of the issues at hand. Moreover, women possessing those particular qualities and strength of character were less likely to be selected by the men who did the choosing. 'It was', she said, 'a great object-lesson of the absolute instability and insecurity of any citizen's rights that women may gain, however well they may employ those opportunities, until they have achieved the great fundamental right, which is both the basis and protection of every other, the Parliamentary franchise.'

Jane Connolly, headmistress at Aske's School, Hatcham and president of the Association of Headmistresses advised members to 'take your full share in the public educational work of the day' and by 1904 forty of the association's members had been invited to serve on education committees, including Sara Burstall in Manchester and Mary Macrae in Nottingham.[2] A further step forward was taken when, through the Qualification of Women (County and Borough Councils) Act 1907, qualifying women were allowed to stand for election onto the councils. The first to be elected was the same woman who had been the first elected to the London School Board: Elizabeth Garrett Anderson, in her home town of Aldeburgh, Suffolk. Adding to her list of firsts, on 8 November 1908 she became the first female mayor in England.

In the meantime, the new education legislation was followed by action. Some education authorities were slow to move (as had been some authorities after the 1870 Elementary Education Act); the 1902 Act did not specify the future direction of educational development, only empowered the LEAs to subsidise education 'other than elementary' out of the rates. Nonetheless, new secondary schools were established at an ever-increasing rate. Some new schools were mixed and under the leadership of headmasters, but many were single-sex schools and the development of the new County Girls' Schools owed much to their headmistresses. Many were young and had been educated at the girls' schools and universities in the 1890s; some had served on the staff of these pioneer schools and they joined a network of similar women, maintaining and developing the ethos of girls' education in which they had trained.[3] The expansion of secondary schools offered these women an opportunity just as they were embarking on their new careers and they seized it with an almost missionary zeal. Salaries also improved so that by 1905 a typical rate was £300 with a £1 capitation payment for every pupil in excess of 100.

Existing schools facing financial troubles were taken over by the LEAs. Falmouth County School, founded in 1887 and run by a limited company with fifty-six shareholders and only seventeen pupils had grown to a roll of eighty by 1908. This, apparently, was too much for the shareholders to bear and the company went into liquidation. The county council bought it and combined it with the local pupil-teacher centre to form a new school. Other pupil-teacher centres formed the basis of new county schools and began with a nucleus of the pupil teachers as their first pupils. Other financially stretched existing secondary schools were incorporated into local provision; the endowed Orme Girls' School at Newcastle under Lyme was one, Maidstone and Rochester was another.

The relationship between headmistress and LEA was not always easy. Experienced headmistresses were naturally sceptical of secondary education being guided by education committees whose members often had 'no more than elementary education'. Inexperienced but spirited new headmistresses were also uncertain about the relationship, finding officialdom overbearing and tending to resist or ignore it. One young head was upbraided for closing her school for a couple of days, without official leave, in order to quell an epidemic of colds and coughs; another, forewarned of a visit from the school inspector, sent the whole school to the swimming baths and told the inspector there was no one home when he turned up. As with any new scheme, in order to succeed, adjustments had to be made on both sides. Some authorities were rigidly bureaucratic; some headmistresses needed protection from their own follies. The local officials were new to their jobs and also prone to mistakes, upsetting parents and teachers alike. Sometimes it needed the headmistress – often a key figure and a link between the various bodies – to take her share in building up confidence and trust to gain respect and understanding among her neighbourhood. Headmistresses of existing girls' schools supported teaching staff in the new rate-aided schools; they offered practical knowledge, experience and encouragement, even though the new schools presented competition to their independent schools with fees at half the rate. The Association of Headmistresses formally accepted heads of the new schools to their membership from 1906, something that might have led to deep division but instead created a fresh 'assertion of unity and equality' among the women. With its wide variety of backgrounds, convictions and local issues, it produced a lively intercommunication of ideas that were to influence girls' education for years to come.[4] There would be many heated discussions with the authorities, but the women who taught were not only carrying the education of girls to new levels but taking in part in a national venture that would impact on future generations of children.

Chapter 13

Education for Girls: The Capacity to do Things

It was the work of other women that created the foundation on which future generations of women would flourish. Josephine Butler, co-founder of the North of England Council for Promoting the Higher Education of Women, writing in *The Education and Employment of Women* in 1868, stressed that women's education, far from being one of intellectual progress only, was a question of deep moral importance, 'entering far into the heart of society, affecting the best interests of men as well as those of women'. There was work on every side waiting to be done by women: 'the work of healers, preachers, physicians, artists, organisers of labour, captains of industry', as well as for the women who would serve and bridge the gulf between the classes now presenting a 'grave obstacle to social and political progress'. She cited the words of Francis Newman who noted that, chiefly through education, 'the increased influence of women will keep in check the liquor traffic, and other abominations which men too readily excuse', and added that the primary education of all generations of men rested in the hands of women.

While many women chose to teach – it was still the primary professional occupation for women – either at elementary, secondary, technical, vocational or university level, thus enabling and inspiring their sisters onward to fulfilling careers, others seized those presented opportunities and forged a path for women of successive generations to follow.

In December 1875, the NLCS published its first issue of *Our Magazine*, a school journal with news, examination successes, and contributions from pupils past and present. It is still in existence though now called *The North Londoner*. Included in its pages was a section 'concerning old pupils' where information about the achievements of 'old girls' was regularly reported. An examination of these records from 1901 to 1910 provides interesting examples of just how far opportunities for secondary school-educated girls had expanded in the thirty years following the Endowed Schools Act, particularly for those born after the mid-1860s.

The educationalists

Naturally, many had become educationalists themselves, with the July 1909 edition listing twenty-eight former NLCS pupils as headmistresses, several them at the new county and borough secondary schools. As with their chief inspirer Frances Buss, many would be principals in their own right, but others, such as Dora Barham BSc, who had been head of large private girls' school in London before being appointed headmistress of the Middlesex County Secondary School for Girls at Palmer's Green, would only be chief assistant to a headmaster at the new co-educational schools. Other women were listed as assistant mistresses, form mistresses and mistresses of the wide range of subjects now being taught to girls: science, mathematics, classics, history, languages, physical education, music. Several were teaching alongside former classmates, which must have created a sense of common purpose and camaraderie. One interesting entry that demonstrates the still-held-by-some belief that a little education would go a long way in finding a good husband was the news that Florence Stanger was engaged in private teaching of a special kind: 'Miss Stanger's pupils are "in society", and she reads chiefly English with them and such subjects of general interest as are likely to be useful for conversational purposes.'[1]

Some girls had become missionaries, taking education to Africa, China and India. Bessie Perry was now married and with her husband on missionary work 'among the Indians' in British Columbia, Canada in 1907. Several others were teaching the practical skills of domestic science at technical colleges, schools of cookery and polytechnics.

Three former NLCS girls were named on the 1901 list of recognised teachers at London University: Catherine Alice Raisin DSc teaching geography and geology at Royal Holloway; Hannah Robertson BA, teaching the theory and practice of education at Bedford College; and Kate Mary Warren teaching English language and literature at Westfield College. They were also listed as members of the various boards of studies and as examiners. A fourth, Nina Georgine Rimington Taylor, was listed in January 1909's *Our Magazine* as being a recognised teacher of pedagogy (the method and practice of teaching) at St Mary's, Paddington. Nina, a solicitor's daughter, born in 1876, had an amazing career in girls' and women's education. In 1902, she was noted as being second mistress to Edith Aitken (see later) at her girls' high school in Pretoria, and by 1905 she had moved to Johannesburg to teach. She was back in the UK in 1907, appointed lecturer in moral science at the Cambridge Training College and from there she moved to St Mary's College, Paddington. The 1921 census reveals she was headmistress at Grimsby Girls' High, but it seems she returned to London a few years later, to lecture at Avery Hill Training College, a women-only (until 1959) college established in 1906 by London County Council to train teachers for its schools. Nina's younger sister, Eva Germaine, gained a scholarship to Royal Holloway and graduated from London University with first-class honours in chemistry in 1903. She taught chemistry at Burton upon Trent School for Girls and at a convent school in Oxford, but in 1906 became a geography student at Oxford University and spent time as a research assistant at the university until once again returning to teaching, as a lecturer at Clapham Training College for Teachers, the Froebel Institute, East London College (later Queen Mary College), and Birkbeck College.[2] In 1929, Eva gained a DSc in geography (London), and was appointed chair of geography at Birkbeck College in 1930, the first woman to hold such a position in the UK. Here she remained until her retirement in 1944, after which she became professor emeritus. Recognised as a great scholar and brilliant lecturer, many honours were conferred on her, including The Royal Geographical Society's Victoria Medal in 1947 and honorary fellowship in 1965. She continued her passion for geography, publishing three books[3] between the ages of 75 and 87.

Of course, it was not just girls from NLCS who achieved recognised teacher status at London University, though in the male-dominated list of 1901 there are just 26 women out of more than 600 lecturers. It is interesting to note that their subjects include topics previously thought too taxing for women's brains: chemistry, physics, geology, zoology, applied mathematics, ophthalmology, Latin and classics.

The scientists

Catherine Alice Raisin

Lecturing and examining in the faculty of science at London University was Catherine Alice Raisin DSc (Geology and Zoology). Catherine was born in 1855 and became a trailblazer for women in geology, being the first woman to study the subject at University College London (UCL) in 1875 and the first woman head of geology at Bedford College in 1890, where she remained until her retirement thirty years later. Out of fifteen heads of department at Bedford in 1901, there were just two women, the other being Beatrice Edgell MA. Catherine ran three departments simultaneously: geology; botany; and geography, as well as being on various committees and publishing twenty-four research papers.

Margaret Elizabeth Buchanan

Another former NLCS pupil was Margaret Elizabeth Buchanan, born in July 1865, who qualified as a pharmacist in 1887, serving an apprenticeship under her father and studying at the Pharmaceutical Society's School of Pharmacy in Bloomsbury Square.

Her first post was as a hospital dispenser and she noted, in 1892, that 'it is becoming recognised by the public and the trade that women can be both business-like and well-trained scientifically, the number of lady-pharmacists will doubtless increase as the field further opens up.' Having the courage of her convictions, she founded the Association of Women Pharmacists in 1905 and in 1908 wrote that women should not accept lower pay than men for doing the same job. She founded the Margaret Buchanan School of Pharmacy for Women at Gordon Hall, Gordon Square, later purchasing a pharmacy at Clapham Common where her students could gain practical experience, working either mornings or afternoons, alongside their studies. It is clear she was an inspiration for other girls wanting to pursue a scientific career.

Elsie Seville Hooper

Elsie Seville Hooper BSc, born 1879, a NLCS girl, studied pharmacy under Margaret and in 1901 registered as a chemist and druggist, eventually owning two London pharmacies. She too encouraged female apprentices to the profession. By 1908, she had been appointed demonstrator in chemistry and assistant lecturer at Portsmouth Municipal College; she became a Fellow of the Institute of Chemistry and later taught at what had become the Gordon Hall School of Pharmacy between 1920 and 1942, becoming the school's joint proprietor. Like many of that cohort of women, she was very much in favour of Votes for Women and joined a group of female pharmacists marching in the 40,000-strong Women's Coronation Procession on 17 June 1911.

Gertrude Holland Wren

Gertrude Holland Wren, born 1885, was another of Margaret Buchanan's successful protégées, gaining numerous medals at the Pharmaceutical College, being the first woman to be awarded the Pereira Medal – the 'Blue Riband' of pharmacy – and being appointed Research Scholar by the Pharmaceutical Society in 1908. The scholarship meant she could carry out a year's research work on chemistry as specially applied to drugs. That November, Gertrude, described in the newspapers as a 'plucky young London girl', was appointed demonstrator at the Pharmaceutical Society's School of Pharmacy, another first for a woman. By 1915, with more than 200 qualified women pharmacists. the *Lady's Pictorial* was advocating pharmacy as a career for women, but noted: 'As in all professions, what the woman chemist can make depends mainly on her energy, her ability, and her use of the "opportunities at hand".'

The inspirers

Edith Aitken

Edith Aitken, born in 1861, was a pupil at NLCS before studying science at Girton, where she gained a first class in the Natural Sciences Tripos (but, of course, no degree) and, when the idea of girls learning the subject was in its infancy, taught science at Manchester High School for Girls (1882–3); Nottingham Girls' High School (1884–7); and Notting Hill High School (1887–92) before returning to NLCS to teach. Speaking at the Science Teachers' Conference in January 1901, Edith argued that the education commonly given to girls and the acquirement of the usual feminine accomplishments, or 'parlour tricks', were no longer adequate, and that some scientific instruction ought to be superimposed upon general education. She must have been an inspiring teacher as a number of girls who came under her tutorship in the years before she left in 1902 to take up a headship of a girls' school in Pretoria went on to have stellar scientific careers.

Ethel Sargant

Ethel was born in 1863 and, like Edith Aitken, was an inspiration to younger girls wishing to pursue their studies in science. Like Edith, Ethel too was a pupil at NLCS before going to Girton in 1881 to study natural sciences. It is very likely that they knew each other well and it was probably at Edith's invitation that Ethel returned regularly to the school to give presentations to its science club, founded in 1890. Her work as a botanist, particularly on the anatomy of seedlings as well as her theory of the origin of monocotyledons, made a valuable contribution to the increasing knowledge on plants and she was soon recognised by being one of the first of fifteen women elected Fellows of the Linnean Society on 15 December 1904, when its constitution was amended to admit women – 'a matter,' she said, 'for congratulation to all women.' Just two years later, she was the first woman elected to its council. The 1901 and 1911 censuses note her as living 'on her own means' in Reigate – she was looking after her elderly mother and invalid sister – and this limited any academic teaching career she may have had, but it did free up her mind for research. After their deaths, she moved to Girton and in 1913 she was elected president of the botanical section of the British Association for the Advancement of Science at its annual conference, the first woman to occupy the chair. That same year, she was also elected president of the British Federation of University Women (following in the footsteps of Sara Burstall and Eleanor Sidgwick) and was soon spearheading the collation of a register of university women to ensure their education was utilised for national service during the First World War. Her death in January 1918, before the war had ended, was a shock and it was thought that her hard, extended work on the register had brought on the stroke. That she was an advocate for the education of women is evident from this quote from 'The Inheritance of a University', a piece she wrote for *Girton Review* in 1901:

> The great inheritance, then, of the Universities is the tradition of learning for learning's sake. And in this inheritance women have been allowed a share. It was claimed for us by our founders when they established Women's Colleges at Cambridge and Oxford. We have reaped the first fruits of their wisdom. Sooner or later an account will be required of us. It is not enough that our graduates can point with pride to their achievements in the Finals. These may satisfy their college, but the University asks how many women trained in her schools are adding to the sum of knowledge. For the torch of research is handed on as the Fiery Cross once was in the Highlands.[4]

The inspired

Four women who came under the influence of Edith and Ethel and really made their marks were Barbara (known as Ally at school) Tchaycovsky, b. 1876; Gabrielle Louise Caroline Matthaei, b. 1876, Agnes Robertson, b. 1879, and Marie Stopes, b. 1880. Apart from Barbara, all were botanists first, with Gabrielle investigating the role of photosynthesis and carbon fixation; Agnes specialising in plant phytomorphology and anatomy; and Marie in palaeobotany, the study of plant remains in their geological context.

Barbara Tchaykovsky

Barbara was born in Long Island, New York to Russian parents; the family came to the UK shortly after her birth. She was head girl at NLCS before gaining a scholarship to Bedford College in 1894, graduating as BSc in 1897. From there she studied medicine at the London School of Medicine for Women graduating MB BS in 1906. Three years later, having obtained the Diploma in Public Health of Cambridge University in 1908, she took an MD degree and became the first woman to win the University Gold Medal in State Medicine and was appointed an assistant Medical School Officer under London County Council. The job was part-time in order for her to devote her time to bettering the welfare of mothers and children – although she also worked closely with Sylvia Pankhurst for the suffragette movement. In 1912, she founded the Dental Clinic for School Children of Harrow and District and three years later the Wealdstone Day Nursery and, in association with it, the first baby clinic and ante-natal clinic. She later helped the former Wealdstone UDC to establish the first municipal baby clinic in the district. and urged the formation of a special Maternity and Child Welfare sub-committee of the Public Health Committee, on which she served for over twenty years, pouring out her energy and means for its support.

Gabrielle Louise Caroline Matthaei

Gabrielle studied at Newnham from 1895, focusing on botany in part II of the Tripos examinations. She worked part-time as a demonstrator of chemistry in the Balfour Biological Laboratory for Women, established by Anne Clough and Eleanor Sidgwick in 1884, and the income from this helped pay for her post-graduate research into plant physiology; she published various papers with the highly prestigious Royal Society on 'Vegetable Assimilation and Respiration' and the effect of temperature on carbon-dioxide assimilation. In 1905, aged 31, Gabrielle married Albert Howard, newly appointed imperial economic botanist to the government of India, and together they continued their research on crops, arguing that plants should be studied in relation to their habitats, and ran a fruit experiment station at Quetta, now part of Pakistan, between 1912 and 1919. Gabrielle became the second imperial economic botanist to India in 1913. The couple supervised the planning and construction of the Institute of Plant Industry at Indore, India's first agricultural research institute, now Indore College of Agriculture. Shortly before their planned retirement and return to England, Gabrielle died suddenly in Genoa in August 1930.

Agnes Robertson

Agnes was only 15 when she published her first piece of research in the NLCS magazine in 1894. Her academic career began in seriousness at UCL where she gained a BSc in 1899, before gaining a scholarship to Newnham where she studied for a degree in natural sciences, graduating in 1902 (again, not being awarded a degree due to being a woman, and not being allowed to join practical classes with men in the university's laboratories). She worked with Ethel Sargant for a year before returning to UCL for further research, through the Quain Studentship in Botany – £100 a year for three years – being awarded DSc in 1905. While studying at Newnham, Agnes had met Edward Alexander Newell Arber, a university demonstrator in palaeobotany, and they married in 1909. Once back in Cambridge, Agnes continued her research at the Balfour Laboratory. She was awarded a Research Fellowship from Newnham College in 1912 and, inspired by Ethel Sargant, focused her research on the anatomy and morphology of the monocot group of plants. Her first of several books on botany, *Herbals: Their Origin and Evolution*, was published the same year. After the early death of her husband, in 1918, Agnes continued her research, but recognition for her outstanding contribution took some time. It eventually came when, aged 67, she became the first women botanist (and only the third woman) to be a Fellow of the Royal Society. Two years later (1948) she became the first female recipient of the Linnean Medal from the Linnean Society of London. Awarded annually, there is still only a handful of women in its list.

Marie Charlotte Carmichael Stopes

Probably the best known of the women scientists listed here, Marie Stopes's name has been carried worldwide through her birth-control clinics, but the first records of her scientific achievements were in another field entirely. After NLCS, Marie studied botany and geology at UCL, graduating after just two years with a first-class BSc in 1902. The NLCS magazine noted she had gained a gold medal for Advanced Botany, and in 1904 wrote that she had obtained the degree of PhD (Botany) at the University of Munich, after only nine months' work in Germany, remarking that 'her knowledge of German was not great when she began work there, so that the fact that she headed the list is all the more creditable.' The same issue also notes she had been awarded a Gilchrist research scholarship (for women to undertake a year of study) by the University of London. In October 1904, she was appointed Assistant Lecturer and Demonstrator in Botany at Owen's College, Manchester, the first woman appointed on the university staff, Owen's College having been hitherto closed to women. According to NLCS and University of London records, Marie gained her DSc in Botany in 1905, one of the youngest women to do so. After presenting a paper on 'Coal Balls found in Coal Seams' at the British Association in 1906, Marie was sent to Japan by the Royal Society to further her research into fossil botany, sailing in July 1907. There she stayed for around eighteen months, entering most of the coal mines and obtaining many new and important fossil plants. As the NLCS reported in 1909: 'She was, of course, the first woman to do anything of the sort in the country.':

> I visited places where no European ever set foot before, the unknown region of Yezo and even the squalid villages of the superstitious, semi-civilised Ainus, and yet was always treated with the utmost deference. The Japanese are really an admirable race – more so in many ways than our own. Not once did I feel that I was not allowed to do certain things on the ground that I was a woman. Directly I came back to England I found myself imprisoned in a net of prejudices. I am in fact so much in love with Eastern customs that I still eat with chop-sticks. I should have adopted the kimono as a dress, but somehow or other European women look ridiculous in it.
> *London and China Telegraph*, Monday, 29 March 1909

She was appointed a Fellow of UCL in February 1910 and later that year was commissioned by the Geological Survey of Canada to examine the Fern Ledges, a geological structure on the Bay of Fundy at St John's, New Brunswick. While en route to the work, she met fellow researcher Reginald Gates in St Louis and, in true whirlwind Marie Stopes fashion, was engaged to him in two days and married within three months. This was the catalyst for her change in direction. Although she continued her palaeobotany research, Gates's apparent impotence spurred her into annulling her marriage and drafting her first book, *Married Love or Love in Marriage*. The book was eventually published on 26 March 1918 and was an instant success. Marie was able to put her theories into practice when she married Humphrey Verdon Roe, who had helped finance the book, on 16 May. This marked the beginning of the end of her palaeobotanical career and the start of her more extraordinary and enduring contribution to society.

The writers and artists

Of course, women had already been established as writers and artists but these three former NLCS pupils deserve a mention for their contributions to women's life opportunities.

Netta Syrett

Baptised Janet, Netta was born in March 1865, one of nine surviving children of Mary Ann and Ernest (a draper by trade). She was a boarding pupil at NLCS from 1876 before going to Cambridge Training College for Women Teachers, where she gained her certificate of proficiency in the Theory, History and Practice of Education in 1889. That perhaps teaching was not her real ambition, although it is noted she enjoyed the job and was a good teacher, may be gleaned from her noted occupation – journalist and author – on the 1891 census. Her first short story, *A Birthday*, was published in *Longman's Magazine* in March 1892, while she was still teaching, and it was the first of many short stories published in various magazines. Her first novel, *Nobody's Fault*, published in 1896, was perhaps drawn from life as it described the plight of the daughter of tradespeople given a refined education, who finds herself adrift from the class of her birth, struggling to find a creative and personal identity. Bridget Ruan, the protagonist, despairs that the hard-working existence of a teacher excludes the opportunity to experience life, asking her old teacher friend Miss Miles, 'What have you done all your life?' 'I went to a high school, and got a scholarship to Girton, and then I went to a training college, and then I came here,' is the reply. 'I've always worked hard, but I've been rewarded, of course. I've had several scholarships, and I'm a successful teacher.' That was not going to be enough for Bridget, it seems, nor Netta. She became a successful author, publishing a novel per year until retiring in 1939, mostly on the themes of women's struggles for recognition and emancipation, as well as plays and several children's books. Her *Portrait of a Rebel* (1929) was made into a Hollywood film, *A Woman Rebels*, with Katharine Hepburn in 1936, but it was not a box office success.

Jessie Mothersole

Described in her later years as a Christian Science Practitioner, Jessie was born in 1873 and after attending NLCS, trained at the Slade School of Fine Art for five years from 1891, winning many awards and prizes. She continued her studies at the studio of Henry Holiday and in 1902 *Our Magazine* reported that she was doing very important work for the well-known artist in stained glass and enamels. She was still working with him in 1905 and carrying out his designs for stained-glass windows, one of which depicted 'Literature, Arts and Sciences in Ancient Greece' and was to be placed at a museum in Preston. On Christmas Day 1907, Jessie left for Egypt for a three-month visit and it was probably at this time that an earlier interest in archaeological drawing became more of a focus. After publishing, with the Religious Tract Society, a book on the Scilly Isles in 1910, illustrated with her own watercolours, her attention turned to British archaeology. In 1920, she walked and sketched the entire length of Hadrian's Wall, engaging with archaeologists who were making their excavations as she made her journey, and later exhibited a series of the watercolours she had made. The notes she made on her adventure became the basis of another self-illustrated book, in which she reflected on the stories associated with the wall, its construction, the ideals of leadership exhibited by figures like Hadrian, and the enduring impact it had on those who followed its course, capturing the conversations she had with local people and recording their lives during that period for ever. The book, *Hadrian's Wall*, published in 1922, was the first of her illustrated books on archaeology and travel, in what was a male-dominated profession.

Janet Robertson

Janet, born 1880, was the daughter of artist Henry Robertson and younger sister of Agnes the botanist. She was one of a number of women miniaturists leading a revival in the artform in the early twentieth century, and a talented watercolourist. *Our Magazine* details her yearly successes at the Royal Academy exhibitions and notes her other exhibitions, including at London County Council's Central School of Arts and Crafts (where she showed enamelwork and jewellery), Walker Art Gallery, Liverpool and the Royal Society of Miniature Painters. Her watercolours were mainly of landscapes and her miniatures usually portraits, including one of

Agnes at the Royal Academy's exhibition of 1907. She described herself on the 1939 register as a Travelling Portrait Painter, but it is clear she was more than this. The new edition of Charles Kingsley's *Water Babies*, published in 1906 by Clarendon contained five full-page illustrations by Janet.

Winifred Christine Stopes

Like Janet Robertson, Winifred was the younger sister of a scientist. Born in 1884, she was Marie's junior by four years and is listed in 1911, living with Marie and Reginald, as a hand bookbinder, though she had retired ten years later and died in 1923 after a long illness. NLCS records detail how talented she had been as a leatherworker and bookbinder. She became a member of the Women's Guild of Arts after its establishment in 1907, when the founding members had been denied membership of the Art Workers' Guild. It was also conceived as an alternative for female artists to the Guild of Handicraft – another organisation that excluded women from its membership (until 1964).

Educated sisters

Was there sibling rivalry for success that spurred girls from the same family to higher things? Or were they supportive of each other? Netta Syrett's sisters Nellie and Mabel also wrote short stories and contributed to the *Yellow Book*; both were artists, Mabel designed fabrics and both illustrated some of Netta's books. Another sister, Kate, who had attended Bedford College before studying art in Paris, created costumes for Netta's plays. Winifred Stopes's obituary mentions her passion for botany rather than her bookbinding. Jessie Mothersole's older sister Kate Elizabeth became a missionary and *Our Magazine* notes she had returned to Persia to work under the Church Missionary Society at the end of 1905, having spent five months in England on account of her health. She died in Persia in 1907. Another sister, Frances Ann, became an assistant teacher in a secondary school.

Agnes and Janet Robertson's younger sister Margaret gained the Clothworkers' scholarship to study English at Somerville and then the Gilchrist scholarship to train at the Cambridge Training College in 1904. In 1906, she was appointed as mistress at Mary Macrae's Queen Elizabeth Grammar School in Mansfield but left at Christmas 1907 'intending to take a short holiday and then get teaching in London'. During this 'holiday', she did a little work in connection with women's suffrage campaign, and she decided to give up teaching and work for 'The Cause', joining the National Union of Suffrage Societies where Millicent Fawcett appointed her as by-election organiser in Manchester in July 1908. She was among the many former pupils (and mistresses) of NLCS who joined the 10,000-plus women (led by Sophie Bryant) in a procession from the Embankment to the Royal Albert Hall on 13 June 1908. On the 1911 census, having completely embraced the cause, she is listed as 'Organising Secretary Manchester and District Federation of Women's Suffrage Societies'. Jessie Mothersole, Marie Stopes and many other former NLCS pupils were active campaigners, several joining the University of London Woman's Suffrage Society.

One family of sisters, inspired by their headmistress, was the Lett family of Wakefield who had attended Wakefield Girls' High School under Gertrude McCroben. Norah Kathleen (b. 1878), Olive Mary (b. 1882), Phyllis (b. 1884), Hilda (b. 1885) and Eva (b. 1887) were the daughters of a surgeon and his wife who never saw their daughters' success, both dying in the early years of the twentieth century. Norah had qualified as a teacher by 1901 but was later secretary to the British Embassy in Rome. Phyllis and Hilda became musicians: Phyllis a contralto soloist who performed many times with Elgar, and Hilda a distinguished violinist. Olive trained as a gymnastics teacher, becoming a teacher at the Chelsea Training College, where she trained other women to become gymnastics instructors These women were considered among the elite in their field and in huge demand as professional teachers in girls' schools, just as physical exercise for girls was becoming part of the curriculum. Eva, the youngest and most academic, quietly influenced the lives of other women. After graduating from Cambridge, she gained a teaching diploma and became a lecturer at St Hild's College, Durham. From there she became vice principal of Dudley Training College until 1921, then principal of the Physical Training College, Dartford – a women-only college founded by Swedish-born, physical education instructor and women's suffrage advocate, Martina Sofia Helena Bergman-Österberg. In 1930, Eva was appointed principal of Ripon Diocesan Women's Teacher Training College, astonishingly the first woman to hold the post. She remained there until August 1945, when she was compelled to retire through ill health. In addition to her role as college principal, Eva had held offices at both the Ripon Diocesan Conference and Diocesan Education Council, been vice president of the Ling Association (a PE association founded by a group of Dartford College graduates in 1899), and had been a member of the Board of Administration for Yorkshire Training Colleges, governor of Skellfield School for girls, manager of Ripon Holy Trinity Day Schools, a governor of Ripon Modern School, and president of the Ripon Business and Professional Women's Club. She passed away in a nursing home in Winchester on 30 November 1945, aged only 58. In tribute to her life, the Bishop of Ripon, Dr G.C.L. Lunt, said at her Winchester funeral:

> Under her leadership the training college has gone from strength to strength, and in her last two terms as principal she was seeing a vision for future developments and busily working out detailed plans for bold future policy,

though she knew full well that it would not be hers to see these plans take material shape. It was by a miracle of superb courage that she remained at her post all through last term, carrying on her work with her usual patience and thoroughness, giving her best to staff and students alike, too deeply concerned about their well-being to have any leisure for thought of herself. Her own unswerving loyalty to her charge and to Him from whom she received it drew out from staff and students alike a fine and abiding loyalty and has enhanced and deepened the traditions of the college and made of it a fellowship which those who have received their training here continue to value all their lives. She had strong reserve and did not easily make a multitude of friendships, but those whose privilege it was to work with her year by year came to realise the richness and depth of friendship which were hers to give. A deep spirituality and an inspiring self-discipline were balanced by a subtle and fragrant sense of humour. The name is legion today to those who as teachers or homemakers in every part of the country are conscious that their lives are forever the richer for the influence of her life upon theirs. She brought great gifts to her life work, but the greatest gift all was herself, and that she freely gave.[5]

Eva was typical of the thousands of women in education who dedicated their entire lives to the betterment of children's and girls' education enabling those girls, now educated, to actively pursue their own aspirations, goals and passions.

The first British-born female MP

Of course, there was much still to do: equality of pay was years away (it was agreed that women teachers would be paid the same as men in 1955, but it was not implemented until 1961; other women had to wait until Barbara Castle (ex BGGS) pushed through the Equal Pay Act 1970 – and we still have a gender pay gap; equality of opportunity had to be fought for (the marriage bar meant many experienced women teachers had to forgo their careers once married), but at least, eventually, there were a few women able to make their voices heard as MPs. Interestingly, the third woman to be elected as an MP (after Countess Markievicz and Viscountess Astor) and the second to take her seat in the Commons, was a Yorkshire lass from an ordinary background, Mrs Margaret Wintringham (née Longbottom). Maggie, as she was known, was born in 1879 in the hamlet of Oldfield just 4 miles west of Keighley. Her father, David, was headteacher at Bolton Road School, Silsden and she attended this elementary school before going to Keighley Girls' Grammar School, the first endowed girls' secondary school in the country. Like many girls of her era, she took the best opportunity available to her and trained as a teacher, at Bedford Training College, becoming a kindergarten teacher and eventually headmistress of a school in Grimsby. In 1903, she married Thomas Wintringham, a local timber merchant, and thus her teaching career ended, although she continued to work on behalf of women and was an active member of the Grimsby Women's Liberal Association; the papers reported that in North Lincolnshire there were 'many institutes which exist for women, and which are monuments to her energy and grit'. Thomas was elected to parliament as MP for Louth in June 1920, following the sudden death of the incumbent MP. Tragically, Thomas also died suddenly, in the Commons' reading room, on 8 August 1921, and in the by-election that ensued, his widow was elected as the Liberal MP. It was no sympathy vote; polling was close with Margaret winning 8,333 votes and the Conservative and Labour candidates 7,595 and 3,873 respectively. And so the ordinary lass, who, had it not been for education would never been able to aspire to such heights, became the first British-born woman elected to parliament. Described as an active parliamentarian, she emphasised the need for expenditure on education, health and housing – typically seen as women's priorities – and in 1924 was a leading supporter of the Guardianship of Infants Bill, which aimed to equalise women's rights of access to their children with men's; she was also involved in campaigns to extend the franchise to women on the same basis as men, something that eventually came to pass in 1928. Margaret worked closely with Nancy Astor – they were the only two women in the Commons until 1923 – and was the unofficial co-ordinator of the eight women MPs when six more joined their ranks that year. Although she was re-elected in 1922 and 1923, the Liberal Party had a disastrous election in 1924 and Margaret lost her seat, along with 127 other Liberal MPs. Her work in politics continued through various organisations until her death in 1955.[6]

***

That continuous push for improvements in education for women by women throughout the nineteenth century was to pave the way for successive generations of women to thrive, each taking further steps from the apex of their predecessors' achievements. There would be countless future further reforms in education, but the foundations built by women were secure.

The Duchess of Atholl, speaking at the BGGS Golden Jubilee in June 1925, put it succinctly. Under the headline, 'Education for girls: The capacity to do things', *The Leeds Mercury* reported her address: 'If you can go from school feeling you are not afraid of work, one of the greatest fears life can hold is gone from you,' adding that 'although the work women had done during the war and the bold suffrage movement before that had helped, it was the improvement in women's education in the last fifty years that was at the fundamental root of the enlarged opportunities women enjoyed today in professional and public life.'

Of course, they could not have done it entirely without the help and support of some great men. Lady Sarah Byles, one of the chief movers and shakers in raising funds to establish BGGS, speaking at the same event, acknowledged the contribution of the late William Edward Forster, the borough's former MP:

> No statesman of his day realised so fully the place and duty of women in education, and in the schemes under his Endowed Schools Act he ensured full scope for women on the governing bodies and in his Elementary Education Act he made women eligible for election on the new School Boards.[7]

But it was the women who did the hard graft. To those women – too numerous to mention individually – whose struggle, strife and sheer determination enabled subsequent generations of girls and women to take education and the opportunities it creates for granted, we give our recognition and heartfelt thanks.

Appendix 1

Examinations of Pupil Teachers in each Year of their Apprenticeship

General Rules. In the subjects marked with * girls need not be examined, but in every year they will be expected to show increased skill as sempstresses, and teachers of sewing, knitting, etc.

Year 1

1. In writing from memory, the substance of a more difficult narrative.
2. In arithmetic, the rules of 'Practice' and 'Simple Proportion,*' and in the first rules of mental arithmetic*.
3. In grammar, in the construction of sentences, and in syntax.
4. In the geography of Great Britain and Palestine.
5. In the Holy Scriptures and in the Catechism, with illustrations by passages from Holy Writ, in Church of England schools, the parochial clergyman assisting in the examination.
6. In their ability to give a class a reading lesson, and to examine it on the meaning of what has been read.
7. In the elements of vocal music, in this and in succeeding years, when taught from notes.
8. In their ability to drill* a class in marching and exercises; and to conduct it through the class movements required for preserving order.
9. Girls should also be able to instruct the younger scholars in sewing and knitting.

Year 2

1. In composition, by writing the abstract of a lesson*, or a school report.
2. In decimal arithmetic*, and the higher rules of mental arithmetic. Girls will not be required to proceed beyond the rule of 'Compound Proportion' in this year.

3. In syntax and etymology*.
4. In the geography of Great Britain, of Europe, the British empire*, and Palestine.
5. In the Holy Scriptures, Liturgy, and Catechism in Church of England schools, more fully than in the preceding year, the parochial clergyman assisting in the examination.
6. In their ability to examine a class in reading, in the rudiments of grammar and arithmetic; and, during the examination, to keep the class attentive, in order and in activity without undue noise.

Year 3

1. In the composition of the notes of a lesson on a subject selected by the Inspector.
2. In the elements of mechanics*, or in bookkeeping.
3. In syntax, etymology, and prosody*.
4. In the geography of the four* quarters of the globe. Girls in the geography of the British Empire.
5. In the outlines of English history.
6. More fully in the Holy Scriptures, Liturgy, and Catechism, in Church of England schools, the parochial clergyman assisting in the examination.
7. In their skill in managing and examining the second class in grammar, geography and mental arithmetic.
8. The girls should have acquired greater skill as teachers of sewing, knitting, etc.

Year 4

1. In the composition of an account of the organisation of the school, and of the methods of instruction used.
2. In the first steps in mensuration*, with practical illustrations; and in the elements of land surveying* and levelling*.
3. In syntax, etymology, and prosody*.
4. In the *geography of Great Britain as connected with the outlines of English history. Girls in the geography of the four quarters of the globe.
5. More fully in the Holy Scriptures, Liturgy, and Catechism, in Church of England schools, the parochial clergyman assisting in the examination.
6. In their skill in managing and examining the first class in grammar, geography, and mental arithmetic, and in giving *a lesson to two or three classes grouped together.

Year 5

1. In the composition of an essay on some subject connected with the art of teaching.
2. In the rudiments of algebra*, or the practice of land surveying* and levelling*.
3. In syntax, etymology, and prosody.
4. In the use *of the globes, or in the geography of the British empire* and Europe*, as connected with the outlines of English history. In this year girls may be examined in the historical geography of Great Britain.
5. More completely in the Holy Scriptures, Liturgy, and Catechism, in Church of England schools, the parochial clergyman assisting in the examination.
6. In their ability to give a gallery lesson, and to conduct the instruction of the first class in any subject selected by the Inspector.

Appendix 2

Qualifications of Stipendiary Monitors in each Year

Year 1

1. To read with fluency, ease and expression.
2. To write in a neat hand, with correct spelling and punctuation, a simple prose narrative, slowly read to them.
3. To write from dictation sums in the first four compound rules of arithmetic, to work them correctly, and to know the tables of weights and measures.
4. To point out the parts of speech in a simple sentence, and to give the rules of its construction.
5. To have an elementary knowledge of geography.
6. In Church of England schools, to show a general acquaintance with the Scriptures; the parochial clergyman, in this and the succeeding years, assisting in the religious examination.
   In other schools, the managers will certify, in this and succeeding years that the religious knowledge of the stipendiary monitors is satisfactory to them.
7. In schools where vocal music is taught, he should have commenced instruction from notes, and should give proof of improvement in each succeeding year.
8. Girls to teach sewing and knitting in this and succeeding years.

Year 2

1. To write from memory, with correct spelling and punctuation, the substance of a simple prose narrative, read carefully to them two or three times.
2. In arithmetic; to write from dictation sums in Practice, and to work them correctly.
3. In grammar, to parse more difficult sentences, and give the rules of their construction.
4. To know the geography of Great Britain and Palestine.

Qualifications of Stipendiary Monitors in each Year

5. In Church of England schools, to give illustrations of the Catechism from the Bible, and to show a more complete acquaintance with the Scriptures.
6. To give a class reading-lesson, and examine it on the meaning of what has been read.
7. Girls to be able to cut out clothes.

Year 3

1. To write from memory the substance of a longer and more difficult prose narrative, and to show greater skill in composition.
2. In arithmetic, to write from dictation sums in Simple Proportion and Simple Interest, and to work them correctly.
3. In grammar, to be able to parse sentences, with a thorough knowledge of the rules of syntax.
4. To know the geography of Great Britain, Europe, and Palestine, and that of the outlines of the four quarters of the globe,
5. In Church of England schools, to possess a more extensive knowledge of the Holy Scriptures, and of the Liturgy and Catechism.
6. To examine a class in the rudiments of grammar, geography, and arithmetic.

Year 4

1. To prepare the notes of an oral lesson on a subject selected by the Inspector.
2. To work correctly sums in decimal arithmetic, and to show an acquaintance with the simple rules of mental arithmetic.
3. In grammar, to be examined in etymology.
4. To know the geography of the four quarters of the world, and especially of the British Empire.
5. To have a general knowledge of the outlines of English history.
6. In Church of England schools, to show a more perfect knowledge of the Holy Scriptures, Catechism, and Liturgy.
7. To examine the first or second class in grammar, geography, and arithmetic, and to give it an oral lesson, keeping the class attentive, in order, and in activity without undue noise.

Appendix 3

Education Code 1882: Teacher Classifications

CHAPTER III.

Teachers. Classes of Teachers.

31. The teachers recognised by the department are
    (a) Pupil teachers
    (b) Assistant teachers
    (c) Provisionally certificated teachers
    (d) Certificated teachers
    (e) Evening school teachers.
32. Lay persons alone are recognised as teachers in day schools.

Pupil teachers.

33. A pupil teacher is a boy or girl engaged by the managers of a public elementary day school on condition of teaching during school hours under the superintendence of the principal teacher, and receiving instruction out of school hours.
34. The conditions of the engagement of a pupil teacher are set forth in detail in the form of a Memorandum of Agreement given in the Appendix. No departure from this form is allowed.
35. A pupil teacher must be of the same sex as the principal teacher of the school in which he or she is engaged. In mixed schools under masters, female pupil teachers may be engaged, and may receive instruction from the master out of school hours on condition that some respectable woman, approved by the managers, be invariably present during the whole time that such instruction is being given.
36. The engagement of a pupil teacher can only begin at the beginning of the school year.

37. A pupil teacher must be not less than fourteen years of age at the beginning of his or her engagement.
38. A pupil teacher is required at the beginning of his or her engagement, and at the end of each school year during the same, to produce the certificates and pass the examination specified in the Fifth Schedule. The inspector informs the managers of the time and place at which the pupil teachers examination will be held. Pupil teachers whose success at the examination for admission to a training college is announced before the date of the examination for the end of the last year of their engagement are not required to attend the latter examination.
39. The length of the engagement is ordinarily four years but may be three or two provided
    (a) that the candidate passes for admission the examination fixed for the end of the first or second year; and
    (b) that the end of the reduced term of service falls beyond the completion of the candidate's eighteenth year.

Candidates.

40. A candidate for engagement as pupil teacher may be employed for a year of probation, provided that he or she
    (a) be over thirteen years of age at the beginning of the school year
    (b) be presented to the inspector at his annual visit; and
    (c) pass an examination in the three elementary subjects and two class subjects according to Standard V or VI.
    The memorandum of agreement prescribed, for pupil teachers may not be executed for a candidate during the year of probation.
41. At the end of the year of probation a candidate, in order to be engaged as a pupil teacher, must pass an examination in the three elementary subjects and two of the class subjects, according to a standard higher than that taken in the preceding year.
42. The number of pupil teachers recognised by the Department must not exceed three for the principal teacher and one for each certificated assistant teacher.
    For the purposes of this article a candidate employed under article is reckoned as equivalent to a pupil teacher.
43. The Department is not a party to the engagement, and confines itself to ascertaining, on the admission of the pupil teacher and at the end of each school year, whether the prescribed certificates are produced and the prescribed examination is passed.

44. Whatever other questions arise upon the engagement may be referred to the Department (provided that all the parties agree in writing to be bound by the decision of the Department as final), but otherwise must be settled as in any other hiring or contract.
45. At the termination of their engagements pupil teachers are free to choose their employment. If they wish to continue in the profession of elementary school-teachers they may, under the conditions stated in the following articles, become
    (a) Students in training colleges
    (b) Assistant teachers
    (c) Provisionally certificated teachers.

Examination for Admission to Training Colleges.

46. An examination of candidates for admission into training colleges is annually held at each college in summer, commencing at 10 a.m. on the first Wednesday after the 2nd July.
47. The examination extends to all the subjects in which pupil teachers during their engagement are required to be examined.
48. The candidates are selected and admitted to the examination by the authorities of each college, on their own responsibility, subject to no other conditions on the part of the Department than that the candidates. (a) will be more than eighteen years of age on the 1st of January next following the date of the examination; or (b) are or have been pupil teachers who (i.) have successfully completed their engagement; or (ii.) will do so before the next following examination.
49. The candidates who pass the examination are arranged in three classes in order of merit.

Assistant Teachers.

50. Pupil teachers who have passed satisfactorily either the examination for the end of the last year of their engagement or that for admission to a training college may be recognised as assistant teachers in public elementary schools.
51. Graduates of any University in the United Kingdom, women over eighteen years of age who have passed University examinations* recognised by the Department, and persons who have passed the examination for admission to a training college may be recognised as assistant teachers.

*The examinations recognised at the current time are: The Oxford Local Examination for senior Students; the Oxford Local Examination for Women over eighteen;

the Cambridge Local Examination for Senior students; the Cambridge Higher Local Examination; the University of London Matriculation Examination; the Durham Examination for senior Candidates not members of the University; the Dublin Senior Examination for Women; the Edinburgh Local Examination for Senior Certificate; the Glasgow Local Examination for Senior certificate; the Aberdeen Local Examination for Honours Certificate; the St. Andrew's Local Examination for Senior Certificate.

Provisionally certificated teachers.

52. Pupil teachers who have passed satisfactorily the examination for the end of the last year of their engagement, or obtained a place in the first or second class in the examination for admission to a training college may, if specially recommended by the inspector on the ground of their practical skills as teachers, be recognised as 'provisionally certificated teachers in charge of small schools' (see Art —).

    The summary of the inspector's report informs the managers whether or not each of the pupil teachers who have attended the examination for the end of the last year of their engagement will be recognised as a provisionally certificated teacher.
53. No certificate is issued to provisionally certificated teachers.
54. Provisionally certificated teachers cease to be recognised as such after the completion of the twenty-fifth year of their age.

Certificated teachers.

55. Teachers, in order to obtain certificates, must be examined and must undergo probation by actual service in school.

Examination.

56. Examinations are held annually in December at each training college, and at such other centres as may be necessary.

Syllabus of Examination.

A syllabus of the subjects of examination, which are different for male and female candidates and for first and second year's students, may be had on application to the Secretary, Education Department, Whitehall, S.W.

Candidates for Examination.

57. The examination for certificates is open to (a) Students who have resided for at least one year in training colleges under inspection; or (b) Candidates who being upwards of twenty years of age have either (1) been employed for not less than two years as provisionally certificated teachers; or (2) served as assistant teachers for at least twelve months in inspected schools under certificated teachers, and have in either of such institutions obtained a favourable report from an inspector on their skill in teaching, reading, and needlework (women).
58. Candidates who at the time of the examination are not teachers in schools under inspection must be recommended by the authorities of their college, or by the managers of the school in which they last served.
59. The names of all candidates, not being students in any training college, must be notified to the department before the 1st day of October preceding the examination.
60. Candidates, not being students in any training college, may, at their option, take the papers of the first or second year's students.
61. A list is published showing the successful candidates of each year, whether students or not, arranged in three divisions.

Probation.

62. Candidates for certificates, after successfully passing their examination must, as teachers continuously engaged in the same schools, obtain two favourable reports from an inspector, with an interval of at least one year between them; and if the first of these reports be not preceded by service of at least six months since the examination, a third report, at an interval of at least one year after the second report, is required. If the second (or third) report is favourable a certificate is issued. Teachers under probation are considered as certificated teachers to all intents and purposes.

Certificates.

63. Certificates are of three classes.

Certificates of First and Second Classes.

64. Candidates who at the examination of December, 1883, or any subsequent examination, shall pass successfully in the subjects for second year's students will receive certificates of the second class, which can be raised to the first class by good service only.

Revision of Certificates.

65. Certificates of the second class are open to revision at the end of ten years from the date of their issue, according to the intermediate reports.

Certificate of Third Class.

66. Candidates who at the examination of December 1883 or any subsequent examination, shall pass successfully in the subjects for either first or second year's students will receive certificates of the third class.
67. Certificates of the third class do not entitle their holders to have the superintendence of pupil teachers. Assistant teachers holding certificates of the third class enable additional pupil teachers to be employed under Article 42.
68. Certificates of the third class can be raised to a higher class only by a subsequent examination in the subjects for second year's students. A teacher cannot be re-examined for this purpose more than once in every two years.

Certificates obtained by Examinations held before December 1883.

69. Candidates who at any examination before that of December, 1883, have passed successfully in the subjects for either first or second year's students but have not yet received certificates, will at the end of their probation receive, if they obtained a place in any of the first three divisions, certificates of the second class; if they obtained a place in the fourth division, certificates of the third class.

Rating of Certificates issued before 1st of January 1871.

70. Certificates of the first or second class issued before the 1st of January 1871, are rated as of the first class.
71. Certificates of the third class, or upper grade of the fourth class. and infant school certificates of the first class, issued before the 1st of January 1871, are rated as of the second class. Such certificates will be open to revision at the end of ten years from the date of their issue, or of their last revision.
72. Certificates of the lower grade of the fourth class and infant school certificates of the second class issued before the 1st of January. 1871, are rated as of the third class.
73. Certificates issued between the 1st of January, 1871, and the date at which this code comes into operation continue to be rated in the same class as heretofore.

Appendix 4

Endowed Girls' Schools Established 1871–1903

Town	Endowment	Year established	Age range of girls taught
Keighley	Drake and Tonson's	1871	Not stated
Burton on Trent	Allsopp's	1872	8–17
Newcastle under Lyme	Orme's	1872	8–17
Ambleside	Kelsick's	1873	10–17
Bedford	Harpur's	1873	Not stated
Greenwich	Roan's	1873	7–16
Hoxton, Middlesex	Aske's Hospital	1873	Not stated
Ilminster	Endowed School	1873	Not stated
Leicester	Wyggeston's	1873	8–17
Stamford	Browne's	1873	8–17
Uffculme	Ayshford's	1873	8–17
Wallingford	Bigg's	1873	7–16
West Ham	Bonnell's	1873	7–15
Westminster	Greycoat Hospital	1873	7–15
Westminster	St Martin in the Fields	1873	7–16
Great Crosby	Harrison's	1874	8–17
Kingston upon Thames	Tiffin's	1874	7–16
Taunton	Huish	1874	7–15
Totnes	Grammar and Municipal Charities	1874	Not stated

Endowed Girls' Schools Established 1871–1903

Town	Endowment	Year established	Age range of girls taught
Bradford	Girls' Endowed School	1875	Not stated
Bristol	Queen Elizabeth's and Red Maids	1875	Up to 15
Bristol	Colston's	1875	Up to 15
Camberwell	Dulwich College	1875	Not stated
Exeter	Maynard's	1875	10–19
London	St Paul's	1875	Not stated
London	Lady Eleanor Holles	1875	8–16
Loughborough	Endowed Schools	1875	Not stated
Mansfield	Queen Elizabeth Grammar	1875	Not stated
Reading	Kendrick's	1875	7–16
St Helen's	Cowley	1875	8–17
London, St Pancras	North London Collegiate and Camden	1875	Not stated
Wakefield	Girls' High	1875	8–18
Warwick	King's	1875	Up to 16
Westminster, Holborn	St Clement Dane's	1875	8–18
London	Burlington	1876	7–18
Thetford	School and Hospital Foundation	1876	7–15
Newcastle upon Tyne	Allan's	1877	7–16
Tiverton	Middle Schools	1877	7–16
Birmingham	King Edward VI	1878	Not stated
Canterbury	Simon Langton	1878	7–16
Coggeshall	Sir Robert Mitcham	1878	7–16
London, Islington	Dame Alice Owen's	1878	Up to 15
Louth	Grammar	1878	8–17

Town	Endowment	Year established	Age range of girls taught
Wells	Blue School	1878	Up to 16
Ipswich	Endowed Schools	1881	7–16
Gloucester	United Endowed Schools	1882	8–16
Watford	Endowed Schools	1882	Up to 16
Lincoln	Christ's Hospital	1883	8–17
London, Poplar	George Green's	1883	6–16
Manchester	High School	1884	Not stated
Southborough in Tonbridge	The Holme Foundation	1884	Not stated
Pendleton, Manchester	High School	1885	Not stated
London, Hackney	Skinner's	1886	8–17
Maidstone, Kent	Grammar	1886	7–17
Rochester, Kent	Sir J. Williamson's Mathematical School	1886	7–17
Salisbury	Godolphin	1886	Not stated
Skipton	Petyt's Charity	1886	8–17
Berkhamsted	Grammar	1887	Not stated
London, Lewisham	Grammar	1887	9–16
Oldham	Hulme Grammar	1887	8–17
Barnet	Queen Elizabeth's	1888	Not stated
Dewsbury	Wheelwright's	1888	8–17
Hitchin	Grammar	1888	8–17
Ashby de la Zouch	Grammar	1889	Not stated
Tadcaster	Dawson's	1889	Not stated
London	Christ's Hospital	1890	Not stated
Taunton	Bishop Fox's	1890	7–16
Framlingham, Suffolk	Mills' Grammar	1891	8–16

Endowed Girls' Schools Established 1871–1903

Town	Endowment	Year established	Age range of girls taught
London	Central Foundation	1891	7–17
Mansfield	Brunt's	1891	Up to 16
North Manchester	High School for Girls	1892	Not stated
London, Deptford	Addey and Stanhope	1893	Not stated
Walsall	Queen Mary's	1893	10–17
Kirkham, Lancashire	Never Built	1898	8–17
Wigton, Cumberland	Grammar	1898	8–18
Bury	Grammar	1899	8–18
London	St Saviour's and St Olave's	1899	8–17
Leeds	Girls' Grammar	1901	8–19
London	Godolphin and Latymer	1903	7–18

Source: Fletcher, Sheila Margaret, 'The part played by civil servants in promoting girls' secondary education 1869–1902; some aspects of the administration of the Endowed Schools Act'. (Appendix XII: Secondary Schools Established by Schemes Made Under the Endowed Schools Acts. 1869–1903)

Appendix 5

Girls Public Day Schools Company Schools in 1894

School	Year Established	Headmistress
Bath	1875	Miss Firth
Blackheath*	1880	Miss F.M.A. Gadesden^
Brighton*	1876	Mrs A. Luxton
Bromley*	1883	Miss Heppel
Carlisle	1884	Miss Beevor
Clapham High	1875	Miss A.A. O'Connor^
Clapham Middle		Miss Wheeler
Croydon*	1874	Miss D. Neligan^
Dover	1888	Miss Frost
Dulwich	1878	Miss Cooper
East Putney*	1893	Miss Huckwell
Gateshead	1876	Miss Moberley
Newcastle on Tyne Preparatory		Miss Moberley
Hackney and Clapton	1875	Vacant
Highbury and Islington	1878	Miss M.A.A. Minasi^
Ipswich	1878	Miss Youngman
Kensington (formerly Chelsea)*	1873	Miss A. Hitchcock
Liverpool*#	1879	Miss Cannings^
East Liverpool#	1891	Miss Silcox
Maida Vale	1878	Miss Andrews^
Newton Abbot	1881	Miss Ridley
Norwich*	1875	Miss L. Gadesden
Nottingham*	1875	Miss M.E. Skeel^

Girls Public Day Schools Company Schools in 1894

School	Year Established	Headmistress
Notting Hill and Bayswater	1873	Miss H.M. Jones^
Oxford*	1875	Miss Soulsby
Portsmouth*	1886	Miss Ledger
Sheffield*	1878	Mrs E. Woodhouse
Shrewsbury*	1885	Miss Gavin
South Hampstead*	1876	Miss Benton
Streatham Hill and Brixton*	1887	Miss Tovey
Sutton*	1884	Miss Duirs
Swansea	1888	Miss Vinter
Sydenham*	1887	Miss I.C. Thomas^
Tunbridge Wells	1883	Miss Julian
Weymouth	1880	Miss Blagrave
Wimbledon*	1880	Miss Hastings
York	1879	Miss Chambers

Preparatory Departments were attached to Bath, Brighton, Bromley, Clapham, Croydon, Dulwich, Gateshead, Ipswich, Kensington, Liverpool, East Liverpool, Maida Vale, Norwich, Nottingham, Oxford, Portsmouth, Sheffield, Shrewsbury, Streatham Hill and Brixton Sydenham, Tunbridge Wells, Weymouth and York High Schools.

*Still a member of the Girls' Day School Trust
#Merged in 1912
^ attended 1887 conference at Uppingham

Endnotes

Chapter 1

1. Joyce Valerie Ireland, 'Education of Poor Girls in North West England *c*.1780 to 1860: A Study of Warrington And Chester'
2. https://www.bronteschoolhouse.com/history
3. Ibid.
4. Eileen E. Meades BA, *A Brief History of St Mary's Hall, Brighton 1836–1956*, p.7
5. Ibid., p.8
6. Ibid., p.9
7. www.smhassociation.org/registers
8. Meades, *A Brief History of St Mary's Hall*, p.11
9. Census, 1861
10. https://www.smhassociation.org/registers
11. Elizabeth Patchett had been at boarding school in York with another famous Calderdale woman: Anne Lister of Shibden Hall
12. Claire Harman, *Charlotte Brontë: A Life* (Penguin, London, 2015), p.160
13. Ibid., pp.190–91

Chapter 2

1. Histpop.org: The Online Historical Population Reports Website
2. Katie Green, 'Victorian Governesses: A Look at Education and Professionalization'. University of Toledo, 2009
3. United Kingdom. Third Report. Royal Commission on Scientific Instruction and the Advancement of Science. Report, 1873, xxi. Via https://education-uk.org/documents/devonshire/devonshire.html#03
4. Lady Henrietta Stanley, 'Personal Recollections of Women's Education', *The Nineteenth Century*, August 1879, pp.308–321
5. *Liverpool Mail*, Saturday, 18 May 1850
6. 'Co-operation Among Governesses', *Work and Leisure: A Magazine Devoted to the Interests of Women* No. 1 (1881): 224

7. Josephine Kamm, *How Different from Us: A Biography of Miss Buss and Miss Beale* (Bodley Head, London 1958), p.20
8. Ibid., p.21
9. Ibid., p.28
10. Ibid., p.33
11. *Echo (London)*, Tuesday, 2 January 1877
12. Ancestry: 'UK, Registers of Births, Marriages and Deaths at Sea, 1844–1890'

Chapter 3

1. Minutes by the Committee of Council on Education, Dated 25th August, and 21st December, 1846: (1) General; (2) Regulations Respecting the Education of Pupil Teachers and Stipendiary Monitors – Support of Normal Schools, Council Chamber, Whitehall, 25th August, 1846. Via www.education-uk.org/documents/cce/minutes

Chapter 4

1. Jane Martin, 'To "blaise the trail for women to follow along": sex, gender and the politics of education on the London School Board, 1870–1904'. University College, Northampton, 1999

Chapter 5

1. Jane Martin, 'To "blaise the trail for women to follow along"
2. Rosemary T. Van Ardell, 'Victorian Periodicals Yield Their Secrets: Florence Fenwick Miller's Three Campaigns for The London School Board', *History of Education Society Bulletin*. (History of Education Society. 1986)
3. Oxford Dictionary of National Biography
4. Jane Martin, 'To "blaise the trail for women to follow along"
5. Obituary, *Western Daily Press*, Friday, 8 August 1902
6. *London Evening Standard*, Wednesday, 21 July 1880
7. *School Board Chronicle*, 30 March 1878, via Martin, Jane, 'To "blaise the trail for women to follow along"
8. *The Governess*, 17 November 1883, p.138. (via Martin, Jane).
9. *School Board Chronicle*, 14 April 1877; 24 February 1881. (via Martin, Jane).
10. Florence Fenwick Miller, *Autobiography: An Uncommon Girlhood* (c. 1900).
11. *South London Press*, Saturday, 15 June 1878
12. *London Daily Chronicle*, Thursday, 13 November 1879

Chapter 6

1. Trevor R. Phillips, 'Certificated Women Teachers in The National Union of Elementary Teachers, 1870–82', *History of Education Society Bulletin*, Autumn 1992
2. St Luke's National School, Chorlton-on-Medlock, Manchester. Logbooks, Manchester Archives
3. *Manchester Courier*, Tuesday, 9 December 1873

Chapter 7

1. Huddersfield School Board, Triennial Report, 1874
2. *Huddersfield Daily Examiner*, Tuesday, 23 February 1875
3. Ibid., Tuesday, 13 April 1875
4. Mount Pleasant Infants' School Logbook, West Yorkshire Archives
5. Ibid.
6. https://hansard.parliament.uk/Commons/1898-06-17/debates
7. https://hansard.parliament.uk/Commons/1900-06-14/debates. He added, 'I would support the State spending a million of money in educating our teachers. After all, what would a million of money be, spent in that way, when we can spend forty or fifty millions on war? One million, if properly administered would be ample to train our juvenile apprentices by having them sent to secondary schools.'
8. Linda Mahood, 'Elementary Teaching as Toil: The Diary and Letters of Miss Eglantyne Jebb, a Gentlewoman Schoolmistress', *History of Education*, 35:3, 321–343, (2006)
9. Ibid.
10. www.cambridgeppf.org/people-with-blue-plaques.html

Chapter 8

1. Sheila Margaret Fletcher, 'The part played by civil servants in promoting girls' secondary education 1869–1902; some aspects of the administration of the Endowed Schools Act'. A Thesis submitted for the Degree of Doctor of Philosophy, Bedford College, London, 1976
2. Schools Inquiry Commission Minutes of Evidence Part II, 1 November 1865
3. Ibid., 17 April 1866
4. Ibid.
5. Ibid., 30 November 1865
6. Kamm, *How Different From Us*
7. Schools Inquiry Commission Minutes of Evidence Part II, 19 April 1866
8. Ibid.
9. Ibid.

10. Fletcher, 'The part played by civil servants in promoting girls' secondary education'
11. Appendix V. Report of Schools Inquiry (Taunton) Commission 1868

Chapter 9

1. Appendix V. Report of Schools Inquiry (Taunton) Commission 1868.
2. *Bradford Observer*, Thursday, 12 January 1871
3. Report of meeting on 9 October, *Yorkshire Post and Leeds Intelligencer*, Tuesday, 10 October 1871
4. *Leeds Mercury*, Monday, 10 June 1872
5. 1901 Census

Chapter 10

1. *Educational Times*, Monday, 1 April 1878
2. *Stamford Mercury*, Friday, 17 June 1887
3. Malcolm Tozer, 'Thring's "favourite wish": Uppingham High School for Girls, 1888–1893', *Rutland Record*, vol. 32, 2018, pp.363–72
4. Ibid.
5. In 1887, she was asked to join an Education Department committee looking at the pupil-teacher system chaired by the chief inspector of schools, Thomas Wetherherd Sharpe. Only three women were asked: Hughes, Lydia Manley of Stockwell Training College and school inspector Sarah Bannister. The committee's report resulted in a policy that, by the end of the century, caused the closure of the pupil-teacher centres that had been established
6. 'Miss Day's Account of Her Life', www.mhsg-times.co.uk/article
7. Ancestry: 'London, England Royal Holloway and Bedford College Student Registers, 1849–1931'

Chapter 11

1. The Bryce Report (1895) Report of the Royal Commission on Secondary Education
2. https://archives.lse.ac.uk
3. *The Queen*, Saturday, 4 October 1890
4. Bradford Girls' Grammar School Jubilee Chronicle 1875–1925
5. Yorkshire Ladies' Council of Education: https://ylce.org/
6. Bryce Report: pp.429–30 Appendix
7. *London Evening Standard*, Saturday, 27 April 1895
8. *Surrey Mirror*, Friday, 26 February 1943, Obituary

Chapter 12

1. *Bath Chronicle and Weekly Gazette*, Thursday, 19 December 1901
2. *Our Magazine*, North London Collegiate School Archives
3. Nonita Glenday and Mary Price, *Reluctant Revolutionaries: A Century of Headmistresses 1874–1974* (Pitman, London 1974)
4. Ibid.

Chapter 13

1. *Our Magazine*, March 1904
2. Oxford Dictionary of National Biography: www.oxforddnb.com
3. *The Mathematical Practitioners of Tudor and Stuart England* (1954); *The Haven-Finding Art: A History of Navigation from Odysseus to Captain Cook* (1956); and *The Mathematical Practitioners of Hanoverian England* (1966)
4. The British Federation of Women Graduates: https://bfwg.org.uk/bfwg2/wp-content/uploads/2024/04/Ethel-Sargant.pdf
5. Gaynor Haliday, *Struggle and Suffrage in Wakefield: Women's Lives and the Fight for Equality* (Pen and Sword, Barnsley, 2019)
6. Journal of Liberal History: https://liberalhistory.org.uk/history/margaret-wintringham-1879-1955
7. Bradford Girls' Grammar School Jubilee Chronicle 1875–1925

Bibliography

Books

Butler, Josephine E., *The Education and Employment of Women* (Macmillan, London, 1868)

Dent, H.C., *The Training of Teachers in England and Wales, 1800–1975* (Hodder and Stoughton, London, 1977)

Glenday, Nonita and Mary Price, *Reluctant Revolutionaries: A Century of Headmistresses 1874–1974* (Pitman, London, 1974)

Haliday, Gaynor, *Struggle and Suffrage in Wakefield: Women's Lives and the Fight for Equality* (Pen and Sword, Barnsley, 2019)

Harman, Claire, *Charlotte Brontë: A Life* (Penguin, London, 2015)

Hubbard, Louisa Maria, *Work for Ladies in Elementary Schools* (Longman, London, 1872)

Kamm, Josephine, *How Different from Us: A Biography of Miss Buss and Miss Beale* (Bodley Head, London, 1958)

Meades, Eileen E. BA, *A Brief History of St Mary's Hall, Brighton 1836–1956*

Miller, Florence Fenwick, *Autobiography: An Uncommon Girlhood* (c. 1900)

Pratt, Edwin A., *A Woman's Work for Women: Being the Aims, Efforts and Aspirations of 'L.M.H.' (Miss Louisa M. Hubbard)* (G. Newnes, London, 1898)

Various, *Education in Bradford Since 1870* (Educational Services Committee, Bradford Corporation, 1970)

Documents/Archives

Bradford Girls' Grammar School Jubilee Chronicle 1875–1925, West Yorkshire Archives

The Bryce Report (1895) Report of the Royal Commission on Secondary Education Vols 1–20

Huddersfield School Board, Triennial Report, 1874

Mount Pleasant Infants' School Logbook, West Yorkshire Archives

Report of Schools Inquiry (Taunton) Commission, 1868

Schools Inquiry Commission Minutes of Evidence, 1868

St Luke's National School, Chorlton-on-Medlock, Manchester. Logbooks, Manchester Archives

United Kingdom. Third Report. Royal Commission on Scientific Instruction and the Advancement of Science. Report, 1873, xxi.

Theses

Campbell-Day, Mary, 'Mary Gurney (1836–1917) and the reform of English female education'. University College London Institute of Education, 2024

Fletcher, Sheila Margaret, 'The part played by civil servants in promoting girls' secondary education 1869–1902; some aspects of the administration of the Endowed Schools Act'. Bedford College, London, 1976

Green, Katie, 'Victorian Governesses: A Look at Education and Professionalization'. University of Toledo, 2009

Ireland, Joyce Valerie, 'Education of Poor Girls in North West England c.1780 to 1860: A Study of Warrington And Chester'. University of Central Lancashire September 2005

Martin, Jane, 'To "blaise the trail for women to follow along": sex, gender and the politics of education on the London School Board, 1870–1904'. University College, Northampton, 1999

Journal Articles

Boucherett, Jessie, 'Endowed Schools: Their Uses and Shortcomings (1862)', *The Education Papers* (Routledge 2013)

Butler, Rev. G., 'Education Considered as a Profession for Women', *Women's Work and Women's Culture: A Series of Essays* (1869).

'Co-operation Among Governesses', *Work and Leisure: A Magazine Devoted to the Interests of Women* 6. no, 1 (1881)

Mahood, Linda, 'Elementary Teaching as Toil: The Diary and Letters of Miss Eglantyne Jebb, a Gentlewoman Schoolmistress', *History of Education*, 35:3, (2006)

Our Magazine, 1901–1911, North London Collegiate School Archives

Phillips, Trevor R., 'Certificated Women Teachers in The National Union of Elementary Teachers, 1870–82', *History of Education Society Bulletin*, Autumn 1992

Robinson, Wendy, 'Teacher Training in England and Wales: Past, Present and Future Perspectives'. *Education Research and Perspectives* Vol. 33, No. 2, (2006), University of Exeter

Stanley, Lady Henrietta, 'Personal Recollections of Women's Education', *The Nineteenth Century*, August 1879

Tozer, Malcolm, 'Thring's "favourite wish": Uppingham High School for Girls, 1888–1893', *Rutland Record*, vol. 32, 2018
Van Ardell, Rosemary T., 'Victorian Periodicals Yield Their Secrets: Florence Fenwick Miller's Three Campaigns for The London School Board', *History of Education Society Bulletin*. (History of Education Society. 1986)
Wloch, Anna, 'The Development of Teacher's Education in England in the 19th Century', University of the National Education Commission Krakow, 2019
Wolstenholme, Elizabeth C., 'The Education of Girls, Its Present and Its Future', *Women's Work and Women's Culture: A Series of Essays* (1869)

Newspapers

Avis's Birmingham Gazette
Bath Chronicle and Weekly Gazette
Bradford Daily Telegraph
Bradford Observer
Brighton Gazette
Bristol Mirror
Burton Chronicle
Cambridge Chronicle & Journal
Carlisle Journal
Dewsbury Chronicle
Dundee Courier
Echo (London)
Educational Times
Evening Mail
Gloucester Journal
The Governess
Hampstead News
Hastings and St Leonard's Observer
Huddersfield Daily Examiner
Huddersfield Chronicle
Illustrated London News
Inverness Courier
Leeds Intelligencer
Leeds Mercury
Liverpool Mail
London Daily Chronicle
London Evening Standard

Manchester Courier
Manchester Times
Newcastle Chronicle
Northern Whig
North Londoner
The Queen
Sheffield Daily News
South London Chronicle
South London Press
Stalybridge Reporter
Stamford Mercury
Surrey Mirror
The Tablet
Taunton Courier & Western Advertiser
Western Daily Press
Western Times
Yorkshire Post and Leeds Intelligencer

Websites

Ancestry UK: www.ancestry.com
The British Federation of Women Graduates: https://bfwg.org.uk
The British Newspaper Archive: britishnewspaperarchive.co.uk
Bronte House School: www.bronteschoolhouse.com
Cambridge Past, Present & Future: www.cambridgeppf.org
Education in the UK: The History of our Schools, Colleges and Universities: https://education-uk.org
Girton College: www.girton.cam.ac.uk/pioneering-history/the-great-scheme
Hansard: https://hansard.parliament.uk
Hughes Hall, Cambridge University: www.hughes.cam.ac.uk/about/news/addressing-need-for-over-a-century/
Internet Archive: https://archive.org
Journal of Liberal History: https://liberalhistory.org.uk
Lady Margaret Hall College: www.lmh.ox.ac.uk
London School of Economics: https://archives.lse.ac.uk
Manchester High School for Girls Times: www.mhsg-times.co.uk
Maria Grey College Archives, Brunel University: www.brunel.ac.uk/life/library/ArchivesAndSpecialCollections/Maria-Grey-College-Archives
Newnham College: https://newn.cam.ac.uk/about/history
North London Collegiate School: http://northlondoncollegiateschool.cook.websds.net

The Online Historical Population Reports Website: Histpop.org
Oxford Dictionary of National Biography: www.oxforddnb.com
Spartacus Educational: https://spartacus-educational.com
St Mary's Hall (Brighton) Archive: www.smhassociation.org/registers
Whitelands College, University of Roehampton: www.roehampton.ac.uk/student-life/colleges/whitelands/history/
Yorkshire Ladies' Council of Education: https://ylce.org

Index

Acland, Thomas Dyke, MP, 124
Adams, Mary Bridges, 70
Aitken, Edith, 191, 194
Allcott, Thomas, 81, 95, 100
Allen, Ellen, 153, 158
Anderton, Anna Beatrice, 179
Apprenticeship of Pupil Teachers and
    Stipendiary Monitors, 40
Armitage, Ella S., 162–3
Ashworth, Anne Frances, 63–4
Aske's School, Hatcham, 188
Association for Promoting the
    Higher Education of Women in
    Cambridge, 176
Association of Assistant Mistresses, 172,
    174–5
Association of Headmistresses, 5, 147,
    150, 158, 172–3, 175, 186, 188–9
Association of the Education of Women
    in Oxford, 176–7
Association of Women Pharmacists, 193
Avery Hill Training College, 191

Balfour Biological Laboratory for
    Women, 196
Balfour's Education Act, 186
Banks, Charlotte Stanley, 159–60
Barham, Dora, 191

Beale, Dorothea, 34–5, 73, 108, 117,
    120, 123–4, 127, 145, 147, 149,
    157, 172–4, 181
Becker, Lydia, 57, 62, 79
Bedford College, 116–17, 120, 153, 156,
    161, 175, 185, 191–2, 195, 200
Bedford Girls' High School, 158
Bedford Girls' Modern School, 149,
    152, 158
Bedford High School for Girls, 153
Bedford Training College, 202
Beisiegel, Mary, 149
Bennett, Mary Amelia, 146
Besant, Annie, 70
Birkbeck College, 192
Blackmore, Miss M.M., 172–4
Board of Education Act 1899, 186
Bodichon, Barbara Leigh, 73, 118,
    125, 153
Booth, Mary Ann, 94
Boucherett, Jessie, 73, 118
Bradford Girls' Grammar School,
    3, 135, 143, 147, 149, 151, 158,
    169–70, 173
Bradford Ladies' Educational
    Association, 131–4
Branwell, Aunt Elizabeth, 14–15
Bray, Bertha Ann, 100–101

Index   233

British and Foreign School Society for the Education of the Labouring and Manufacturing Classes of Society of Every Religious Persuasion (British Schools), 2, 16, 32, 40, 61
British Federation of University Women, 194
Brontë Sisters
  Anne, 14
  Charlotte, 4, 7–10, 12, 14–15, 18
  Elizabeth, 7
  Emily, 8, 14
  Maria, 7
Brontë, Patrick, 7
Bryant, Sophie, 154, 156, 161–2, 201
Buchanan, Margaret Elizabeth, 192
Burdett Coutts, Angela Georgina, 2, 47–9, 50–52, 54–5, 77, 134
Burrans, Amelia Hannah, 55, 103–104
Burrows, Annie, 22, 24–5
Burstall, Sara Annie, 156, 188, 194
Burton upon Trent School for Girls, 192
Buss, Frances Mary, 33–5, 71, 117, 120, 122–3, 138–140, 143, 145, 147–9, 154, 156, 181, 191
Butler, Josephine, 36, 128, 190
Buxton, Dorothy Frances, 116
Byles, Harriett, 133, 170
Byles, Mary Anna, 171
Byles, Sarah Ann, 68, 133, 159, 170, 204

Cambridge and Oxford Examinations, 26
Cambridge Training College for Women Teachers, 154, 157, 172, 174, 177, 185, 191, 198, 200

Camden School, The, 33, 138, 141, 143, 147
Carter, Catherine Elizabeth, 13
Carter, Susan Margaret, 13
Cavendish, Lady Frederick, 136, 161
Chelsea Training College, 201
Cheltenham Ladies' College, 35, 73, 108, 117, 123, 154, 157, 159, 172–3, 175, 178, 185
Chessar, Jane Agnes, 70–71, 79
Church Schools Company, 145, 160–61, 170
Clapham Training College for Teachers, 192
Clement, Agnes Gertrude, 159–60
Clough, Anne Jemima, 73, 128, 131, 141, 153, 196
Cockhill, Elizabeth, 12
College of Preceptors, 71, 166
Committee of Council on Education, 40, 49, 55, 66
Connolly, Jane, 188
Cowan Bridge School, 5–6
Cowell, Alice, 70, 79
Creak, Edith Elizabeth Maria, 181
Crofton Hall School, 8, 117

Davenport Hill, Rosamond, 70, 74, 76, 79
Davies, Emily, 62, 66, 70, 73, 79, 118–122, 125, 141–2, 153
Davison, Emily Wilding, 143
Day, Elizabeth, 147, 155–6, 158, 172–5
Day, Elsie, 147
Derby Training Institution for Schoolmistresses, 53
Derrick, Caroline C., 147

Dibdin, Eugenie, 70
Dilke, Margaret Mary, 70
Domestic Economy Congress, 79

Edgell, Beatrice, 192
Education Code, 2, 76, 78, 80, 96, 99, 103, 107, 167
Education Acts
   Elementary Education Act 1870, 60–1
   Endowed Schools Act 1869, 128, 134, 137–8, 161, 190, 204
   Secondary Education Act 1902, 145, 186
Elder, Constance, 70
Elford, Marion, 138, 147
Elliott, Rev. Henry Venn, 8, 34
Eve, Margaret Anne, 70

Factory Act 1833, 40, 92
Falding, Caroline Sarah, 159
Fawcett, Millicent, 200
Fellows of the Linnean Society, 194
Female Middle-Class Emigration Society, 37
Fenwick Miller, Florence, 47, 70, 74–5, 79, 85–8, 90, 149, 187–8
Floyer, Louisa Ayscoghe, 77
Forster, William Edward, 1, 60, 128, 132–3, 137, 147, 170, 204
Fraser, Jesse, 101

Garrett, Dr Elizabeth, 62, 70, 73–4, 79, 188
Garrs, Nancy De, 5
Girls' Public Day School Company (GPDSC), 135, 140, 142–6, 157–8, 161–2, 166, 172–3, 181

Girton College, Cambridge, 146, 153, 156–8, 161, 170, 194, 198
Gladstone, Helen, 145
Glover, Edith, 70
Glynne Jones, Dilys, 162
Gorst, Sir John Eldon, 106–108
Gott, Louisa, 101
Governesses' Benevolent Institution, 28–32, 37
Governesses' Mutual Assurance Society, 28
Grey, Maria, 63, 139–40, 142–3, 154, 172, 174, 185
Grimsby Girls' High School, 191
Gurney, Mary, 141, 143, 172–3

Hadland, Selina, 147, 153
Haliday, Elizabeth, 92, 94, 100, 104
Haliday, Louisa, 99, 101, 104
Hargood, Mary Elizabeth, 176
Hastings, Frances, 70, 79
Heathcoat, Miss Eloisa, 35
Heger, M. Constantin, 14
Heger, Mme Zoë, 14
High Schools Company for Girls, 146
Hobhouse, Arthur, 129
Homan, Ruth, 70, 80, 85
Home and Colonial School Society's Training College for Schoolmistresses, 71–2, 122
Hooper, Elsie Seville, 193
Horsfall, Edith, 159
Hubbard, Louisa, 108–11, 113
Huddersfield School Board, 63, 94–6, 100–102
Hughes, Elizabeth Phillips, 156, 172, 174
Huth, Marian, 63

Incorrigible Truants Committee, 81
Industrial Schools Committee, 76, 80–1, 84–5
Ingelow, Jean, 33

Jane Eyre, 17
Jebb, Eglantyne, 111–16
Jebb, Eglantyne Mary, 116
Jebb, Geraldine Emma May, 116
Jex-Blake, Sophia, 33, 73–4
Johnson, Bertha, 176–7
Jones, Harriet Morant, 147, 172
Jones, M.M., 159

Keighley Girls' Grammar School (Drake and Tonson's), 131, 202
Kennedy, Catherine Lucy, 135, 157, 162, 168
Kennedy, Marion Grace, 176–7
King Edward VI High School for Girls, 138
King, Gertrude, 120
King's College, 3, 29, 31
Kitchener, Frances A., 162, 164
Knox, Isa, 118
Kyberd, Susan, 120

Lady Margaret Hall, Oxford, 112, 155, 161
Lawrence, Hon. Agnes Maude, 70
Lawrence, Miss, 159
Lawrence, Susan, 70
Le Geyt, Alice, 142
Lee Warner, Eleanor, 162, 166
Lee, Agnes Y., 149–50, 152
Leeds Girls' High School, 134–5, 157, 168, 170
Leeds Ladies' Educational Association, 134
Leeds School of Cookery, 134
Lett Sisters
    Eva, 192, 201–2
    Hilda, 201
    Norah Kathleen, 201
    Olive Mary, 201
    Phyllis, 201
Linnean Society of London, 197
Liverpool Governesses' Institution, 32
London Institute for the Advancement of Plain Needlework, 77
London School of Medicine for Women, 74, 195
Ludlam, Ann, 6
Lumby, Amy, 172, 175
Lupton, Edith, 68
Lyttelton, Lord, 119, 128–9

Macrae, Mary, 188, 200
Maitland, Agnes Catherine, 177–8, 186
Maitland, Emma Knox, 70, 76, 85
Manchester Girls' High School, 155, 194
Manchester's Governesses' Institution, 35
Mangnall, Richmal, 117
Manley, Lydia, 113–14
Margaret Buchanan School of Pharmacy for Women, 193
Martin, Frances, 120
Mary Datchelor Girls' School, 175, 185
Marylebone Central Classes for Training Pupil Teachers, 167
Matthaei, Gabrielle Louise Caroline, 195–6
Maurice, Rev. Frederick Denison, 29
Maurice, Mary Atkinson, 30, 33

McCroben, Gertrude, 158, 171, 201
McKee, Ellen Courtauld, 70
McKillop, Mrs, 159
McMillan, Margaret, 68
Mellor, Hannah Exley, 105, 112
Mellor, Mary, 100
Metropolitan Board Mistresses' Association, 82, 87
Miall, Miss K., 159
Miall-Smith, Hilda Caroline, 70
Middlesex County Secondary School for Girls, 191
Mill, John Stuart, MP, 73
Milton Mount College, 147, 153
Morant Jones, Harriet, 147, 172–4
Morten, Honnor, 70, 85
Mothersole, Jessie, 199–201
Müller, Henrietta, 70, 74, 78–9, 81
Mundella, Anthony, 60, 77–8

National Association for the Promotion of Social Science, The, 118
National Education League, 57–60
National Education Union, 58–60
National Society for Promoting the Education of the Poor in the Principles of the Established Church throughout England and Wales, 2, 43–5, 108
National Society for Women's Suffrage, 74
National Union for the Improvement of Education for Women of all Classes, 141
National Union of Elementary Teachers (NUET), 91–2, 95–6
National Union of Teachers, 91, 167

Newnham College, Cambridge, 112, 145, 149, 153–5, 157–9, 161–2, 166, 170–1, 177, 181, 196
Newsome, Carrie, 103–104
North London Collegiate School for Girls (NLCS), 3, 33, 71, 73, 117, 138–40, 143, 148, 156–8, 173, 178, 181, 190–201
North of England Council for Promoting the Higher Education of Women, 128, 131, 190
Norwich Training College, 167
Notting Hill High School, 147, 172, 194
Nottingham Girls' High School, 194

Oakwell Hall, Birstall, 12–13
Olney, S. Allen, 172, 176
Orme Girls' School, Newcastle under Lyme, 189

Palmerston, Viscount, Prime Minister, 119
Pillow, Margaret Eleanor, née Scott, 167–8
Porter, Mary Eliza, 35, 120, 131, 135–6, 143, 147, 149–54, 158–9
Portsmouth Municipal College, 193
Powell, Helena Langhorne, 157
Power Cobbe, Frances, 73, 117–18
Procter, Adelaide Anne, 33

Queen Elizabeth Grammar School, Mansfield, 200
Queen's College, Harley Street, 9, 28, 31–2, 34–5, 117, 153, 155
Queen's Scholars, 43, 46–7, 50, 56
Queen's Scholarship, 45, 55–6, 103, 106–107, 167

Ragged Schools' Union, 2
Raisin, Catherine Alice, 191–2
Rayner Parkes, Bessie, 73, 118
Reed, Sir Charles, MP, 78
Reid, Elizabeth Jesser, 117
Reigate County School for Girls, 180
Richardson, Mary Eliza, 70, 74
Ricketts, Catharine Maria, 63
Rigg, Ellen, 6
Roberts, Margaret Elizabeth, 158–9
Robertson Sisters
  Agnes, 195–6
  Hannah, 191
  Janet, 199–200
  Margaret, 200
Robinson, Canon H.G., 129
Roby, Henry, 120–1, 129, 139
Roe Head School, Hartshead, 10
Royal Commissions
  Elementary Education (Taunton/ Schools Inquiry Commission) 1868, 119, 126, 135, 138, 150
  Elementary Education (Cross) 1887, 79
  Secondary Education (Bryce) 1895, 161–2, 168, 181, 183, 185
Royal Holloway College, 143, 154, 159–61, 191–2

Sallitt, Jessie Amelia, 170
Salt, Catherine, 132
Salt, Sir Titus, 132–3, 170
Saltaire Girls' School, 151
Sargant, Ethel, 194, 196
Schlesinger, Mary, 132
Scott, Alice Townley, 159
Scrutton, Thomas, 84

Sharples, Hannah, 94
Shires, Annie, 101
Shum, Caroline Meta, 63–5
Sidgwick, Eleanor Mildred, 161, 194, 196
Simcox, Edith Jemima, 70, 74, 78
Slade School of Fine Art, 199
Smith, Eleanor Elizabeth, 63, 66, 120–22, 125
Soames, Laura, 145
Social Science Association, 118–19
Somerville College, Oxford, 66, 153, 158–9, 161, 170, 176–7, 186, 200
Springman, Ann, 32
St Elphin's School for Clergymen's Daughters, Warrington, 157
St Hugh's College, Oxford, 154
St Mary's College, London, 157, 191
St Mary's Hall, Brighton, 8, 13, 28
Stanger, Florence, 191
Stanley, Lady Henrietta of Alderley, 32, 43, 78, 143, 153
Stanley, Lynulph, MP, 78
Stocker, Mary Ida, 152, 170
Stockwell Training College, 44, 55–6, 113–14
Stopes, Marie, 195, 197–8, 201
Stopes, Winifred Christine, 200
Strongitharm, Sophia, 36–7
Surr, Elizabeth, 70, 74–5, 79, 81–2, 84, 87
Syrett, Netta, 198, 200

Taylor, Eva Germaine, 192
Taylor, Helen, 70, 73, 79, 81–5, 87–9
Taylor, Nina Georgine Rimington, 191
Taylor, Sarah Jane, 101

Tchaycovsky, Barbara (aka Ally), 195
Temple, Jennetta Octavia, 66–8
The Teaching of Common Things, 51
Thring, Reverend Edward, 148

Uppingham School, 3, 148
Upton House, Homerton, 82
Upton, Misses Sarah & Martha, 12

Waite, Eliza, 101
Wakefield Girls' High School, 134, 154, 158, 171, 201
Warren, Kate Mary, 191
Waterford, Lady Louisa, 6
Webster, Julia Augusta, 70, 74, 89
Westfield College, 191
Westlake, Alice, 70, 73–4, 78–81, 87

Whitelands Training College, 44, 46, 48, 51, 53, 55–6
Wilson, Rev. William Carus, 7
Winterbotham, Henry, MP, 128
Wintringham, Margaret, 202
Withiel, Marion, 172, 175
Wollstonecraft, Mary, 1
Wolstenholme (-Elmy), Elizabeth Clarke, 73, 120
Wood, Mary Hay, 157
Woods, Alice Augusta, 172–4
Wooler, Miss Margaret, 10, 13
Wren, Gertrude Holland, 193
Wright, Alice Mary, 70

Yorkshire Ladies' Council of Education, 162, 171–2